100
QUESTIONS
EVERY
WORKING
AMERICAN
MUST ASK

CAROLANN BROWN

Dearborn
Financial Publishing, Inc.

Dedication

To Paul, Allyson, Michael, Dad and Rose
with all my love
and
in loving memory of
my mother

This publication is designed to provide accurate and authoritative information in regard to the subject matter covered. It is sold with the understanding that the publisher is not engaged in rendering legal, accounting or other professional service. If legal advice or other expert assistance is required, the services of a competent professional person should be sought.

Managing Editor: Jack Kiburz
Cover Design: S. Laird Jenkins Corporation
Interior Design: Publishing Services, Inc.

Published by Dearborn Financial Publishing, Inc.®

Printed in the United States of America

96 97 98   10 9 8 7 6 5 4 3 2 1

Library of Congress Cataloging-in-Publication Data

Brown, Carolann Doherty, 1946–
    100 questions every working American must ask / Carolann Brown.
        p.   cm.
    Includes index.
    ISBN 0-7931-1582-5 (paper)
    1. Finance, Personal.   2. Retirement—Planning.   3. Pensions.
4. Career changes.   I. Title.
HG179.B74637   1996
332.024—dc20   95-40560
                                                            CIP

Contents

CHAPTER 3 ◆
Providing for Family Needs   57

CHAPTER 4 ◆
Preparing for Emergencies   77

CHAPTER 5 ◆

Planning for Retirement   105

CHAPTER 6 ◆

Investing Retirement Funds   127

CHAPTER 7 ◆
Protecting Your Pension   145

CHAPTER 8 ◆
Profiting from Your Employee Benefits   165

CHAPTER 9
Making Job Transitions 179

Preface

Every day hardworking Americans throw thousands of dollars away. In fact, we turn away money from our employers and the government. We borrow from all the wrong places, we pay credit card interest instead of tax-deductible interest, we pay too much in taxes and we do not save enough money. Worse yet, we throw away benefits and perks from our employer that could make our lives richer and less stressed. Instead, we try to increase our wealth by working harder, working overtime and adding second jobs, even though we can choose better ways to expand our income through workplace benefits.

We face an overwhelming number of decisions at work, such as how to select insurance plans, health care plans and child care benefits; how much to invest in retirement plans; and which investments to select. We must decide when and what type of raises to ask for, and how to handle tax situations. We get so overwhelmed that, instead of evaluating these decisions carefully, we make hasty, ill-informed, stop-gap decisions that, in the long run, only will guarantee a less prosperous lifestyle.

I host several radio call-in shows, and day after day, listeners ask questions about mutual funds and stocks, but seldom do they ask the *most* important questions: How do I take advantage of all my workplace opportunities? When should I use trusts or children's accounts? What are the best ways to save on taxes? How can I protect my investments from large losses? Or how can I take advantage of employer's matching programs, referral and resource programs, dependent savings accounts, pretax saving plans and employee benefits?

Each day, I also work as a financial planner helping American workers reach their financial goals. I have seen some people make mistakes that cost them happiness, safe retirements and even their health. I will show you how to avoid these same mistakes.

In *100 Questions Every Working American Must Ask,* I give you the 100 questions you absolutely must ask and the ready-to-use responses you need to make the most of your employee income and benefits. These questions and answers can make a real difference to your long-term financial health. It will show you how to take your fair share of all the money the government and employers are willing to give away. And it will show you how to handle your most pressing concerns with greater ease.

Like many hardworking Americans, you may feel sandwiched between the demands of your children, your work, your spouse and your aging parents, so you need to have a plan that balances these various demands. In this case, your strategy depends on carefully fitting together a complete puzzle—one that provides for every part of your life. This book will show you how to set up a plan that helps you meet these competing demands and live more comfortably.

Even if you're not a member of the sandwich generation, you're probably coping with other stressful situations in your life. For instance, surveys show that almost 44 percent of Americans are afraid they'll lose their jobs. Given today's very volatile economy, that's a very real fear. In this book, I will reveal some of the warning signals as well as strategies to help you protect your job from a cutback. I will also help you to figure out the best time to negotiate for a raise versus a promotion or more benefits. And I will tip you off to common mistakes people make when changing jobs.

This book also will help you prepare for the future. By 1997, most American workers will have more money set aside in retirement than they have invested in their homes. It makes sense to take this money seriously, but most workers ignore it. They are intimidated by the volumes of information and confusing terminology, such as vesting, integration, 403(b) plans, asset allocation, sector rotation, flexible savings and flextime. We will explore these terms in plain language and how they can benefit you.

We also will focus on ways to build your retirement nest egg during your working years. Participating in the stock market is an important yet small part of what you need to learn about growing your assets. This book will share tips about other investment vehicles, and it will show you how to minimize short-term volatility in your investment portfolio.

Although we can choose ways to get more from our employers and the government, we must remember not to depend too much on them. Social Security ultimately may provide less than a quarter of our retirement income, and fewer and fewer employers still offer pensions. We will examine practical ways to prevent your pension money from eroding and to strive for higher returns. We will also show you alternatives to the bond funds and CDs that appear safe, but can be risky, money-losing ventures.

After reading *100 Questions Every Working American Must Ask*, I hope you'll see many new ways that your future and your family's future can be more secure and brighter, and your workplace more pleasant and rewarding.

ACKNOWLEDGMENTS

For their help and support I would like to express my gratitude and thanks to my husband Paul; my children, Allyson and Michael; my father, Henry Doherty; Marilyn Goldman; Rose Carroll; Nim Marsh; all the Lionettes; the Deramos; Mary Brown; Will, Jane and the Doherty family; Betty-Ann and the Nutter family; Athol Cochran; Ellen, Erin and Mark Rosenthal; *The Providence Journal*; Caroline Carney and Jill Strubbe; Jason and the O'Learys; Sherri Brennam; the Cardillos; Brandom Viera; Sheila Camara.

CHAPTER 1

Managing
Your Paycheck

1 HOW CAN I FIGURE OUT HOW MUCH I REALLY EARN?

You can't tell how much you really earn from your salary alone. Even your paycheck may not tell the whole story. We usually select one job over another because it has a higher salary, and yet, if we select a job based on salary and income information alone, our choice may be shortsighted.

To get a true picture of what we earn, we must look at our total remuneration or your personal bottom line. Total remuneration includes salary, retirement funds, benefits packages, any overtime pay and perks, minus taxes and work expenses. It also includes any so-called soft benefits that cannot be quantified, such as an agreeable work environment, career advancement potential or social contacts. To understand our true pay, we must quantify and place a value on as many of these benefits as possible.

> 33 percent of our pay comes from employee benefits, so it is important to calculate these benefits in any job evaluation.

Look at the total picture. Place a value on your

- ◆ Salary
- ◆ Retirement packages

1

- ◆ Benefit packages
- ◆ Soft benefits

Then subtract your

- ◆ Taxes
- ◆ Work expenses

Remember, too, our comparisons cannot end with adding up all the inflows such as salaries, benefits and pension plans, but we must also factor in the outflows, such as taxes, work-related transportation costs, entertainment expenses and other items that affect the bottom line.

Consider taxes. While all jobs are taxed, each salary and benefits package can have different tax consequences and can affect your take-home pay. Don't assume that your taxes and work expenses are the same with every job. For example, a military officer cannot assume that he will take home the same pay if he switches to a civilian job, because several of the military allowances are tax-free. Nor can you assume that just because two companies quote you the same salary and benefits package, you will net the same pay. The benefits that you receive could be taxable, tax-free or tax-deferred. The salary you pull in from your own business, for example, cannot be compared to what you earn at a large company, because of all the soft benefits and tax deductions that your own business allows.

It is not just what you earn, but what you keep that counts.

> **Salary + retirement benefits + fringe benefits + soft benefits – taxes – work expenses = the bottom line**

You must consider advancement potential, future raises and overtime. One job may pay a little more, but you may not be able to earn overtime, which can make a big difference to the bottom line.

In addition to the normal benefits, your company may offer other unique perks or conveniences. Even little conveniences add up. For example, if you can save time by paying your bills through automatic payroll deduction, then it has value. Time is our most precious commodity, yet too frequently we neglect or underestimate its value.

Other unique benefits might include handymen to do minor home repairs, house sitters to wait for plumbers, in-house laundry and shoe repair services, softball leagues and bowling teams, office parties and picnics or discounts. Some companies will match your charitable contributions, open their phone lines on holidays to employees and community groups or offer on-site exercise facilities. If you use any of these services, then include their value when you do your calculations.

Also consider the soft benefits available to you. A relaxed dress code not only is less stressful, but cuts down on clothing costs, including dry cleaning. A more comfortable work environment might be important to you. At one advertising agency in New York there are oversized chairs, artificial ponds and a little brook running through the office. At another, employees pick up their lap-top computers and portable phones each morning and search for a comfortable area in which to work. Some firms eliminate offices altogether. A chief executive of a Fortune 500 company chose one company over another because there was a better view of the city from his office window. Whatever your preferences, it's important to take these intangibles into consideration.

Don't forget to consider lunch hours and coffee breaks. Having more than an hour for lunch might give you time for errands and exercise. Coffee breaks can provide enough time to catch up on a little bill paying, studying and managing your financial future. Always consider your unpaid free time as well as your paid vacation, personal days and sick leave.

When evaluating the bottom line of any job, make a balance or worksheet for yourself. You can use the following sample balance sheet. You may not know some of the values now, but as we go along you will be able to quantify them more effectively.

Add up the following:

Compensation

Wages   _____

Commissions   _____

Tips   _____

Bonuses   _____

Retirement packages

Employer's retirement plans

Employer's matching contributions
on employee plans

Tax-saving potential on your
retirement plan contributions

Benefits

The value of employee benefits that your
employer pays:

      Life insurance

      Health insurance

      Disability insurance

Savings on group rates for insurance
(If your employer doesn't pay, you may want
to include the amount that you save by
using the company group plan.)

Nonqualified plans

Present value of deferred-compensation
plans

Split-dollar life insurance

Value of severance savings plans

Other nonqualified plan

Tax savings resulting from the use of
nonqualified plans versus cash payments

Fringe benefits

Child care benefits, vouchers

Tax savings on flexible savings account

Tax savings on dependent care accounts

Tax savings on medical care accounts   _____

Resource and referral services   _____

Educational and vocational programs   _____

Adoption allowances   _____

Educational assistance   _____

Time benefits

Vacation time   _____

Sick and personal days   _____

Break and lunchtime   _____

Holidays   _____

Perks

Club membership   _____

Use of dining facilities   _____

Use of company car or truck   _____
    (Caution: only consider the value for your
       use, not for company use.)

Expense account   _____
    (Consider the amount that you would
       normally have to pay at most other jobs.)

Travel vouchers   _____

Parking   _____

Children's scholarship programs   _____

Discount services   _____

Financial planning and accounting
    services   _____

Frequent-flier travel mileage (only
    include after tax benefit)   _____

Other soft benefits

On-site child care facilities   _____

Recreational and social activities   _____

Social and work environment   _____

Conveniences   _____

Matching charitable contributions   _____

Career potential

Overtime potential   _____

Track record of the company for
   advancement potential   _____

Likelihood of bonuses   _____

Incentive programs   _____

Travel rewards   _____

Service awards   _____

Suggestion awards   _____

Participation in company profits

Employee Stock Option Plans (ESOPs)   _____

Profit-sharing programs   _____

Performance pay programs   _____

Once you have listed all the benefits, list all the costs.

Incidental costs

Parking   _____

Commuting expenses   _____

Tolls   _____

Employer-related expenses (i.e., licenses, etc.) _____

Publications, journals, classes, etc.   _____

Union dues   _____

Work-related entertaining not covered
   by employer   _____

Total remuneration   _____

Knowing what you really earn is important when you are comparing jobs, managing your paychecks, managing your retirement and benefits, and when planning for your financial future, your children's future and your estates. Your paycheck is just the beginning of what you earn. When your employer hands you your paycheck, the check is just 60 to 70 percent on average of what he or she is paying on your behalf. The other 30 to 40 percent goes to disability, unemployment compensation, Social Security taxes, insurance, pension plans, benefit programs and fringe benefits.

The real compensation for many workers could typically be broken down as follows:

- ◆ 40 percent to 45 percent—performance pay, commissions, bonuses, incentive pay, stock options, perks and awards (18 percent of that typically in bonuses)
- ◆ 20 percent to 33 percent—benefit and retirement packages
- ◆ 27 percent to 30 percent—average base salary

That is why it is so important to know all your benefits and retirement plans. You need to assess their worth when trying to determine what you really earn.

2 WHAT DO ALL THOSE DEDUCTIONS ON MY PAYCHECK MEAN?

"Who is FICA, and why is he taking all my money?" asks the young waitress on the television sitcom *Friends*. She is suffering from pay-stub shock that takes away the excitement of getting a paycheck. Where does all your money go? Over half the salary for most working Americans goes to taxes and benefits.

The excitement of earning money is dampened by the fact that so much of it disappears so quickly. If you can remember your first paycheck, then you understand the frustration and disappointment when that first payday comes around. Michael was so excited when he got his summer job. He planned to buy a surfboard with his first paycheck. He had figured carefully: two weeks, 80 hours, $5 an hour. He'd have $400 minus a little for taxes. With a little overtime, he'd have his board. Two weeks went by, and he got his check for $287. He looked at the check for what seemed hours and finally asked, "Is this really all I am going to get?" Where **did** all his money go?

It went to federal income taxes, state income taxes, FICA Medicare, FICA OASDI and state disability insurance for a total of $113 in taxes!

Unfortunately, after taxes and benefits our pay stubs may reflect only half of our quoted earnings. Almost 40 percent on average go to various taxes and another estimated 20 to 33 percent go to benefits.

Suddenly, the real world hits us when we look at our paycheck, but we feel we cannot do anything about it, so we just ignore it. But we shouldn't. If you look closely, you may find some ways to make that pay stub look a lot better. Let's examine the typical deductions that are withheld, and make some brief notes on what we can do to improve our pay. Later we will go into more depth on how to grow your paycheck.

Since so much of our hard work goes to paying for these benefits and taxes, it is important to understand them and determine which ones we can control and change.

We can divide deductions into three areas: taxes, retirement and benefits.

TAXES

Today the average American works from January 1st to the middle of May just to pay taxes, so it is crucial that we understand our tax situation.

FICA MED. Usually the first deduction you will see is for FICA MED. This is your Social Security payment for Medicare. In 1995, there is a 1.45 percent tax for the Medicare portion on all your income. This 1.45 percent doesn't sound like a lot, but if you earn $50,000, it is $725, or over an average working period of 40 years, $29,000.

There is not much you can do to reduce this amount and it is likely to get worse in the future.

FICA OASDI. The next deduction you see is also FICA. This time it will be listed as FICA OASDI. This portion pays for old age, survivors' and disability insurance. You will pay 6.20 percent up to $61,200 (1995) of your income. FICA MED and FICA OASDI will add up to 7.65 percent of your gross salary, up to $61,200 (for 1995). Over your lifetime you may pay in $151,760 if you are paying at the maximum levels. If you consider the portion your employer pays on your behalf, you could pay over $300,000 in Social Security taxes. And you should consider your employer's contribution, because if your employer were not paying it on your behalf to the government, it is likely he or she would be giving you some of it. Unlike the Medicare portion, this tax is capped and you will not pay this tax on income over the annual cap. (If you are self-employed, you will pay 15.3 percent of your taxable income into Social Security up to $61,200 and 2.90 percent above that amount.)

What can you do to reduce this amount? Like FICA MED, there is not much you can do. However, if you have changed jobs this year, or if you have two jobs in which your income is over $61,200, you will be able to get a refund for an excess Social Security payment.

What does your 6.20 percent get you? In addition to questionable retirement benefits, you also may be eligible for disability insurance and for aid to dependent children. Ironically, we tend to think of Social Security as retirement income, yet it pays more benefits to children than any other government program and it is a safety net for the country's many disabled.

Federal Income Tax. This is your largest deduction and greatest challenge. It is the most important deduction to reduce. Today the average American pays over 37 percent of their income in federal, Social Security, local, county and state taxes. If you add in real estate, personal property, sales and other taxes, you can easily lose another 5 to 20 percent of your income to taxes. There are also many hidden taxes that sometimes we don't recognize, including taxes on our utility bills, telephone bills, and city and town sewage taxes. How often do we think of taxes when we pump gas? Over one third to one half of the cost are taxes. How often do we think of the hidden taxes when we make a telephone call or buy a loaf of bread? If you add these taxes up, you start to realize how important tax-saving strategies are.

When you look at your tax brackets, remember that they are the marginal rate or the rate you pay on the last dollar earned. It is always important to know this rate, so you can determine if you should work overtime, take a raise or invest in tax-free investments. You also need to know your tax bracket for tax, estate, financial and job planning. As bad as this tax is, however, there are some things you can do to reduce it.

- ◆ Review the tax table for 1995 in Question #8.
- ◆ Check your withholding allowances and make sure you are taking the maximum amount allowed. Call the IRS for *Publication 919* to help calculate the amount you can withhold.
- ◆ Maximize your contributions to 401(k), SARSEP and IRA plans. Your savings and net worth will increase and your taxes will decrease. Although your take-home pay may be less, you are converting what would have been tax dollars into savings for your future! If you just look at your pay stub, you will feel as though you have decreased your earnings. Instead, look at your total net worth, which will increase. By maximizing your pension and retirement, you are increasing your wealth in one of the smartest ways possible, because you are diverting your pay from the government to yourself.
- ◆ Negotiate with your employer for severance savings plans, deferred-compensation plans and split insurance plans instead of taking all taxable income. Consider taking less salary in favor of nonqualified pension plans, participation in ESOPs and other nontaxable benefits. These plans will not only reduce your current taxes, but will create large pools of retirement assets.
- ◆ Use flexible savings plans that allow you to set aside pretax dollars for medical and dependent care.
- ◆ Also consider benefits such as child care vouchers, dining room privileges, trips, car use, expense accounts, parking places, financial and account services and other referral and resource programs. Although these are typically taxable, the reportable amounts may be much lower than if you had to purchase these yourself.

◆ Plan your investments smartly. If you invest in taxable fixed-income investments, place them in your pension and retirement funds. Allocate your long-term capital gains investments (such as aggressive growth funds) to your individual account and your short-term capital gains and balanced funds to your retirement accounts. Long-term capital gains are only taxed at the 28 percent rate, while income from investments such as CDs and Treasury bonds can be taxed at the highest rates (39.6 percent). You want the investments with the higher tax consequences sheltered.

◆ If your marginal tax bracket is 28 percent or above and you are investing in Treasuries, CDs or taxable bonds, consider switching to short-term municipal bonds. Also use tax-free money market funds.

◆ Use appropriate tax strategies, such as saving for your children under their names or gifting securities with large gains to your children or parents. You and they can both benefit when they sell these securities since they may pay taxes at a lower tax bracket and have more disposable income. There are many tax strategies you can use, and we will review these later in more depth.

State Disability Taxes. In addition to Social Security disability, some states have their own disability tax. There is not much you can do about this tax.

State Tax. What you do to reduce your federal taxes will usually reduce your state taxes. If you invest in municipal bonds, select ones from your state or Puerto Rico. That way you will save on both federal and state taxes. Use Treasury securities and U.S. savings bonds that have no state taxes instead of CDs and money market funds.

DEDUCTIONS

401(k) and Retirement Contributions. The first deduction is usually for your 401(k) or other retirement contributions. Although this amount decreases your cash flow, you want this number to be as high as possible, since it is the best way for the average working American to build wealth and save on taxes.

Health Insurance. Another deduction, medical insurance, must be carefully evaluated. With such large differences in the cost for various medical alternatives such as HMOs, PPOs and other health plans, it is important to compare them conscientiously. If you are married, be sure to compare policies and not duplicate coverage.

Supplemental Life Insurance. Many companies will give you a basic life insurance policy equal to one or two times your income. Before you elect for supplemental life insurance, do not assume that your employer's insurance is the best. Shop around and compare it to outside policies. Your employer's policies are usually attractive for older, less healthy employees. If you are young and a nonsmoker, you can usually do better with your own policy. Also make sure that you are not paying for insurance that you do not need. Too often we think of insurance as a way to make our heirs rich, like winning the lottery. Instead we should look at our family's basic needs and provide protection for those needs. If you are single and have no dependents, you may not need any insurance.

Supplemental Disability. This is probably your most important deduction. The chances of becoming disabled are six times greater than those of dying for young workers, yet many workers will have more life insurance than needed and much less disability insurance than needed. This is one supplemental insurance policy you should probably take.

Other Insurance. In addition to life insurance, many companies offer payroll deduction insurance for autos, homes and long-term health care. Although payroll deduction insurance is easy and popular, it may not be the best quality, coverage or price. You may be paying higher premiums than if you purchase the insurance outside your employer's plan.

Other Payroll Deductions. You may also have deductions for savings and direct deposits. Although these will not reduce your taxes, they will make it a lot easier to build your savings nest egg.

Saving Bonds. You might have deductions for savings bonds. If you don't deduct for these bonds, you might want to consider them. Since you can postpone paying federal taxes on the accrued interest for many years, and there are no state taxes, these can be part of a good tax-saving plan.

Flexible Savings Plans.   You can typically save up to $5,000 for child care and $2,500 for medical care on a tax-free basis. We'll discuss these plans more in Question #18.

P.S.   Still wondering what FICA means? FICA is the Federal Insurance Contributions Act, the law that authorized Social Security's payroll tax, and the term is used to note Social Security deductions.

3   HOW DO I KNOW IF THE RIGHT AMOUNT OF TAXES ARE BEING TAKEN FROM MY PAYCHECK?

IRS statistics show that in 1994 and 1995 over 70 million Americans received a tax refund. If you either received a refund or had to pay additional taxes, then you probably did something wrong and need to recalculate your withholding allowances.

The reason we do not have the right amount of taxes withheld from our paycheck is because we do not calculate the correct number of withholding allowances.

When we get a refund, we think we have done a pretty good job of taking all the necessary deductions on our tax return. Instead, it is because we did a poor job the year before in planning our taxes. We gave the government an interest-free loan and gave up the use of that money and the interest we could have earned. For example, in 1994, the average loan we gave the government was over $1,125 and we didn't get paid back until the middle of May of the following year.

The number of allowances we claim tells our employer how much money to withhold from our paychecks to cover our estimated income tax. The more allowances we claim, the less money is taken from our paycheck for taxes. If we claim zero allowances, the maximum amount of taxes will be taken out. Most workers think that their number of allowances corresponds to their number of dependents or exemptions, but that is not always true. This number is determined by:

◆ The number of dependents
◆ Tax credits and other income
◆ Deductions from income

GIVE YOURSELF A RAISE

Plan your allowances carefully. Proper planning will bring you extra income each month rather than giving the state and federal governments your money to use without paying you interest. It's like giving yourself a raise.

- ♦ If you take that extra tax savings each month and invest it, it will allow you to earn more interest or income.
- ♦ If you contribute the tax savings or extra income to a retirement plan, it will reduce your taxable income even more and allow you to earn tax-deferred interest this year instead of waiting until you get your tax refund.
- ♦ If you have credit card debt, you can pay it off with the extra income and save yourself finance charges.
- ♦ You can give the money to a charity and get a tax deduction.
- ♦ You can give it to your children, or just go out to dinner and have fun.

No matter how you use that money, you probably will use it a lot better than the government will!

4 HOW MANY WITHHOLDING ALLOWANCES SHOULD I CLAIM?

One of the first dilemmas you face when filling out employment forms is how many withholding allowances to take on your W-4 forms. Whether you are filling out these forms for the first time or have been working for many years, it is important that you answer them correctly. You want to make sure you are claiming the correct amount of withholding allowances so that you will neither get a refund nor owe too much in taxes.

You need to reevaluate these numbers whenever you get a refund, when you owe additional taxes, when your family status changes or when you have large additions to your income such as inheritance, gambling winnings or capital gains from the sale of a stock.

Call the IRS at 1-800-829-3676 and ask for *Publication 919,* or go to your employer and see if he or she has information on filling in W-4 forms. *Publication 919* will help you compute the number of allowances that you should take.

Basically we calculate our withholdings by adding up the number of dependents we have and then finding the difference between additions and deductions to our income. Start by looking at the deductions that you take on your tax return, lines 23 to 30, and on Schedule A. Write down the amounts you claim for:

♦ Home mortgage interest
♦ Real estate and personal property tax
♦ Predictable medical bills exceeding 7.5 percent of your income
♦ Deductible IRAs
♦ Pension plan contributions
♦ Charitable deductions
♦ Miscellaneous deductions
♦ Deductible alimony
♦ Tax credits
♦ Business expenses
♦ Miscellaneous deductions
♦ Other adjustments you typically take

Then, look at all the additions to your income, such as:

♦ Alimony you receive
♦ Interest earned on investments and bank accounts
♦ Capital gains from the sale of property or investments
♦ Dividends
♦ Taxable educational benefits
♦ Employee benefits
♦ Tips, awards
♦ Prizes, inheritances, gambling winnings
♦ Value of interest-free loans
♦ Business income
♦ Taxable distributions from pensions, IRAs, Social Security
♦ Any other items that increase your adjusted gross income

If you have more deductions than additions to your income, your withholdings should be greater than your number of dependents. You should fill in the worksheet on the IRS *Publication 919* to calculate the correct number of withholdings so that you will pay less taxes each payday.

If on the other hand you have a large amount of nonpaycheck income, you may want to reduce your withholdings to avoid any penalties. Remember:

> **If you claim more allowances, less taxes will be withheld. If you claim less allowances, more taxes will be withheld.**

If it looks like you are overpaying on your taxes and getting a refund, go to your employer immediately and ask to increase the allowances on your W-4 form. If you are underpaying by a small amount, you may be better off waiting and paying on April 15. But if you underpay your taxes by too much, you'll owe penalties, so decrease your withholdings immediately.

To avoid penalties you have to withhold at least the smaller of two amounts:

1. One hundred percent of the taxes you paid last year if you earned less than $150,000, or 110 percent of the taxes you paid last year if you earned more than $150,000

OR

2. Ninety percent of this year's taxes.

Consider decreasing your withholding allowances so that you will not have a penalty for paying too little taxes when an event occurs that is likely to increase your taxable income such as:

◆ You get divorced.
◆ You inherit large sums of money.
◆ You sell your home if there are any capital gains.
◆ You do very well in the stock market.

On the other hand, if events occur in your life that are likely to decrease your taxes, then increase your withholdings. Events such as:

◆ A new child
◆ Marriage

♦ A bigger mortgage
♦ A contribution to a deductible IRA or pension plan
♦ Large medical bills

 5 **HOW MUCH DO WORK-RELATED EXPENSES REALLY CUT INTO MY PAY?**

Work-related expenses have a dramatic impact on your actual take-home or net pay. Your real income is what you have left after all the money you spend to keep your job and all the subtle costs of working are considered. Work-related expenses include travel, licensing costs, business journals, educational costs, parking and all the other costs necessary to keep your job, such as day care, the extra costs of eating out and clothing. Include subtle costs which you would be unlikely to spend money, such as networking, entertainment and social engagements that are not tax-deductible. Maybe you golf to bond with clients instead of golfing for your own pleasure. If so, think of this as a work-related expense.

Don't just guess at these numbers. At first glance they may not seem substantial, but try and quantify them as much as possible. Although we are often aware of commuting time, we seldom quantify it and include it in our equations. Quantifying these numbers can be enlightening.

For example, Linda Morris was offered a $2,000 raise to transfer from her Providence, Rhode Island, office to a Newport, Rhode Island, office. So she took the raise. Who wouldn't? She now has more than an hour commute and a toll bridge to cross each way to her new job instead of a 30-minute commute to her old job. You might think that extra hour-a-day commute is worth the $2,000. But is it really?

If Linda quantified her commute in dollars, she would have achieved a very different picture of her actual bottom line. At two dollars a day for bridge tolls, she must add $520 a year for extra commuting expenses. With an extra 20 miles a day commuting each way, she needs to calculate a cost for this extra mileage and wear and tear on her car. If she uses IRS values of 30 cents for those extra miles, she will have to add $12 a day for extra wear and tear, maintenance, oil, insurance and gas. Even using a more conservative cost of 15 cents a mile, she incurs another $6 more a day than if she went to her old job. Her expenses increase another $30 a week or over $1,560 a year in extra car costs. But in addition to the extra car expenses and bridge tolls, there has to be some value placed on Linda's extra hour of commuting. If we work with conservative numbers and value commuting time at just $5 an hour, the cost for this time is an extra $25 a week. This extra $1,300 in forsaken income, in addition to the extra $1,560 of car expenses and tolls of $520, adds up to $3,380 in additional expenses, which wipes out her $2,000 raise and actually costs her $1,380. If we value her time at $10 an hour, it costs her over $2,680. Also remember **none** of these expenses are usually tax-deductible, and after taxes her raise is less than $2,000.

Too often we spend so much money on commuting, work expenses and subtle costs that our jobs just don't make sense. We should work to·support ourselves and our families, not our jobs! Yet many employees spend so much money on work-related expenses that there is nothing left to spend on themselves.

Maybe the solution for Linda would not be to give up her new raise but to consider carpooling instead. Or maybe she could take the bus, where she could use the time to study, advance her education and make herself more valuable to her employer.

To keep close track of your expenses, consider opening an asset management account. All the major brokerage houses such as Prudential Securities, Merrill Lynch, PaineWebber and Smith Barney and most major banks will have these customized accounts. These accounts provide you checks; categorize your checking and credit card activity such as lodging, travel, food and so forth; give you credit or debit cards; and allow you to borrow and invest in a wide range of securities. Every time you spend money related to your job, you can mark the small code boxes on your checks to keep track of your expenses. Your monthly statement will then break down all your expenses, so that you can get a clear picture of your net cost of working. You may find that your job costs more than you think. Asset management accounts are other tools you can use to track your work expenses and help you make job-related decisions. The best part of these accounts is that you have everything you need on one statement for your taxes, not only your job-related expenses, but also interest income, capital gains and any loan or margin costs. They also give you an automatic line of credit and a checking account that earns high money market interest rates. In addition, the interest or margin rate for borrowing is usually cheaper than with other personal lines of credit.

6 WE HAVE YOUNG CHILDREN AND ARE WORKING FULL-TIME, BUT WE CAN'T GET AHEAD. ARE THERE ANY SOLUTIONS?

Sometimes two incomes just don't add up. Studies in the early 1990s revealed that as much as 56 percent of a second income is consumed by work-related expenses for lower-income families. As families become wealthier, **the amount of work-related expenses actually increases to 68 percent,** because of higher marginal taxes, child care costs, incidental costs and professional expenses. Your pay stub may show an income of $50,000, but what you really have to show for all your hard work may be as little as $16,000 a year!

Today, working parents face the dilemma of balancing work and the needs of young children. It is not new, but more attention is focused on the problem when famous women are in the limelight, such as Marcia Clark, the prosecutor in the O.J. Simpson trial. The cost of working becomes more important, not only in terms of child custody issues such as Ms. Clark's, but also in terms of the bottom line.

To make ends meet, many parents resort to having both spouses work. For many, especially single parents, there appears to be no choice. But could some families be worse off financially when both parents work and place young children in day care? Frequently, parents think work improves their financial situation, only to find they are worse off. The fact is that many are much worse off working, and the decision to work should be evaluated carefully. **Sometimes it just doesn't pay to work.**

As with any financial decision, there are pros and cons of working. Families should create a balance sheet outlining the advantages and disadvantages. Look at the following list of pros and cons, check the ones that apply to your situation and add them to your balance sheet.

ADVANTAGES:

- ◆ Qualifying for earned-income tax credit
- ◆ Accumulation of Social Security credits
- ◆ Seniority (Studies have shown that leaves of absence are detrimental to future advancement and pay.)
- ◆ Career advancement

- ◆ Work experience
- ◆ Credibility
- ◆ Independence from welfare
- ◆ Social contacts
- ◆ Self-fulfillment
- ◆ Opportunity to increase IRA contributions
- ◆ Increased retirement assets (Women live an average of five to seven years longer than men, and their Social Security benefits in 1993, averaging $571.20 a month, were 25 percent lower than those paid to men. Therefore, retirement savings are an extremely important consideration for women.)
- ◆ Prestige
- ◆ Independence (Work allows many of the 17 million divorcees to be free from dependence on alimony.)
- ◆ Pension contributions made on your behalf by your employer
- ◆ Possible reductions in health care or life insurance costs that your policies may offer over those of your spouse
- ◆ Tax benefits resulting from your retirement contributions
- ◆ And, of course, the most obvious advantage: extra income

DISADVANTAGES:

- ◆ Child care costs
- ◆ Loss in scholarship and financial aid resulting from exceeding the limitations on income. It is difficult to get any kind of financial aid if your income tops $60,000 and almost impossible if it exceeds $100,000.
- ◆ Loss in tax advantages for U.S. savings bonds because of higher income. Lower-income families can avoid taxes on U.S. bonds if used for education. In 1995, for example, the amount of income at which the taxpayer will begin to lose a college bond interest exemption is $63,450 for married couples and $42,300 for single people.
- ◆ Extra automobile costs, including gas, wear and tear
- ◆ Household-help expenses
- ◆ Lunch and business entertaining costs
- ◆ Extra trips to fast-food restaurants and eating out with the kids

- Subtle costs, such as the extra costs associated with less time to prepare meals and to shop for bargains. Also include additional clothing costs (business clothes, dry cleaning, etc.). Add 5 to 10 percent of food and clothing budgets as an increased cost of working.
- Increased taxes resulting from lost IRA deductions. If your joint income goes over $40,000 and either spouse has a pension plan, you may lose your ability to deduct your IRAs.
- Increased taxes resulting from marriage penalty. See Question #25.
- Increased taxes resulting from lost exemptions. If your adjusted gross income for 1994, for example, was over $83,850, you need to determine how much of your exemptions will be lost.
- Increased taxes from loss of deductions. If joint adjusted gross income is over certain amounts, some of your deductions may be disallowed. Look at Schedule A of your tax return to find the amount.

After you look at a list like this, you can understand why so many working Americans just can't make ends meet. As you can see, there are many disadvantages as well as advantages to having a second income that can present a conflict for most young working couples. The sad truth is that the major factor that contributes to lower wages for working women is the fewer years they spend in the workforce. Even if a woman's current job does not pay much now, keeping it can have a big impact on the raises and promotions she might receive in the future. However, when women with young children work, 59 percent of them work in low-paying jobs with no sick leave, making it difficult when emergencies arise.

Taxes are another big concern. Don't assume that just because you are a lower-income worker taxes don't affect you. Because of the loss of earned-income credits, dual careers can be even more damaging for low-income couples. Since it can be difficult to calculate the extra taxes, make a comparison of your total tax picture with and without the second income. Complete a tax return for the primary breadwinner. Then complete your actual return. Take the entire amount of additional taxes off the secondary income. This gives you a good idea of your after-tax benefits, the full impact of lost exemptions, decreased deductions, the marriage penalty and other increased tax consequences.

Those who benefit the least are usually men and women with large day care expenses, minimum-wage jobs and minimal possibilities for career advancement. Usually, the benefits of working increase dramatically as soon as child care costs drop and when all the children are in school. Until that time, it may often be of marginal value to work.

As an alternative to work, look at tuition assistance and scholarships that might be available for your children. If you work, you may not qualify for this aid, but if you don't work, you may find you are eligible for a lot of help.

To get a true picture of what you really earn, you need to make up a worksheet and subtract out all your expenses. For many working parents, one income plus one income may not equal two; probably it will be closer to 1.32. With as much as 68 percent of your pay going to expenses, you may question if it is worth working that second job, or overtime, if your spouse is working.

 7 ARE THERE ANY DISADVANTAGES TO PART-TIME JOBS AND JOB SHARING?

More and more workers are looking for alternatives to traditional full-time employment. Job sharing and part-time jobs are attractive alternatives for many employees, but there are disadvantages also.

Job sharing and part-time work have become especially attractive for working parents. They may be single parents, or mothers and fathers who just financially cannot afford to take off several years for child rearing. Although these jobs seldom have the benefits of full-time positions, they may be your only options.

As the economy weakens, more mothers are finding it necessary to join the workforce. The Bureau of Labor Statistics estimates that 58.8 percent of women worked in 1994. Young women of child-rearing age increased their participation in the workforce from 75.1 percent in 1993 to 75.5 percent. Most women will find it difficult to catch up if they take time off in their careers. The old arguments that gender gap caused women to earn less income have been replaced with new studies that show that leaves of absence and time out of the workplace are the greatest factors in lower pay scales and slower advancement for women. However, working part-time and job-sharing programs usually do not allow either men or women to advance in their careers.

When a second full-time job does not add much, investigate some other alternatives such as flexible hours, work at home, job-sharing programs, part-time jobs, multimarketing programs and temporary work assignments. Some of these alternatives may reduce work-related expenses and actually net you more take-home pay.

PART-TIME WORK

The most popular alternative, part-time work, has many emotional and qualitative advantages associated with nurturing a young family. Working part-time may allow you to accumulate Social Security credits, as well as increase family income without incurring some of the child care and household costs that are associated with full-time work. The additional tax burden that occurs with two full-time incomes may be lessened. You may have more time to manage money and investments, as well as save on food preparation and shopping costs.

However, there are many disadvantages to part-time work. There is less career advancement potential and less attractive job alternatives. You may still incur the same transportation and work-related expenses and clothing costs associated with full-time employment while forsaking the higher income and forgoing retirement benefits. If you work less than 1,000 hours, employers can often exclude you from pension plans and other employee benefits.

But part-time work can also be rewarding and improve your financial situation if you use it creatively. You may find working part-time allows you to advance your education. Many community colleges now provide on-site day care centers at minimal costs, so although you may find this to be one more expense at a time when money is tight, you may also find it to be an opportunity of a lifetime. Also, when your income is low, you can qualify for all kinds of financial aid, scholarships, government training programs and sometimes even your part-time employer's tuition assistance programs. If you make the best use of the years you work part-time, whether it is to finish up degrees, advance technical skills, take correspondence courses or just spend time with your family, it may be a better alternative than full-time work.

Sometimes one part-time job and one full-time job may equal higher net income than two full-time jobs.

JOB SHARING

If you can't work full-time and part-time work doesn't allow you to accumulate the retirement benefits you need, then consider job sharing. Job sharing is nothing new, but is increasingly popular as employers seek inexpensive ways to keep employees happy. This hybrid approach to employment allows two or more workers to share the same job. Such arrangements can benefit both employers and employees.

The two or more individuals who share the job may not only feel more in control, but they may be financially better off than remaining in traditional part-time or full-time careers.

Job-sharing arrangements give employees flexibility, and often experience, career advancement and some fringe benefits associated with full-time employment. They also offer the same benefits as part-time employment such as more control over your time and reduced child care costs, while avoiding some of the greatest pitfalls of part-time work, such as lack of career advancement and exclusion from retirement and benefits packages.

Frequently, those with whom you share the job have different goals and needs. One job partner may need fringe benefits; the other may have a spouse with adequate benefits and can willingly forsake them. Often you can juggle hours and responsibilities so that one employee works enough to qualify for the fringe benefits while the other may be able to reduce hours sufficiently to minimize tax consequences and job-related expenses.

There are several new innovative ways to approach part-time employment through job-sharing programs. Job sharing provides many benefits to the employer as well as to employees. When you are trying to convince your employer to accept the idea of job sharing, stress that job sharers can frequently swap hours and fill in when the employer needs someone. In addition, an employer can capitalize on the strengths of both people. An employer may also be able to add on additional hours without having to add on additional benefits packages, especially if job partners can trade off benefits. Your employer will have two capable employees to call upon if he or she needs overtime or extra hours. It also may be an opportunity for your employer to have you train a new employee.

Most job-sharing arrangements require creative and motivated workers. The sharing arrangements usually develop out of the needs of the employees rather than the employer, so it is up to you to package the job yourself and sell the concept to your employer. If you are a working parent, consider a job partnership with college students. Often the job's more important assignments, as well as the fringe benefits, will still rest with the primary employee, and the student can handle the routine and less demanding work, as well as receive less benefits. Many times such arrangements benefit everyone: working parents, employers and students.

You might look for other employees in your situation who may need flexibility. Talk to the personnel department and ask them to keep you in mind when they receive applicants qualified to share your job.

Once you find a job partner, make a list of your responsibilities and assigned tasks, and prove to your employer that all of them will still be handled. Understand the negatives. Know what you are looking for in your job and make a list of what you want. Be careful that the same work-related costs of full-time employment do not apply when you reduce your hours.

8 DOES IT REALLY PAY TO WORK OVERTIME AND LONGER HOURS?

The extra income from overtime can often give us more security and allow us to vacation and spend more quality time with our families. Sometimes working overtime can make us a more valued employee. It may even increase the contributions made to retirement plans, nonqualified plans and perks. If your employer matches your 401(k) contributions, overtime can result in a big bonus in addition to the higher pay scale. If you earn over $61,200 in 1995, you may also find that you no longer have to pay the Social Security FICA OADSI portion on your additional earning (you have to pay the FICA MED, though, on all your income). That means that in addition to overtime pay, you get an extra 6.2 percent of your pay.

Working overtime may appear financially rewarding if you are a salaried employee and getting paid a lot more. For the same amount of work you normally do, you will get paid one and a half or two times as much. For most of us, that is a good deal, but for a small percentage beware! Sometimes you may find there are financial negatives accompanying working long hours and you may want to think again. By the time you get done with taxes and extra work-related costs, overtime may not pay.

There are negatives to overtime also. Overtime can make us the employee who is out of the loop, the one who doesn't show up for the softball games, the office parties and the meetings. The most obvious cost of working overtime is less time for family, hobbies, education, networking and social activities. A less obvious negative to overtime is that we become less productive the more hours we work, and burn out much faster. Workers who reduce the number of hours from 60 to 40 have been shown not only to be much more productive in the hours they do work, but to also have fewer physical and emotional problems. Working overtime can lead to a less multidimensional life.

You also might find yourself pushed into a higher marginal tax bracket. For example, if you are single and your overtime pushes your income up from the 28 percent to the 31 percent marginal tax bracket, you will be paying 31 percent of all your overtime to federal taxes and state taxes where applicable and 7.45 percent to Social Security. Your marginal taxes could increase your taxes to 43.45 percent from 41.45 percent and you will take home only 56 cents of each extra dollar you earn.

Look at the marginal tax table below so you can determine when the overtime pushes you into higher brackets.

1995

Tax Rate	Taxable Income	
	Single Income	Joint Income
15%	$1–$23,350	$1–$39,000
28%	$23,251–$56,550	$39,001–$94,250
31%	$56,551–$117,950	$94,251–$143,600
36%	$117,951–$256,500	$143,601–$256,500
39.6%	over $256,500	over $256,500

If you go over

- ◆ $40,000 joint income, you may lose part of your IRA deductions.
- ◆ $60,000, you may lose part of your ability to get financial aid for educational benefits.
- ◆ $83,800, you may lose some of your exemptions.
- ◆ $111,800, you may lose some of your deductions on schedule A.
- ◆ $63,450, you may lose the ability to cash in your U.S. savings bonds tax-free for your children's education.

It may still be financially worth working overtime, but plan carefully and reevaluate the effects on other benefits.

CHAPTER 2

Increasing Your Real Income

9   **AM I THROWING MONEY AWAY BY NOT PARTICIPATING IN MATCHING-DOLLAR PROGRAMS?**

Yes. If you do not participate in matching programs you are throwing dollars away! With matching programs your employer contributes a percentage of your contributions to retirement plans. If a stranger offered you $1 for every dollar you put in your savings account, would you do it? Or if you knew a guaranteed way to double your money, would you try it?

Matching programs in retirement plans such as 401(k)s and SARSEPs (Salary Reduction/Simplified Employee Pension Plans) are ways that you can often double your money with little or no risk.

Your employer does not always have to match your contribution, but usually will do so to entice you into contributing. To qualify as a retirement plan, 401(k) plans will require a certain percentage of worker participation and so companies will usually offer as high a matching amount as needed to entice employees to participate in the plans.

Sometimes employers will match as much as dollar for dollar. This means you double your money the first year. In addition you will defer your federal and state taxes on the amount you contribute, possibly postponing 39.6 percent of your federal taxes and even as high as 45 percent for both state and federal taxes on the money you contribute.

Let's assume you earn $25,000 a year and are single, you are in the 28 percent federal marginal tax bracket and the 5 percent state tax bracket, and for every dollar you put into your 401(k), your employer will match $1. Your $1,000 contribution immediately increases to $2,000. You will be paying taxes now on $24,000 not on the $25,000 that you earn. You defer $330 in taxes. For simplicity's sake, we will assume there are no other factors to consider when calculating taxes. These contributions are not tax-free but tax-deferred and you will have to pay the taxes when you withdraw the funds. But now you have $2,000 working for you and earning tax-deferred interest. At 10 percent you will have $200 of interest in your 401(k). But there is more. Your $330 in current tax savings can earn interest also. After taxes it earns $22. Your total current benefits equal $2,552.

If you didn't put your $1,000 in your 401(k), you would only have about $670 after taxes. Even if you saved this and earned the same 10 percent interest or $67, you wouldn't be able to keep it all, and you would have to pay taxes on the $67. Saving outside the plan, you would only have approximately $45 in after-tax earnings. On interest alone, the 401(k) pays you an *extra* $155 the first year.

WATCH WHAT HAPPENS TO THE SAME $1,000 WITH A MATCHING CONTRIBUTION IN A RETIREMENT PLAN AND OUTSIDE A RETIREMENT PLAN.

In a 401(k)
$1,000 in
↓

+ $1,000 matching contribution
+ $ 330 tax-deferred savings
+ $ 200 interest earned on contributions
+ $ 22 interest earned on tax savings

↓
$2,552 out

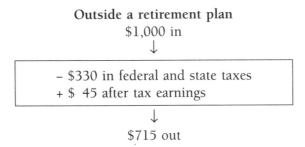

Outside a retirement plan
$1,000 in
↓

– $330 in federal and state taxes
+ $ 45 after tax earnings

↓
$715 out

The magic of matching contributions in 401(k)s and SARSEPs can lead to almost three and a half times as much current assets for the same amount of money, and depending on your tax bracket when you retire, more than twice as much.

Sometimes your employer may offer very little, and you may not feel the matching contribution is worth it. Even if your employer offers as little as 25 cents for each $1 you contribute, that in itself equates to a 25 percent return on your investment that year. Wouldn't you be happy if you could get 25 percent interest on a savings account?

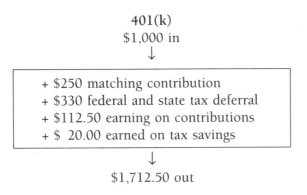

401(k)
$1,000 in
↓

+ $250 matching contribution
+ $330 federal and state tax deferral
+ $112.50 earning on contributions
+ $ 20.00 earned on tax savings

↓
$1,712.50 out

Even if your employer matches only 25 cents for every dollar, you still come out with more than the $715 you would have outside a retirement plan.

There is a catch, however. There always is when something looks too good to be true. When you pull the money out of tax-deductible retirement plans, you will have to pay taxes on your contributions. If your tax bracket is lower, you will actually experience true tax savings. But even if your tax bracket is the same, you will come out ahead, for postponing the taxes allows you to earn money on that tax-deferred income. Because everyone's situation is unique, have your tax adviser calculate the actual tax consequences for you.

Another disadvantage to 401(k)s is that most restrict your investment choices so you do not have the liquidity, freedom and selection of investments that you do when you save outside the plan. SARSEPs are similar to 401(k) plans, but are only for small companies with less than 25 employees. These plans allow you to select any investment you want, so you have more investment diversification. Also, for the very wealthy, contributing too much could result in an excess penalty when you pull the money out. In addition, some states do not have income taxes and some don't allow you to deduct these contributions from your state taxes. However, for most of us, it's important not to miss out on such opportunities. Take 401(k) magic seriously. Some general rules to remember when saving money:

◆ Save two months in emergency funds.
◆ Save in 401(k)s to the maximum possible.
◆ Save in IRAs, but only after you have made the maximum contributions to your 401(k).
◆ Save on taxes. Save in tax-sheltered accounts.
◆ If your plan has a matching element, save at least up to that amount. If you don't, you will be throwing away free money.
◆ If you have large credit card debt, pay that off before you contribute more than the matching amount.

Ideally, it's best to always save as much as possible in pension and retirement plans, but frequently we need the cash flow and can't. Contribute to these plans as much as possible. It's worthwhile to note that 60 percent of 401(k) plans allows you to borrow money in an emergency, so unlike some other retirement plans, you may have access to these funds.

10 SHOULD I PARTICIPATE IN AUTOMATIC SAVINGS PLANS?

As a country we have one of the lowest savings rates in the world. Though the savings rate was up in 1995 to 2.9 percent, on average our savings rate is around 2 percent.

Why do we save so little? Critics blame our tax system, saying it does not give us enough incentives to save. I'm not sure about that. I think most of us just don't know what incentives there are, and many are so complicated that we do not understand them. Others say it is because baby boomers look at their parents who seem to be able to survive on Social Security and pensions and assume they can do the same. In countries without Social Security and retirement systems, like Japan, most workers assume that they will be responsible for their own retirement, and the savings rate has been as much as five to six times as high as that in the United States.

But even if we realized that the government and our employers would probably not be able to provide for us in retirement, would we save more? Most analysts think not. They claim Americans want immediate gratification and do not have long-term horizons, that they live for today and do not think about the future. Others feel that we can't afford to save; after taxes and basic insurance there is just nothing left. No matter what the reason, most of us find it difficult to save. Something always comes up and we forgo our savings plans. However, we must save, and we can no longer rely on our employers, families or the government to provide for us in emergencies and retirement. We can't even be sure that we will receive anticipated Social Security benefits.

Social Security is changing for the worse.

- Retirement benefits are being taxed more, up from 50 percent to 85 percent.
- Cost of living indexes (COLAs) that allow benefits to keep up with inflation, will gradually be reduced.
- You won't be able to retire as early as previous generations. You will have to work longer to qualify for full benefits.

Since we will have to work longer, receive smaller benefits and pay more taxes on those benefits, we can no longer expect Social Security or other retirement benefits to provide a secure future. Most of our retirement income must come from our own personal savings. The savings rate in the United States is so low that **96 percent of Americans will not have a financially secure retirement.**

There is a way to save that is easy and rewarding: the automatic payroll deduction savings plan offered by your employer. If you did not sign up when you were first hired, you should go to your benefits department and ask about payroll deduction plans.

By doing it automatically, rather than trying to force ourselves to regularly put something aside each payday, we are more likely to continue saving month after month. Financial planners have discovered that automatic payroll-deduction plans not only are the easiest ways to save, but they also create the greatest likelihood of continuity in savings. If savers start with a small amount and increase it over the years, after a while most do not even notice the reduction in their paycheck and hardly miss that money set aside for their future.

Start small, then increase the deduction as you grow comfortable with it. For example, start by saving $25 a month. After several months, you should be able to readjust your budget and spending habits to live without the $25. Once you get comfortable and learn you can live without the $25, then you can increase the amount to $35. At first you might notice, but you will be surprised at how soon you adjust.

Is it worth it to save a little a month? **YES!** If you save as little as $50 a month for 20 years, you will have $28,633 (at an 8 percent effective annual yield). Save $100 a month and you will have over $57,266! This means at retirement, if you just spent the interest on your savings, you could have an extra $4,581 a year in income. If you continue for 30 years, it could be over $141,761 and you could add an additional $11,341 a year to your retirement income. If you save $100 a month for 41 years at 12 percent, you will be a millionaire.

11 WHEN IS THE BEST TIME TO SIGN UP FOR BENEFITS AND SAVINGS PLANS?

Immediately! Sign up as soon as possible, on the very first day of work, on your very first job. If you start early enough, even small amounts of money can increase your wealth. Start with $75 a month, or $900 a year at age 22, and you may retire a millionaire.

LET TIME DO THE WORK

By saving early, you let time and compound interest do the work. If you are young and you save $42 a month or $500 a year in retirement accounts, you can look forward to a financially rewarding future. If you started saving when you were 17 years old and saved $42 a month in retirement plans, you could be a millionaire or close to it by retirement. If you earn 11 percent, you will have over three quarters of a million dollars at age 65. If you earn 12 percent, you can retire a millionaire. All for $42 a month! If you save $2,000 a year in a tax-deferred account, you will have over $4.3 million! A million dollars will not be worth as much, but it sure beats being poor.

Saving early also means contributing money to a savings plan earlier in the year rather than later. If you invested $2,000 for 35 years on January 1st instead of December 31st each year, at an interest rate of 10 percent, you could earn $40,000 more upon retirement.

My husband and I were able to take advantage of an early savings plan to help our daughter Allyson ensure a comfortable retirement income. When Allyson graduated from college, she went immediately into doing volunteer work at homeless shelters in Los Angeles, Guatemala and then Mexico. As a volunteer she earns only $75 a month! As a student, she spent the bulk of her time working in volunteer programs. As parents we were proud of her, but we became painfully aware that Allyson would never have a well-paying job and never have any kind of retirement or future security. Our only hope was to contribute as early as possible to an IRA for her. The maximum you can contribute to an IRA is 100 percent of a wage earner's income up to $2,000, and since Allyson's income was only $900 a year, that was all we could gift to her IRA. Doesn't sound like enough to retire wealthy on, does it? However, $900 a year can accumulate. If we can continue to add $900 for ten years in a good mutual fund that averages 12 percent a year, she will have $17,680. If we never add another dollar and the money is left to compound until Allyson retires, in 37 years it will grow to over 1.1 million dollars ($1,170,978).

Even if she works the rest of her life for a below minimum wage salary, if inflation isn't high, our total contribution of $9,000 will lead to a financially solvent retirement. Of course, the wild cards are inflation and the rate of return we can earn. Still, at least it gives us some hope that someday she will have some retirement income.

Automatic savings programs work because money you do not see and keep separate from your everyday checking account is likely to grow year after year untouched.

12 HOW DO I KNOW WHICH SAVINGS PLANS ARE BEST FOR ME?

There are many good employer-sponsored savings programs. Before you choose your saving plans, determine how much time you have to save and your goals. Many of us have a variety of time frames and goals. If this is true for you, you should participate in several different savings programs. Here are a few commonsense steps to make savings easier:

- ◆ Make a time map, listing different events in your life for which you have to save.
- ◆ Determine how long you can wait before you pull out your savings.
- ◆ Determine how much savings you will need for each event, i.e., car purchase, house repairs, children's education, an emergency fund and so forth.
- ◆ Divide your savings into three categories:
  1. Short-term emergency funds (usually two months' worth of income)
  2. Intermediate savings for items such as children's education, houses and autos
  3. Long-term retirement savings

SAVING FOR LONG-TERM GOALS AND RETIREMENT

- ◆ For retirement savings, look at all the pension and retirement options available to you, such as 401(k)s, IRAs, SARSEPs, other pretax pension programs and deferred-compensation plans. Ninety-five percent of large companies (companies with over 5,000 employees) offer these plans. As we have already discussed, these plans and IRAs are usually the best types of savings programs for retirement.
- ◆ If your retirement is many years away, consider growth-oriented investments such as aggressive growth stock funds, international funds, value funds, index funds, as well as natural resource and blue chip funds. Your age and how long you

can save is the first factor in determining where you invest. Although the value of the stocks will fluctuate more than CDs, guaranteed accounts and bank savings accounts, historically stocks have returned much higher yields. The volatility diminishes in importance over the long run. We will look at these investments in much more depth in Chapter 6.

◆ If you are retiring soon, start shifting to more income investments and consider Guaranteed Insurance Contracts (GICs) and guaranteed funds.

◆ Most importantly, use employer-sponsored savings plans whenever possible. Ask your employer to sign you up. It is simple, and you will be on your way to building a healthy financial future with maximum simplicity.

INTERMEDIATE SAVINGS

◆ For savings between one to ten years, sign up for automatic savings plans that send funds to mutual funds or U.S. savings bond programs.

◆ If the savings are for five years or less, stay with safer, more balanced mutual funds, CDs, Treasury notes, municipal bonds, asset allocation and utility funds.

◆ If the savings are for events in five to ten years, you may want to add 50 percent to more growth-oriented stock mutual funds.

One of the most popular employer-sponsored savings options is the U.S. savings bond program. This is one of the easiest and safest ways to invest. There have been many changes in these bonds lately, but they remain attractive savings for goals in the five- and ten-year range. Because of recent changes in calculating the interest rates, these bonds are no longer so attractive for short-term emergency savings, but they are still appropriate for your intermediate savings plans.

Find out the current rates for savings bonds by calling 1-800-487-2663, or ask your employer or local bank for the Treasury Department brochure. You can also write the Bureau of Public Debt, Division of Customer Services, Washington, DC 20239 (202-874-4000). For information on rates on older bonds, ask for Form PD 3600 from The Bureau of the Public Debt, Parkersburg, WV 26106.

SHORT-TERM SAVINGS

◆ For your emergency fund, save two months in money market or Treasury bills. For short-term emergency funds, the important thing to remember is that you want these funds to be *liquid, easy to get at and risk-free.*

◆ For medical expenses of less than one year that you can predict, sign up for flexible savings accounts (FSAs). FSAs allow you to set money aside for medical and child care expenses. These plans are especially attractive because they allow you to save on a pretax basis.

◆ For predictable child care expenses, also sign up for your employer's flexible savings accounts. We will talk a lot more about these in Question #18, but they are a great way to save for regular medical and dependent care expenses.

◆ For predictable events, invest in brokerage CDs or short-term municipal bonds and Treasury securities.

13 WHEN SHOULD I ASK FOR A RAISE?

When you are trying to negotiate a raise, several important factors should be considered. Many good books have been written on topics such as: how to ask for raises; how to meet with management; how to prepare yourself; and how to negotiate. We will discuss instead **when** to ask for a raise and **what** type of raise to ask for.

◆ **Look at the economy.** When the economy is improving, it is usually a good time to ask for a raise. Consider how your company fits into the economy, and if the current economic picture will help the profit margins.

◆ **Look at your company's profits.** Is your company growing and improving in profitability? If yes, then this may be a good time to go for that raise. If you cannot negotiate a cash raise, consider stock options. In growing companies, these can be your best choice.

◆ **Look at the unemployment numbers and layoffs.** If there are large pools of unemployed, it is difficult to ask for a raise, especially if you have skills that can be replaced easily from the unemployed ranks. However, if you feel you add value to the company, ask for that raise, but do it in a way that might not cost your employer much initially.

- ◆ **When other employees are getting raises.** If the rest of the employees are getting raises and you are at least as competent as the average employee, then this could be a good time to move. If there is an increase in wages in the economy at large, then you may also find your employer more likely to offer raises.

- ◆ **When inflation is increasing.** Your employer is less likely to be concerned about cost constraints if inflation is increasing, and if he or she can pass the cost of giving you a raise onto the consumer.

- ◆ **Look at unions and their ability to get big increases.** If you are not in the union, your company may believe it is important to minimize the disparity between nonunion and union workers. So, after the union gets its raises, it might be a good time for you to ask for one.

- ◆ **After an apparent success.** After you receive some strong recognition, a reward, a favorable public-relations piece, a new educational degree or complete a training course, it's always a good time to pave the way for a raise by making sure your employer is aware of your success.

- ◆ **When competitors are giving raises and when the industry is profitable.** If your company's competitors are giving raises, in order to retain employees and reduce turnover, your employer may be willing to give a raise.

WHAT TYPE OF RAISE SHOULD I ASK FOR?

Match your raise to your company's profit potential. Remember, even when the economy or profits do not look that great, you can still ask for a raise. Just match the type of raise to the circumstances.

- ◆ **When your company is facing weak profits.** If the company's profits have just fallen miserably, and you are the one who can actually improve your company's productivity level, ask for a performance raise instead of a straight salary raise.

- ◆ **Executive turnover.** If your company is going through a major turnover with a lot of its best people jumping ship, you may want to negotiate a substantial deferred-compensation package instead, showing your commitment to the company and your willingness to prove your loyalty to it. When your company wants loyalty, it also may be willing to give restricted stock.

◆ **Weak economy.** When the economy is weak and profits are erratic, you may find your employer afraid to give raises but he or she may be willing to give a one-time bonus, a deferred-compensation plan, incentive packages or stock options.

◆ **Profits are volatile.** If you cannot ask for a raise because company profits are very volatile—up one year, down the next—then ask for a bonus. In volatile times employers do not like to commit to long-term pay increases, but may be willing to give a one-time bonus that they can renegotiate later.

◆ **Employees costs are high.** Your employer may not want to increase all the other benefits costs, Social Security costs, unemployment costs and retirement packages that go with a salary increase. If you cannot negotiate a salary increase in these situations, consider nonqualified plans or a tax-deferred compensation plan. This can be even more attractive for you. A raise may actually hurt your after-tax income, but a retirement plan that is not taxable now could enhance your total wealth. You may find a tax-deferred plan is more attractive to both you and your employer. Ask your tax adviser to run some comparisons for you.

◆ **When cash-poor and your company is struggling**, ask for stock options instead of cash. When the company wants you to be more responsive to its needs, it may be willing to offer profit-sharing programs.

◆ **When the economy is strong and your company is healthy.** When your company is doing well and has large profits, cash and wage increases are likely alternatives.

HOW MUCH OF A RAISE SHOULD YOU ASK FOR?

Find out what typical raises are in your company.

◆ Look at others in your position with the same amount of time on the job.

◆ Ask fellow employees. Although many are afraid to divulge such information, if you make it a two-way street, it is easier to get the information. If you are an executive for a major corporation, you should have no trouble comparison shopping. The information is public.
◆ Look at industry pay scales.
◆ Look at Department of Labor reports at the library.

14 SHOULD I ASK FOR A RAISE OR FOR MORE BENEFITS?

Save taxes, take benefits instead of cash.

Often one of the best ways to reduce your taxes is to negotiate with your employer to take benefits packages instead of pay increases. Work closely with your tax adviser and evaluate the pros and cons of various benefits packages.

The type of raise you should negotiate will not only depend on what you want, but also on the economy. If the economy is weak, you may want to negotiate performance pay as mentioned previously. But when the economy is weak, you may find your employer more amenable to nonqualified plans and benefits rather than raises.

Before you ask for that raise, be sure you understand what you want it for. If it is to generate immediate income, then cash may be the best alternative. If, however, you want a raise because you feel you deserve it, or because under new government rules your retirement plans have been cut, or to increase your wealth and net assets, or to start saving for a healthy retirement, or for your children's education, then you should take a second look and consider benefits instead of cash.

Many employee benefits are nonnegotiable and must pass strict IRS rules. But other perks and benefits can be given to select employees in lieu of cash.

If your taxes are high and you want to increase your total worth, not your current paycheck, consider nonqualified plans, deferred-compensation plans, split-dollar insurance plans, ESOPs and severance savings plans. If you have special family needs, you may want to consider negotiating company-sponsored family moves, dining privileges, etc.

Nonqualified Plans. These retirement plans can allow you or your employer to contribute money that will grow tax-deferred. Although you don't get tax deductions from your pay as you would with qualified plans, these plans can be very attractive.

Since the new tax laws only allow contributions for profit-sharing, money purchase, 401(k) and other retirement plans on income up to $150,000, many high-income employees have seen their contributions decrease substantially. In the past, the income limits were $236,000. These changes have created a flood of new nonqualified plans, excess plans, supplemental retirement plans, target plans and so forth. Even if you are not in the top income levels, you may find one suitable to your current needs.

Deferred-Compensation Plans. If you don't need the money now, but are trying to build a future nest egg, consider deferred-compensation plans. These plans allow you to postpone bonuses and pay increases until you retire. Not only do they minimize current income taxes, but your funds grow much quicker and you build a much larger nest egg since these funds grow tax-deferred.

These plans may be difficult to negotiate for they are not tax-deductible for your employer. However, if it is in lieu of a salary raise, your company may consider it, especially when profits are low and tax deductions are not important to your company.

Be careful. These plans are not under your control, and if your company falls on hard times, the plans are exposed to your company's creditors. If you have a lot of faith in your company's future health, opt for deferred-compensation plans. If you believe your company is vulnerable to bad times, take the cash.

Performance and Incentive Programs. If raises are difficult to come by because of hard economic times for your company, negotiate a performance bonus or performance-based pay instead. It is common for senior executives to receive as much as 45 percent of compensation based on performance pay. Companies feel comfortable with this concept, since they get what they pay for. Performance pay was only 21 percent in 1985, and increased to 37 percent by 1989. By 1993 it was 45 percent, and it is still growing.

Severance Savings Plans. If you are afraid of losing your job, consider severance savings packages. Athol Cochrane, CLU, an authority on retirement planning, explains that under IRS code 419 (A), your employer can set up plans to put aside as much as 20 percent of your income in case of cutbacks or forced early retirement. If you feel your job is at risk and that you may be caught in a cutback, these plans are very attractive. They are one of the best-kept benefits secrets and a way to prepare for terminations, cutbacks, poor economic conditions, etc.

These plans fund early-retirement packages and severance pay packages and can add security to your life without increasing your taxable income.

Many of these plans are not funded and management may terminate them. Frequently, the funds are placed in rabbi trusts (named after a case involving a rabbi's retirement trust) that protect the assets from management changes. These plans, as all insurance plans, do not pay off unless the risk you are insuring for occurs, so you must be involuntarily terminated for them to pay off.

Split-Dollar Insurance. This perk used to be for highly compensated employees only, but now even lower-income employees can utilize it. These policies allow you to build a large nest egg, often larger than any other single method. You and your employer split the premium costs of a large insurance policy. At termination, you and your employer also split the value of the policy. Your employer gets the premiums back, and you get a flexible retirement package. There is no limit to these plans, and your funds grow tax-deferred in either a whole life policy or variable life policy. You can take the funds out before you reach 59½ without penalty since the withdrawals are considered loans.

Company Stock. In lieu of wages or as part of your salary, your company may offer you stocks. This can be attractive if you work for a young, growing company. But it can also be risky, if stocks are offered when the company is facing hard times or bankruptcy. Or you may be given an option to buy stock within a certain time frame. Sometimes these options or stocks come with restrictions and if you do not stay with the company for a certain amount of years, you will lose these stocks (called golden handcuffs). You may also be given an option to purchase the stocks at a discount, typically 15 percent.

You may want to consider taking Employee Stock and Option Plans (ESOPs) instead of cash, especially if you work for a growing profitable company. You have to pay taxes when you exercise options or sell them, but you may be able to gift them to your children and family members or even charities, and avoid much of the tax.

If you have company stock and you know you will be spending money on college expenses for your children or your elderly parents, don't sell the stock to raise funds. Instead, have your company transfer the stocks to your child or parent. If they are in lower tax brackets, you can save as much as 30 percent, maybe even 44 percent in taxes.

Excess Plans. Because of the tax codes and recent tax changes, highly compensated employees may have a much smaller percentage of income allocated to retirement plans than lower-paid employees. In order to balance out this inequity, many employers will contribute to special retirement plans to restore benefits to previous percentage levels. Other plans can target a certain amount of income for you to receive in retirement. These plans can run into trouble, however, if your employer goes bankrupt and creditors come after the assets.

Supplemental Executive Retirement Plan. In addition to current income, you may face a 15 percent excise tax on excess qualified plan accumulations. Typical retirement plans may not work for you. With Supplemental Executive Retirement plans, your employer agrees to provide death, disability and retirement benefits that are usually funded through insurance policies. Such insurance plans allow you to take out income without 10 percent penalties for early withdrawals and no excise tax for excessive distributions. In addition, the income grows tax-free until you receive it.

15 CAN SOME EMPLOYER BENEFITS PLANS REALLY MAKE ME RICH?

One of the easiest ways to assure wealth and a comfortable retirement is to start saving in pension and retirement plans. And if you are lucky enough to work for a successful company and participate in their stock purchase and stock option plans, you can increase your wealth considerably.

Over the years I have met countless hardworking Americans with good jobs who, year after year, contributed to pension plans, participated in stock option and stock purchase plans and have become extremely wealthy. If a gentleman who has worked for a major railroad for 30 years keeps saving at the rate he is saving now, he will retire with pensions and related stocks of over $2 million. Is he a senior executive with a high-paying job? Not really. In fact, he just started making over $55,000 this year. Saving the maximum in pensions and retirement plans and being fortunate enough to work for good companies bring you the greatest financial rewards. It is one of the reasons why you should be selective when picking the companies for which to work. If you have the choice of working for a good company that lets you share in its future with stock options, versus a weaker unexciting company that offers better pay, choose the good company with stock and participate in stock option plans.

While some benefits can make you rich, you have to be selective. The most likely benefits to increase your wealth are stock option plans, split-dollar insurance, pension plans, performance pay, stock-matching plans and nonqualified retirement plans. But they are also the riskiest, so use common sense and work with your tax and financial advisers. You may even need to work with your legal adviser for some of these benefits.

16 ARE ESOPs RISKY?

Yes. But they still should be looked at and probably be a part of your financial plan.

ESOPs have gained a lot of publicity because of the failures of Eastern Airlines and Pan-Am and the troubles at Avis. As the economy weakens, more ESOPs will fall upon hard times. ESOPs are only as good as your company. If your company goes out of business, you can lose a large part of your savings, and possibly end up with little or no retirement funds. If you work for a strong healthy company, such as Kellogg's or Coca-Cola, then your ESOP can be an extremely attractive way to make you wealthy.

An ESOP is usually set up as a profit-sharing plan in which annual contributions to each employee's account is made in the form of company stock. The amount of stock you receive depends on how profitable your company is. If the company is very profitable, you will receive more stocks. If the company is not profitable, you may receive nothing.

Typically, ESOPs combine money purchase plans for 10 percent with profit-sharing plans for 15 percent. These funds grow tax-deferred until you withdraw them at retirement.

Sometimes your entire employer's contribution to your pension may consist of company stocks, your money purchase plan as well as your profit-sharing plan. This can be dangerous. If you have a large amount of your net worth invested in company stock, then you should consider diversifying the rest of your assets. Even if you are invested in profitable companies such as IBM, you may find that even the best of the best companies can fall on hard times.

ESOPs are an ideal way for cash-strapped companies to reward their employees. Also, such plans can create a sense of partnership between you and your employer. You are much more likely to stay with a company that you feel a part of, or own a share in, through an ESOP. E-Systems, a large electronics manufacturer, saw its turnover rate drop 36 percent after two years into its ESOP plan.

The key is picking the right employer. It is the most important decision you can make when it comes to financial rewards. The best companies usually are those that are at the forefront of technology, positioned in growing markets and have a clear, well-defined niche. They can also be small companies that have great management and a clever idea. Recently, Toledo's Textile Lather Corporation, with 300 employees who were worker-owners, sold their company. They all earned tens of thousands of dollars, averaging up to $60,000 each.

But there also are the ESOP horror stories, such as those employees who lost the bulk of their retirement and wealth when Eastern Airlines collapsed.

Thousands of large and small companies offer ESOP plans. You may find these plans being used as qualified retirement plans in which your funds compound tax-deferred. If your company pays a large dividend, this can be attractive. If, however, you work for a young growth company, it would be more attractive to have such low-taxed stocks in individual accounts and more income-oriented investments in your pension.

ESOPs do not have to fulfill the requirements for diversification that most pension plans must. ESOP trusts are similar to conventional profit-sharing plans, except that they generally are invested in qualifying employer securities. A typical profit-sharing plan may include CDs, GICs and mutual funds, but an ESOP plan will usually have the bulk of its investments in your company's stock. With these plans, you, the employee, are assuming the risk for poor performance of your company. These plans are not defined-benefits plans that guarantee an income for life and assume all the investment risks.

When you retire or reach the age of 59½, you can take the stocks out in a lump sum or roll them over into an IRA and take monthly or regular distributions.

What if you leave before you are 59½? If you are vested, the stocks will still be yours, but if you do not roll them over into an IRA, you will have to pay a 10 percent penalty for early withdrawal. The stocks will be treated as ordinary income, so you will also pay federal and state income taxes on them. Be especially careful if you take out large sums at a time, for you may not qualify for ten-year averaging, and such distributions can easily push you into higher marginal tax brackets. These plans are treated just like any other retirement plans.

Vesting schedules also apply to your ESOP as to other retirement plans. Before you consider changing jobs, check the vesting dates and hold off on that move if you are not quite vested yet.

HOW DO I KNOW WHAT
MY ESOP IS WORTH?

You should receive a statement from your employer showing the number of shares that you have in your plan. This statement will also show you your vesting dates and the market value of the stock. Every day the market value changes, so the easiest way to calculate your current value is to multiply the number of shares by your vested percent by the stock price.

For publicly traded companies, it is easy to get the stock price by looking up the price in any large newspaper. However, private companies are much more difficult to evaluate. You will have to look at periodic independent audits. Then, you will have to evaluate if the company's bottom line appears better or worse since the last audit.

There are several types of stock ownership programs:

◆ *Incentive Stock Options.* Incentive stock options may be better for executives than nonqualified plans. These are taxed when you sell at the maximum capital gains rate of 28 percent versus ordinary income tax rates that can be as high as 39.6 percent. You usually have to hold them for two years, and their sale might trigger the alternative minimum tax, but still the timing of the sale of these stocks can make them very attractive.

◆ *Nonqualified stock options.* The gains on these shares are taxed as if they came out of a retirement plan at ordinary income rates.

◆ *Performance Stocks and Options.* These are used to help motivate workers to think about the company's profits. They are given out gradually as the corporate goals are met.

◆ *Stock Option Transfers.* These allow you to pass any unexercised options to someone else without paying gift or estate taxes and therefore are very attractive for high–net worth employees.

17 WHAT CAN I DO TO REDUCE THE TAXES TAKEN FROM MY PAYCHECK?

It's not what you make that counts; it's what you keep. If you live in New York or Connecticut, you have to work three hours and nine minutes each day just to pay your taxes. An average American has to work two hours and 46 minutes just to pay taxes. In 1985, you only had to work two hours and 38 minutes, but in 1945 you only had to work for one hour and 59 minutes. As taxes keep going up, we are seeing more and more pressure on wages to stay down. Review the tax-saving tips in Question #2:

◆ Claim all the withholding allowances that you are allowed.
◆ Contribute the maximum in any 401(k)s, SARSEPS or retirement plans.
◆ Sign up for pretax saving accounts if you have child care and day care expenses.
◆ Contribute to nonqualified plans and IRAs. Even though you will not see the difference in your paychecks, you will see it on your tax returns.
◆ Participate in deferred-compensation plans.

◆ Negotiate with your employer any tax-free benefits, non-qualified plans and other tax-sheltered alternatives in lieu of cash raises.
◆ Time your bonuses and raises.
◆ Have financial, estate and tax plans.
◆ If you have appreciated company stock and know you will be spending money either on college expenses for your children or caring for your elderly parents, don't sell the stock to raise funds. Instead have your company transfer the stock to your child or parent. If they are in lower tax brackets, you can save as much as 30 percent, maybe even 44 percent in taxes.
◆ Gift your lowest-cost basis stock, probably your oldest. Make sure that when you transfer the stock, you keep records for the IRS of the exact shares you are selling, the dates they were purchased and the certificate numbers if possible. If you are married, you can give up to $20,000 to each person.
◆ Gift your company stock rather than cash to charities. If you tithe or give regularly to a church or charity, you can save substantial amounts by gifting stock rather than cash. By gifting stock, you have more to give charity, avoid capital gains taxes and reduce the risk of having all your assets exposed to your company stock.
◆ If you are lucky enough to have large amounts of company stock, consider the possibility of setting up a charitable remainder trust. These trusts allow you to gift the stock to the charity's trust. You can draw income out of the trust for as long as you or your beneficiary live. In addition, you avoid all capital gains, get a charitable deduction and receive income, sometimes even more than you would have if you sold the stock. Let's say you have $200,000 of company stock that has doubled over the years (that's very likely, good stocks double in value every six to seven years). You sell the stock, pay $40,000 in taxes and you are left with $160,000 to invest in 8 percent government bonds. Your gross income is $12,800 a year before taxes. Instead, if you gifted the stock to a charity, the charity can sell it, keep the $200,000 and invest in the same 8 percent bonds. Then it can give you $16,000 a year in income. In addition, you will save substantial amounts on your taxes, not only because you didn't have to pay the $40,000 in

capital gains taxes, but also you may get a substantial deduction for a charitable gift.

18 HOW DO FLEXIBLE SAVINGS ACCOUNTS DECREASE MY TAXES?

You can reduce your taxes and give yourself a raise by letting your employer help you pay your medical bills. Remember April 15th? You probably had neat little piles of medical receipts that you collected all year long. You thought you could write them off and save on taxes. When buying glasses, or running to the orthodontist, or filling prescriptions, you cringed at the cost, but at least you thought it would help at tax time. But now you discover you were wrong! If they don't add up to more than 7.5 percent of your adjusted gross income, there is no write-off.

Suddenly, you are painfully aware that the tax changes enacted over the past few years have eliminated many of your deductions and write-offs. Even if you are in a low tax bracket and use the standard deductions, you won't get to write off all those medical expenses.

What about day care? Again, the higher your income, the less you can write off and the tax credit may be of minimal benefit.

There is a way to get tax relief for these medical expenses and dependent care expenses if your employer has an FSA. Since over 60 percent of large companies have these plans, it is likely you will be able to take advantage of one of the most overlooked of employee benefits.

If your company doesn't have an FSA, discuss the possibility with your employer or benefits department. Except for administration costs, which can be minimal, these accounts are some of the most inexpensive benefits an employer can offer. Most employers will make these plans available if workers express an interest in them. Even smaller companies can implement these accounts inexpensively.

An FSA offers you an opportunity to set aside pretax dollars to pay for medical and dependant care expenses. Since you don't pay taxes on these dollars, you have more money to spend and you are, in effect, giving yourself more disposable income or a raise. An FSA is simply a pretax saving account that your employer arranges for you. Each month your employer deducts the amount you designate from your paycheck.

Let's look at the pros and cons of participating in an FSA:

Pros: Tax savings!

- On a pretax basis you can save up to a combined total of $7,500 for medical and dependent care ($5,000 maximum for dependent care).
- You have to earn $11,538 at a 35 percent tax bracket to pay $7,500 of medical bills. But in an FSA you only need to earn $7,500, so you get $4,038 gross income to spend. It's like getting a raise!
- Payments are easy through automatic payroll deductions.
- Filing claims are simple and you get paid immediately, unlike typical insurance claims.

Cons:

- You must plan carefully. If you overestimate your expenses and save too much, you will have to forfeit the unused funds. For example, if you save $7,500 but only incur expenses of $7,000, then you must forfeit $500.
- You must sign up and make a commitment in the previous year, sometimes before you have a good idea of what your next year's expenses will be.
- You cannot change the amounts during the year.
- You must have two separate accounts, one for medical FSA and one for dependent care FSA, and unfortunately you can not move funds from one to the other.
- Your total contributions may be reduced by the cost of medical coverage. For example, if your medical plan costs $69 a month or $828 a year, your maximum annual amount may be only $6,672 for other expenses. In addition, if your income is over certain limits, the allowed dependant care contributions may be lowered.
- Since these contributions reduce your income, if other benefits are based on income, they may also be reduced. In addition, since there is no Social Security paid on these contributions, it may actually reduce the Social Security benefits you ultimately receive. If you are close to retirement, this

should be a consideration. However, if you are young, usually a dollar saved today is worth more than a Social Security dollar that may never be paid many years from now.

◆ Since these accounts receive special IRS treatment, they can't be changed unless there is a change in your family status.

Because of the tax savings, these plans are beneficial, but the possibility of forfeiting excess payments and the reduction of future Social Security payments make it important to evaluate contributions carefully.

19 HOW CAN I MAKE SURE I AM NOT MAKING COSTLY MISTAKES ON MY TAXES?

There are thousands of mistakes that workers make on their tax returns. You should sit down with a tax adviser, maybe an independent tax consultant rather than your accountant, and go through your return to make sure you are not missing out on valuable tax-saving strategies as well as making errors on your return.

To start, here is a list of simple things you can look for yourself. You don't have to understand all the calculations to catch some of these errors, just the overall concepts.

1. **Not receiving a refund.** This past year, 92,200 Americans never received over $54 million in refunds because they did not notify the IRS of address changes or they forgot to include their addresses. The refunds also got lost in the mail. The average refund was over $586.
   Solution: If you don't receive your refund within nine weeks of filing, call the IRS.

2. **Failure to deduct IRA contributions.** Many times, taxpayers assume they can't deduct their IRA contributions because they have pensions. That is not so. If you have joint income under $40,000 and single income under $25,000, you can still get a full deduction. You can get a partial deduction if you are filing jointly and your income is between $40,000 and $50,000 and you are single with income between $25,000 to $35,000. If your IRA is nondeductible, you may still want to contribute because

of the tax deferral, but you should maximize your contributions to deductible 401(k), SARSEP or 403(B) plans first.

Solution: On your 1040 form, look at line 23a for your deduction and line 23b for your spouse's deduction. If you are entitled to a deduction, make sure it is listed. If you are not entitled to the deduction, make sure you have contributed the maximum to deductible retirement plans first.

3. **Miscalculation of mutual fund gains or losses.** Often we pay too much taxes on mutual fund sales and swaps because we forget to add the reinvested dividends into the cost basis. For example, if you purchased $10,000 of a small company fund such as Aim Aggressive five years ago, your $10,000 may have grown to over $30,000. Thus, you have $20,000 in gains, and in the 33 percent tax bracket, your taxes are $6,600. Correct? No. If you have been reinvesting the dividends, your taxable gain is much less. You do have $20,000 more than you invested, but over the years you have been paying taxes on the capital gains distributions and income. Let's say on a fund like this you had over $10,000 in taxable distributions. If you have reinvested these dividends back into the funds, they are added to your cost basis.

> Your cost – $10,000 – original price
>   plus $10,000 – cost of the reinvested distributions
>   = $10,000 – taxable capital gains
> your taxes = $3,300

If you did not add the cost in of your previously taxed dividends and capital gains distribution, your taxes would be $6,600. As you can see, there is a tremendous difference in taxes if you calculate your cost basis accurately.

Solution: Always add reinvested dividends to the cost you paid for your funds.

4. **Paying taxes on tax-free funds.** Many times we have 1099 reports for various funds and may not realize that some of these funds are tax-free and may include them on our returns, and year after year pay taxes on this tax-free income.

Solution: Review your 1099s before turning them over to your accountant and note tax-free income. Look at schedule B and make sure that any tax-free funds that are listed are noted as such. They should be used for calculation of Social Security, state taxes and alternative minimum taxes, but not for federal taxes.

5. **Tax-free and tax-deferred investments in retirement plans.** Don't put tax-free investments in IRA or retirement accounts. If you do, you will have to pay taxes on them when they come out. Since retirement plans are tax-deferred, it is redundant to place tax-free municipals and tax-sheltered annuities in pension plans.
   Solution: Place your highest-taxed investments in IRAs and retirement plans, and those investments with low taxes, long-term capital gains, tax-free income and tax-deferred income in non-retirement taxable accounts.

6. **Paying double on capital gains.** Sometimes, since reading 1099 information from mutual funds or a brokerage firm is confusing, ordinary dividends are incorrectly listed on both part II of Schedule B and on Schedule D. You end up paying taxes twice.
   Solution: Look at your Schedule B, part II, line 7, and make sure you subtract any amounts that are capital gains.

7. **Not deducting interest on debt.** The IRS has eliminated the ability to deduct debt on credit cards, but if you are borrowing money, you should consider using margin accounts with debit cards at your brokerage firm, since this debt is tax-deductible.
   Solution: If you have credit card debt, you should always consider ways to convert it to tax-deductible investment interest.

8. **Inability to write off large medical bills.** Because your bills must be over 7.5 percent of your adjusted gross income, you may not be able to write off your medical and dental expenses and insurance premiums.
   Solution: If you find you cannot write off these expenses, consider a pretax medical savings account or flexible saving accounts at work. If the bulk of the expenses are for your children, consider filing separate returns for them.

9. **Forgetting deductions on K-1 accounts.** If you own oil and gas partnerships, make sure you are deducting the IDC and depletion allowance from the income that shows on your K-1. One of the errors with these investments is to include much more income than you need to from these investments. Many computer

tax programs assume you have already deducted the IDC and allowances and do not include a worksheet for you to subtract them.

Solution: Follow the instructions on your K-1 and make sure that if you are allowed, you subtract any IDC and depletion allowances from the income that shows on the K-1.

10. **Miscalculating child care deductions.** Your child care deductions may be reduced because you are over certain income limits.

    Solution: Look at your child care credits. If you have expenses that you can not write off, consider FSAs or other pretax savings plans.

11. **Lack of communication on financial matters.** We often pay too much taxes because the left hand doesn't know what the right hand is doing. You need both a good accountant and a good financial planner. Too often we pay too much in taxes because we do not have our team work together.

    Solution: You, your spouse if you are married, your accountant and your financial planner should always review your taxes together. Your financial planner may understand investment idiosyncrasies that aren't known to your accountant. Many large companies will offer financial and accounting services to senior executives at the workplace, making it easy to bring everyone together. Otherwise, you have to coordinate the efforts of all your advisers.

CHAPTER 3

Providing for Family Needs

**20** **WHAT CHILD CARE PROGRAMS DO EMPLOYERS PROVIDE?**

Not too many, but the dramatic increase of women in the workforce may change that. Employers are now becoming more sensitive to the needs of families. And as more women move up the corporate ladder, family issues will become more and more important. Even though there is a wide range of opportunities to help with child care, many companies don't participate in all of them. You usually have to ask for these benefits.

On-Site Child Care Centers. Although less than 10 percent of employers offer child care benefits, some companies are making an effort to fill this important need. About 1 percent have on-site child care centers. These centers not only offer convenience, but they also can mean the difference between your ability to work and the need to quit. If your employer does not have such centers, approach other working parents at your company and together create a plan to present to your employer. Most on-site centers are started because parents have been able to prove their value to employers. For starters, you can let your employer know that the convenience of on-site centers can directly influence your productivity.

Employers often have to accept liability for these sites, even if parents pay to cover the costs, so they may be hesitant to act. But with so many working parents, it is likely that you can convince them. Despite this convenience, there are other factors to consider when creating on-site centers. Although the federal government has been a model, making great strides to increase the number of on-site facilities, after the Oklahoma City bombing, parents and employers are somewhat less inclined to request them.

Credit Vouchers. According to the Department of Labor, approximately 10 percent of U.S. companies offer child care benefits, such as credit vouchers or child care credits. These are often part of cafeteria benefit packages and can be applied toward child care costs. Some 12 percent of companies offer top professional and technical employees some form of child care and almost 68 percent offer top employees reimbursement accounts. If you are not a top executive, your chances of getting assistance drops dramatically. Only 6 percent of clerical employees are offered child care benefits. Nevertheless, the number is growing and you should keep careful track of changes in benefits. Your employer may already offer such benefits. When in doubt, ask.

Under IRS rules, companies can offer as much as $5,000 tax-free child care benefits for children under 13. Although these benefits are not for educational costs, they will cover some of your costs for kindergarten or preschool education that act as substitutes for child care.

Flexible Savings Accounts or Dependent Care Accounts. The fastest growing benefits are pretax savings accounts, usually called flexible savings accounts or dependent care accounts.

You can save for dependent care for your children as well as your parents on a pretax basis in these special pretax savings accounts. Saving pretax makes your dollars go further. Many companies allow you to save up to $5,000 for dependent care. Question #18 explores these plans in more detail.

Tax Credits. If you have day care expenses, you may find that you qualify for a tax credit. For one child in 1995, the credit can be up to $720 off your taxes. For two children, it is worth up to $1,440. Remember, tax credits are worth two to three times as much as tax deductions. They come right off your tax bill. The higher your income, the smaller your tax credit is.

Sick Days and Personal Days.   Many employers allow you to accumulate sick days for scheduled events. This can be especially important if you need to take vacation time off during school breaks. You may be able to cover an entire summer's child care needs with both spouses' vacation times and sick days as well as normal personal days.

Backup Emergency Care.   Some companies are leading the way in child care. Dow Jones & Company provides backup child care for their employees. In case of emergencies, the company will provide day care services if the primary day care service is unable to care for the child. If Dow Jones & Company cannot provide the care directly, it will reimburse its employees up to $400 a year for backup emergency care. Also, the company often allows employees to use their sick leave to care for their children.

To look into further options regarding child care, the American Business Collaboration for Quality Dependent Care (ABC Coalition), a group of corporations, has pooled financial resources to address child care.

Referral Services.   Although employers will not give direct advice to employees for fear of liability, many companies offer referral programs such as Life Work that can refer you to the least expensive child care services available in your area. Many have consultants and specialists available to discuss almost any child-rearing problem. In addition, these companies offer lectures, tapes, videos and literature that will walk you through the various stages of child development, from birth through college. Easy access and use of these services may not only make your life simpler and less stressful, but also save you money. They offer safety guidelines for children, first-aid information and questions to ask those who care for your children, and they can show you ways to monitor your children's care and treatment. Your employer will pay anywhere from $2 to $20 for each employee, and you will be able to get hundreds of dollars' worth of free counseling and advice!

Fill-in Care for Holidays.   Summertime is especially difficult for working parents. To relieve the pressures of summer care, some companies offer employees programs during school vacations, such as supervised field trips and activities for children at subsidized rates. Other companies offer free workshops for after-school day care providers. They even offer programs for child care providers on how to enrich the caring experience.

Emergency Swaps.   Many companies allow employees to share leave with other workers in case of medical emergencies. Following the bombing of the federal building in Oklahoma City in 1995, many concerned federal employees gave their annual paid-vacation days to employees involved in the bombing. In desperate situations, you may find that your coworkers can, and will, pitch in.

21 HOW CAN I FINANCE MY CHILDREN'S EDUCATION?

Consider using your employer as a source of savings for your children's education. Ask your human resources representative about U.S. savings bond programs, tuition assistance, company scholarships, automatic savings plans and 401(k) loans.

> Start saving as soon as possible and put compounding on your side.

If you need $50,000 for your new baby's education, and you start saving $50 a month at 12 percent, you would have almost $50,000 when your child turns 20. If you wait until the child is 15, you would have to save $600 a month to reach your goal. By starting early and letting time and compounding of interest work on your side, you only have to contribute $12,000 of your own money. If you wait until your child is 15, it will take $36,000 of your own money. If you wait until your child is 20, it will take $50,000 of your own money.

Automatic Payroll Deduction Plans.   It's hard to save on your own. Let your employer help by using automatic payroll deduction plans that automatically send your savings each month to a mutual fund, bank or brokerage firm of your choice. Usually there are no restrictions on which funds or firms you can use. You can have savings taken out automatically from your paycheck as soon as your child is born.

U.S. Savings Bonds. You can also save through employee automatic savings plans for U.S. savings bond programs. If your income is under certain limits, you may be able to cash in these bonds without tax consequences if used for your children's education. For 1995, the limit was under $63,450 for joint and $42,300 for single parents. If you go above these income levels, then you lose the exemption for college bond interest.

Scholarships. Many companies sponsor tuition assistance programs and scholarships that are available for employees' children. Many of these programs are merit-based, which is important, because most scholarships today are based on financial need. And because many families' incomes appear high on paper, they are disqualified from scholarship programs. Even if your income is high, let's say you earn $60,000, because of the needs of parents and children, large taxes and routine bills, you may not be able to afford to send your children to school, yet there is little financial assistance available.

Custodial Accounts. There are many tax advantages to saving in your child's name. There are two tax levels for children: under 14 and over. When children are under 14 years old for 1995, they can earn $650 a year tax-free in their name. The next $650 is at a 15 percent tax bracket. Amounts earned over $1,300 will be taxed at the parents' tax bracket. Remember, we are talking about the amount of income earned, not the amount invested in your child's name. For example, a married couple can put $20,000 in their child's growth mutual fund and if the taxable income generated on the $20,000 is less than $1,300, your entire tax burden can be less than $100.

Saving in your children's names when they are young can be smart, especially if you save in growth investments that will generate minimal income.

The tax code actually encourages you to invest smartly. When investing for young children, you should lean toward growth because growth investments, such as stock mutual funds, perform better than taxable-income investments, such as CDs and bonds. Since you want to keep the taxes down and since taxes are lower on growth, it is attractive to lean to growth mutual funds for both investment and tax purposes. When the children are older and it is time for them to go to school, you can cash in these growth investments and pay capital gains at the child's tax bracket. Once a child turns 14, he or she will no longer be taxed at your tax bracket, even for amounts over $1,300. At this point you may be able to switch to CDs and bonds without worrying about the higher taxes.

Be careful before you save too much in your children's names. We never really know if the money we put aside will be used for what we planned. I met a young Navy widow who earned less than $17,000 a year, yet every month saved $50 for her son's college fund. When he turned 18, he demanded the funds. Legally, the money had to be turned over to him. He bought a motorcycle, and, two weeks later, died in a motorcycle accident. Ever since then I have been hesitant to recommend saving money in children's names, even if the tax savings makes sense.

Even if your child seems tuned into education, or well behaved, you may want to think twice about placing money in your child's name or in custodial accounts. Over the past 20 years I have seen many children dip into these funds. Ironically, it is usually not the drug-addicted problem child, but rather the more sensitive and giving child.

A young woman, Milly, took all her funds to help a charity. A young man, Rob, dropped out of school and gave his last dollars so he could help a friend start a business. Another young man pulled out funds to help his girlfriend, only to see her leave after the funds were depleted. If you want to make the decision on how the money is to be spent, it may be better to save through your retirement plans or in your name. You may want the tax savings, but the risk of losing control may not be worth it.

It doesn't really matter what your children use the money for, if you are comfortable with their decisions and are aware that eventually they **will** have ultimate control. Once you place funds in your child's name, they must be used for the benefit of your child. However, if you think your children might not use the savings for college, you can place them in less liquid investments, such as real estate, collectibles or insurance annuities. If offspring are clever, they may be able to get the money no matter what you do, but such ploys will make it a lot harder.

◆ **Check the age of majority** in the state in which you are likely to live when your children reach maturity. If it is 18, think twice about putting funds in your children's names. If it is 21, you may feel a little more comfortable since they may have completed most of their education before they can touch the money.

◆ **Financial Aid:** Avoid custodial accounts if you think you can qualify for financial aid when your children go to college. If you save too much for your children's education, you may not be able to qualify for aid. Instead of being rewarded for thinking ahead and saving, you actually can be penalized.

   To be considered for financial aid, children have to put up 35 percent of their assets, but parents only have to put up 5.6 percent. If you plan smartly and start early, families with incomes as high as $100,000 can often qualify for aid, if they have other children or large expenses. A family with an income of $60,000 has a very good chance of getting aid.

◆ **Shift assets out of children's names in their junior year** of high school. If you think you may qualify for financial aid, you may want to start shifting assets out of your child's name at the beginning of the junior year in high school. If you are planning on spending those assets to buy computers or cars for college, do it before January 1st of their junior year since financial aid forms will request information starting then. Go to your child's school counselors when your child is in the 10th grade and start working with them on appropriate packages.

Save in Retirement Plans.   Save through tax-sheltered employer plans such as 401(k)s. Check with your employer now about the possibility of borrowing from your 401(k), money purchase and profit-sharing plans. You want your money to work the hardest for you, so saving without taxes can be just the edge you need to meet your goals. When you borrow from your 401(k), you will be paying yourself back, and you will be paying yourself the interest. If you save $50 a month in a 401(k) for 20 years at 12 percent, it will equal over $45,000. If you save outside retirement plans, it could equal only $28,633.

IRAs.   Another place to get money for your child's education is through retirement savings. If you are in your 40s, you should be saving through IRAs, pension plans and 401(k)s. When you are over 59½ and your children are in school, you won't have to worry about 10 percent penalties for early withdrawal.

Taxes are important when you are pulling funds out of retirement savings. If your income is high, you may find that if you take the pension funds as income instead of a loan, this will negate the ability to qualify for any financial aid. If you borrow the money, you will have to pay it back, but you pay it back to yourself, and you pay yourself interest.

If you are in your 40s with new babies, stash away as much as possible in 401(k)s. If your children will be going to college when you are in your 60s and retired, then IRAs are also fine.

Home Equity Loans.   Sometimes it can be a good idea to borrow from home equity to start your educational funds. If you borrow $10,000 now and deposit it immediately in your child's savings, it will grow year after year with minimal tax consequences, especially if you put it in long-term growth investments. The mortgage interest that you pay is tax-deductible, so you have converted your savings program into a tax-deductible amount.

Invest for Growth.   Saving for children can be the greatest financial burden you have, so do it smartly. Review the investment tips in Chapter 6. Because college costs have been increasing at a rate of 10 percent a year, your savings will have to earn at least that, if you expect to get ahead. You can't leave all your savings in U.S. savings bonds and CDs if you are planning for college many years down the road.

Guaranteed Prepaid Tuition Plans.   Many states have prepaid tuition programs in which you can lock in the current rates of college costs. If you do not think you can earn 10 percent on your investments, these plans may be attractive.

As with any investment, there are advantages and disadvantages to these plans. While the advantages are obvious, consider these factors:

♦ The IRS is trying to pass laws to tax the appreciation in these accounts.

◆ If your child doesn't go to college or to the state schools, you may not get any interest or even all your money back. You have lost the opportunity to invest it somewhere else and earn better interest.

◆ If you saved a sum of money monthly yourself, you would probably have enough to pay for state schools anyhow.

Student Loans.　There are a variety of student loans available, but be careful before you get into too much debt. With college costs increasing, these loans are becoming real burdens for many years to the graduates as well as the parents.

If you are stuck with these loans, try to negotiate with the Student Loan Marketing Association, or Sallie Mae, to allow you to just pay interest the first couple of years, and then increase the payments after your children have stable jobs and can take over the payments themselves. Also consider step payments, in which you pay smaller amounts in the first few years, and then payments increase later.

Sallie Mae will reduce your interest rates if you pay the first four years on time. So make every effort, even borrow if necessary to keep up these payments. You can even have these payments paid directly through automatic payroll deductions or automatic transfers from asset management accounts.

Call Sallie Mae at 1-800-524-9100 for student loan information. Also look into Stafford Student Loan programs.

22　HOW MUCH PARENTAL LEAVE AM I SUPPOSED TO GET?

The federal Family-Leave Act requires that employers allow you to take 12 weeks off for the care of children. Your employer isn't required to pay you for this leave. However, you are guaranteed to have your job waiting for you if the leave is for childbirth, adoption or illness of an employee or a family member.

Many employers don't understand the law, thinking it is only for emergencies. Others think it only applies to mothers and not dads. Few if any realize it is not only for newborns. Others don't even know the law exists. If you have problems and your employer is not aware of the law, call the Department of Labor, which not only will register your complaint, but also get information out to you so you and your employer can review it together.

Some companies offer more benefits and will extend this leave for longer periods of time. Dow Jones & Company adds on an additional 14 weeks for maternity leave. It also allows mothers to work part-time for up to nine months after maternity leave. Unfortunately, only 1 percent of employers pay for this leave and usually only for professional and technical staff.

23 CAN MY EMPLOYER HELP ME TAKE CARE OF MY PARENTS?

As parents live longer, there is a greater likelihood that they will need help from their children. The U.S. Census Bureau estimates that the number of Americans 80 years old and over will be 9.2 million by the year 2000. It is estimated that over a quarter of the nation's population will be over 60 by the year 2030.

And who is taking care of all these senior citizens? According to the Department of Labor, almost 4 million working Americans are caring for their parents while trying to hold down jobs. More than 2.5 million are caring for both their parents and their children.

Increasing longevity is creating an expanding strain on the resources of Social Security and pension plans, as well as on families. Living longer is one of the great benefits of our society. However, it creates several dilemmas for America as a country, especially employers and families. Many baby boomers never planned to assist their parents, and actually planned on inheritances that may never materialize. The anticipated inheritances may be consumed as their parents live longer. As the sandwich generation grows dramatically over the next five years, so will the drains on their financial futures.

Employers are more willing than ever to help, since caring for elderly parents impacts the company's bottom line. Also, those who make the decisions, the senior executives, are at the age where caring for elderly parents is a top priority. Many have already paid off their children's college bills and were looking forward to their own retirements. Instead, they are faced with worrying about their parents' health.

Know your parents' financial situation. Our parents may be poorer than we think. Government statistics show some 80 percent of women face financial problems because of divorce or widowhood. Although 75 percent of elderly poor are women, men also fall into this category; 54 percent of men at the age of 65 are dependent on relatives, friends or charity to survive in retirement. Some options to consider:

Long-Term Care Insurance. Start planning early for the possible health care and nursing home needs of your parents. Many employers will offer long-term care insurance policies for your parents. If your parents have limited funds, Medicaid may pay most of their nursing home expenses. If they are wealthy, they may be able to pay for their own expenses. Ironically, you do not have to worry if your parents have limited funds or if they are very wealthy. However, if they have assets that are worth protecting, and are likely to be dependent on you for financial support, consider long-term care plans that will cover most of the cost of nursing home care and allow them to keep their assets intact.

Shopping around for these policies and then comparing all the benefits and costs is difficult and time-consuming. However, your employer usually has done the shopping for you and has been able to negotiate group rates, so first consider the plans available through your job. You may still have to do a little legwork yourself. Your employer picks policies that are attractive for an entire group of people, not for your unique needs.

Long-term care is very expensive; however, you have to weigh the costs versus the risks. It may be worth spending the money on premiums now so that you will not have to spend the money for expensive nursing home care later. These policies have improved tremendously over the last few years, and offer many attractive features at lower costs than in the past.

When selecting long-term care policies, you need to look at:

◆ Inflation clauses
◆ Waiting periods
◆ Elimination periods
◆ Types of benefits, i.e., at-home, nursing
◆ What you need to start receiving benefits (some policies will require that you be in the hospital first; others will add restrictions, such as two doctors' letters saying nursing home care is necessary, etc.)

Life Insurance Policies. Several life insurance policies have an option that will allow you to pull out funds in case of terminal or long-term illness. You can always borrow the cash value of your policy at any time, but the new option allows you to take out a large chunk of the death benefit before you die.

You will not get the full amount, since there is a time element and a loss to the insurance company if you do. However, these policies can provide large pools of assets that will allow you to get the medical care your parents need to prolong their lives, or at least help them to be more comfortable in their illnesses. Be forewarned, however, many health-care policies and Medicare do not cover extreme, unusual or experimental procedures to prolong life, and none offer adequate nursing home coverage. In addition, most of these life insurance policies will not let you pull out the death benefit unless you are in a nursing home for six months. As with many long-term care policies, a doctor may have to certify that this will be permanent.

If you want long-term nursing home policies, life insurance is usually not a good substitute. Many elderly buy life insurance that allows them to pull out funds in case of terminal illness, but these are not long-term care policies. There have been several complaints against insurance companies for selling life insurance policies to elderly, who believe they are buying nursing home insurance.

Shifting Assets. Often parents move assets out of their names into yours so that they will qualify for Medicaid. It is important to remember that the assets must remain in your name for three years, in most states, before your parents can claim that they have no assets (five years for irrevocable trusts). In the meantime, they will need long-term care for those three years in order to protect you from expenses during that time. If they do not have long-term insurance, and your parents go into nursing homes before the three- to five-year period is over, they will have to deplete their assets to pay for their care, and then ask you to give back the money they gifted to you.

Flexible Savings Accounts. FSAs work for parents as well as for children. If you have expenses related to dependent care for your parents, plan for the expenses through your employer's pretax savings plan. You may be able to save $5,000 each year on a pretax basis for dependent care.

Employee Assistance Programs. Check with your employer about emergency days and programs that are available to help you care for your parents. Many employers will allow you to accumulate personal and sick days so that you can cover planned periods with your parents.

Flexible Hours. More and more companies are willing to offer flexible hours, job-sharing programs and at-home hours to accommodate workers who need to care for elderly parents. Flexible hours have not only cut back on absenteeism, but reduced stress for workers.

Family Leave. Under the Family and Medical Leave Act of 1993, your employer must extend the same job guarantees to you if you take time off for the care of parents as for the care of children.

Resource and Referral Programs. Approximately 25 percent of large companies and 15 percent of small companies provide referral programs as well as support groups to help in times of emergency. Hundreds of companies offer their employees referral and resource programs (R&R), such as the Life Works program from WORK/ Family Directions, in Boston, Massachusetts. These referral services are available for advice on child care and also for the elderly. They can offer information on nursing homes, geriatric care, medical care, adult day care programs, Meals on Wheels and so forth. They are an especially attractive benefit for those whose parents are in different locations. They will put you in touch with local affiliates, supply you with information and referrals and help find your parents the appropriate care. Your company usually foots the bill.

Consider Reverse Mortgages. If your parents have a home and they need extra income, this might be a viable alternative. Many times through your employer referral systems, you can find out information about these mortgages. Simply stated, they are a loan taken a little at a time, month after month, against the equity on a house. Each month your parents will receive a check. When their home is sold, there will be less equity and fewer dollars remaining for inheritances, but such mortgages often allow your parents to stay in their own homes longer.

Plan for Inflation.   Whether you are saving for your own retirement or for your parents, remember that one of the greatest risks is not planning for growth and inflation. Don't be too conservative, and don't leave all your assets in money market funds and CDs. Be more growth oriented. Remember, if you reach the age of 50 and are healthy, you have a good chance to live well into your 80s and possibly even 90s. So plan for the long-term.

Check Your W-4.   When you assume responsibility for your parents, recalculate your withholdings. If your employer can't help you, the government might be able to. You may be able to claim your parents as dependents and write off much of their medical expenses on your tax return. You may even get a tax credit for in-home care. If you help your parents, ask your employer for a W-4 worksheet so you can recalculate your withholdings. Look at the IRS worksheet in Appendix F that explains withholdings. When you are calculating withholdings, consider all those items that will increase your deductions or decrease your taxable income.

Medical Deductions for Trips to Health Facilities.   If you are providing more than half your parents' income or support, you may be able to list them as dependents. When you are using the worksheets and calculating withholding allowances, make sure you also plan for any medical expenses and even transportation to medical facilities that you will be paying for your parents.

Tax Credits.   You may qualify for a tax credit. Usually the maximum is $720 for home care for each of your parents. The IRS will help you, free of charge, to determine if you qualify for the credit.

Direct Employer Assistance.   A growing number of employers are offering direct assistance for employees by contracting with health service agencies. These direct programs tend to be more in-depth and employees are more likely to take advantage of them.

Take Your Parents with You.   If you are afraid to take a new job because you have to leave your parents behind, talk to your employer. Surveys show that the major reason for turning down promotions and transfers is the growing concern for parents. Work/

Family Directions, in a survey conducted by Atlas Van in 1994, says that 64 percent of employees stated this as the reason for refusing to move. This number was up from 53 percent in 1993. Employers are increasingly willing to pay for the move of elderly parents to get top executives to move.

Before You Move, Check Your Parents' Pension Taxes. Be careful about state taxes on your parents' pensions. Even after you move, states such as New York are coming after the taxes on those pension and retirement plans that grew, tax-deferred, while you lived there. Also there are different Medicaid rules in each state. We will discuss this more in Chapter 10.

When You Just Can't Help. If your parents are facing poverty, and neither you nor your employer has resources to help, consider contacting several government agencies. Start with Social Security, then follow up with calls to the Administration on Aging (AoA). Also talk to local welfare offices and call the Association for the Advancement of Retired Persons (AARP) for information on elderly advocates.

Long-Distance Care. Make sure that you know services and support groups available to call when helping your parents from a distance. If you have an elderly parent living alone, make sure you have some emergency procedures to follow if he or she don't check in. If there are no family members to rely on, contact volunteer and community support groups. Get a copy of the local phone book so you know who to call in emergencies.

Keep in touch with your parents' medical team, and stay in touch with your parents' friends and contacts. It is difficult to monitor your parents' emotional as well as physical well-being from a distance, but it often is necessary, so be prepared.

24 CAN I USE SICK LEAVE FOR FAMILY EMERGENCIES?

Today, an increasing number of employers are doing whatever they can to accommodate employees as long as it doesn't cost them anything. Many employers will allow employees to accumulate sick leave and personal days and use them to care for parents, for family emergencies and child care responsibilities.

Check your company's policy. Giving workers flexibility on selecting the days they need to take off, instead of forcing them to create or fabricate illness to use sick leave, makes sense for everyone.

Research this policy as soon as possible. Don't wait until you have an emergency. Those workers who do best in crisis situations are those who plan the best. If you have a plan, and already have thought ahead, you will be able to function much better.

25 WHAT SHOULD I DO WHEN I GET MARRIED?

A generation ago, 75 percent of U.S. households were made up of married couples. Today, the number is down to 50 percent.

We have talked a lot about the benefits that companies offer their workers, and these are especially important to married couples. When you marry, you get hit with what is called the marriage penalty. It is the government's wedding present, except that you are giving the gift to the government. The government likes to see couples marry since they pay more than two single individuals earning the same income.

High-Income Couples.   Not very romantic, but you may want to postpone those wedding bells. If you are getting married late in the year, you may want to postpone your wedding a few more months. When married couples file, they pay higher taxes than do single people. Hopefully, by the time you read this book, Congress will have eliminated "the marriage penalty."

Low-Income Couples.   You also can be hurt if one or both of you were earning under $11,000 a year. If you earn under $11,000, you probably qualify for the earned-income tax credit. Once you get married, you may no longer qualify for this credit.

Steps to take when you get married:

1. Consider life insurance policies. Before you married, there was probably very little need for insurance. If you both feel you can support yourselves easily, you still may not need much. Check to see whose group policies are the least expensive.

2. Recalculate your withholding allowances.
3. Compare pension plans. If one of you has a better plan or a matching contribution plan, you may want to save in that plan first.
4. Reevaluate beneficiary forms. If you want your spouse as your beneficiary, make sure you correct all your IRA, retirement, insurance and any other beneficiary forms that are applicable.
5. Compare health insurance policies and select the best one. Make sure you are not duplicating coverage.
6. Look at tax ramifications and the effects on IRAs, deductions and so forth.
7. Flexible savings plans usually can't be changed, but marriage is one of the exceptions. If you get married, you can ask your employer to decrease or increase the amount.
8. Save as much as possible, 20 percent annually, if you can. Save the maximum you can now, since once you have children, you may no longer be able to. If you save the next five or six years while you are still young, you may be able to discontinue in a few years and still retire comfortably as well as educate your children. Set goals and let your employer help you save.
9. Create a savings plan. Use automatic deposits and preplanned payments and investments.
10. Many marriages start with large credit card debts. Your first rule should be: Do not spend money you do not have. Only go into debt for a home and for true emergencies.
11. Always attend employee benefit meetings at the other spouse's employment. At the very least, read your spouse's benefit package. Plan and discuss your financial goals together before you marry.
12. Get a will.

26 WE'RE A CHILDLESS DUAL-INCOME COUPLE. WHAT CAN WE DO TO REDUCE OUR TAXES AND BENEFITS?

You are in a great position to save and build wealth, but taxes can be one of the greatest detriments for you. As more and more couples postpone having children until their 30s and even 40s, we are seeing a large increase in DINKs, dual-income-no-kids couples. In general, they tend to have intense spending habits and allocate much of their income to entertainment, dining and travel. However, if you find yourself in this category, and are planning on a home, children or a good retirement, you may want to consider the following points.

As mentioned previously, married couples are faced with the marriage penalty, an unfair tax burden. This means you pay more taxes than two single workers do. It doesn't pay for a married couple to file separately, though, unless one spouse has high medical or business expenses. This tax is likely to stay since it will cost the Treasury over 25 billion dollars a year to do away with it.

It's worth noting that the average marriage penalty is over $1,200 and much more for higher-income couples. For example, if one spouse earns $150,000 and the other earns over $100,000, the penalty is over $6,100 more in federal taxes. Congress is now looking at a provision to allow a credit of $145 starting in 1996. That's not really much when you consider that the tax penalty is as high as $5,000 or $6,000 for many working couples.

Short of getting divorced and living together, what can dual-income couples do?

- **Review the tax-saving strategies previously discussed.**
- **Time bonuses carefully.** If possible, plan your bonuses and time both spouses' bonuses so they hit at the best time for tax planning. If you get bonuses every year, both spouses should work with their employers to evaluate other alternative non-taxable benefits.
- **Monitor your spending.** Remember the monitored asset-management accounts that we discussed earlier? Use these types of accounts to keep accurate records of your spending.
- **Save, save, save.** Save in every tax-saving vehicle available to you, for the reasons we've already discussed.
- **Compare tax returns:** Compare filing your tax return jointly and separately. In most cases, a joint return will have the lowest tax consequences. However, if one spouse has high business expenses or medical costs, you may do better filing separate returns.
- **Don't go into debt:** Keep your credit card and unsecured debt down to 15 percent of your take-home pay or net income.

◆ **Buying a home**: Usually one of the highest priorities for dual-income couples is buying a home. It should be, because you need all the tax write-offs possible. Stay within your budget. You should usually keep your mortgage payments to 28 percent of your gross income. You can estimate the cost of your house by multiplying your gross income by one and a half to two and a half. If you have a lot of debt already, you will have to lower your sights or pay off that debt soon. Even the most generous banks do not allow debt payments over 40 percent of gross income for home mortgages.

  You can usually borrow for a down payment from your 401(k)s, but typically that is not a good idea, because you are trading off current spending for future security.

  Make sure you have your credit rating intact. Check with TRW (1-214-235-1200) and Equifax (1-800-685-1111) to see what your credit looks like. Don't wait until it's time to buy. There could be an error on your report that should be corrected as soon as possible.

◆ **Plan your investments together**: Be aware, however, of the difference in financial concerns. When I discuss stocks on my radio show—especially technology stocks and trading strategies—almost all the calls are from men. The same pattern exists with my seminars and columns. When I concentrate on longer-term core stocks or financial planning issues, women start calling, and the responses are almost all from women.

  I have seen couples use these differences to their mutual benefit. For example, Anne tends toward very risk-averse investments. Henry is more risk-tolerant and inclined to trade. Together, they meet in the middle. Anne feels comfortable with Henry's trading as long as he does not dip into that portion of their investments directed toward securing their retirement and children's education. Time and time again, a couple's differences improve the balance and returns in investments. Approach investing and money as a team, picking the strengths from each partner.

◆ **Municipal bond swaps**: Look at some of the tax strategies outlined in Question #2 and some active tax strategies. For example, if you have municipal bonds trusts or individual bonds, always check with your broker about the possibility of swapping these bonds. Usually such swaps create short-term paper tax losses. You may have to pay the taxes back on these when the new bonds mature, but that can be many years down the road, when your tax bracket is lower because possibly only one spouse will be working or you have children.

◆ **Mutual fund switching**: Often you have paid taxes on the reinvested dividends in mutual funds. Consider swapping your mutual funds around so that you can take advantage of the taxes you have paid in the past. See Questions #17 and #19 for more details.

CHAPTER 4

Preparing for Emergencies

27 WHERE CAN I GET MONEY FOR EMERGENCIES?

Save two to three months of income in emergency funds before you buy homes, invest in long-term investments or put money aside in investments that are not liquid. However, if you deplete these funds and need more, there are many other places to access funds. Where you get these funds will depend greatly on the type of emergency. You need different sources for different situations. Where you get money when you lose your job or become ill may be completely different than the money you get for your parents or for your children or for home and car repairs.

In emergencies, first use those assets that are the most liquid and have the least penalties, costs and taxes. Borrow from the lowest-cost sources.

FOR ALL EMERGENCIES

The Government. Look at ways to increase your income. Most emergencies affect your taxes. If they do, you can increase your monthly income immediately. If you are going to have large medical bills, or losses, these will reduce your tax burden. Go immediately to your employer and increase your withholdings to the maximum so

77

that you will reduce your taxes. This may not give you the lump sum you need now, but it will increase your monthly cash flow and allow you to pay back loans more easily.

SHORT-TERM EMERGENCIES

Margin Accounts. Look at inexpensive sources for borrowing. You are in luck if you have any stocks, mutual funds or bonds. Instead of selling these securities, it is much better to borrow against them, especially if you think you will be able to pay back the funds in a short period of time. You can borrow from a brokerage firm at rates that are some of the lowest and also are tax-deductible. What can you borrow against?

◆ If you have Treasuries or CDs, deposit them in a brokerage account. The brokerage firm will use the CDs and government securities as collateral and you can borrow up to 95 percent of the value of government securities. Because these margin loans are tax-deductible, they reduce the cost of your borrowing.

◆ If you have some stocks stashed away in a safe deposit box, take them out and deposit them in a brokerage account. You will be able to borrow up to half their value and pay tax-deductible margin interest in most cases.

◆ If you have company options or stocks that are not restricted, deposit them in a brokerage account and borrow against them.

◆ If you have been sending off a few dollars every month to your local utility to purchase shares in its customer accounts, or any dividend reinvestment program, have the money deposited in your brokerage account. These small monthly amounts add up and are a good source of collateral.

◆ Margin accounts also work for any mutual funds you have. Make sure you ship them off to a brokerage firm and use them to borrow against.

IRAs. For short-term loans, you can borrow from your IRA for 60 days without any penalties.

Credit Cards and Charge Cards

◆ If it is a short-term emergency, consider credit cards. But the rates are so high, you may want to use this as a last resort. Shop around before a crisis arises and find the least expensive rates. Charge all your purchases, but always pay off before the 30 days. You will see your line of credit grow quickly as you establish credit.

◆ Once you establish a line of credit, most credit card companies willingly extend you credit. You may find that one way to avoid the interest charge on your credit card is to transfer the balance to another credit card company before interest is due or within 31 days. You may end up being able to get an interest-free loan for 60 days or even more. Many companies offer you a much lower introductory interest rate for a limited time (usually six months). This may be an attractive way to get inexpensive loans. Let the new company pay off your current debt. Be careful to obey all rules and laws when transferring balances.

◆ I don't like recommending charge cards, because it is an easy way to get into debt. Charge cards are similar to credit cards, except they are usually for individual stores and gas stations. For emergencies you may want to stash away several department store and gas charge cards (they usually have no annual fees). This way you can charge all your basic food, car and housing needs until you're back in shape. As a general rule, if you cannot pay cash, or pay off your cards in 30 days, then don't charge. Easy access to "plastic" is the leading cause of overwhelming debt and is the major cause of financial failure.

Tax Refunds. Get your taxes done as soon as possible and apply for an early refund. If you are due a refund, you can request the IRS to expedite processing your tax return.

Overdrafts. Check into overdraft privileges with your checking account.

Credit Unions. Borrow from credit unions. Make sure you establish a good credit rating early. Credit unions, affiliated with your community or employer, are some of the easiest places to get loans.

Family Assistance Programs. The military and many communities will have family assistance programs where you can get some short-term help.

LONGER-TERM NEEDS

Borrow from Your Children. If you put money aside in your children's names, you cannot legally take that money back for your own needs. However, you may be able to borrow it.

401(k)s. Over 60 percent of 401(k) plans allow loans. Check out these plans because the interest you pay is to yourself. You usually have up to five years to pay these loans off.

Profit-Sharing and Retirement Plans. Ask your employer about borrowing from your profit-sharing and money purchase plans. Many of these plans will allow you to borrow under terms similar to your 401(k). The ability to borrow from these plans is a little more restrictive, but, in most cases, you should investigate.

Lock In Home Equity Rates Now. Most of us know that we can borrow from our home through a home equity loan. The big advantage is that these loans are tax-deductible. If you wait until you have an emergency, interest rates may be very high and you may find it difficult to qualify if you are out of work. So lock in your line of credit when interest rates are low and while you still have a job. These loans aren't as attractive as borrowing from your retirement plans, but they are better than borrowing on unsecured loans.

Insurance. Do not cash in your insurance, but borrow against the cash value of your insurance policy. These loans will have no tax consequences, but if you surrender the policy, you may have taxes due.

Your Bank. Before you need a loan, borrow some funds from your bank and pay back the bank quickly. You want to establish credit so that in emergencies you can borrow easily. When your income is low is when most banks are likely to reject you. If you have already established credit, the loan may be as easy as writing a check on an overdraft account.

Personal Loan Companies and Second and Third Mortgages.
Personal loan companies and second and third mortgages on your home are very expensive and should only be considered if you have a real emergency.

Family.   Borrowing from relatives and friends may be something you cannot consider because such a transaction would make you feel awkward. If you do borrow, you have to pay a fair interest rate or the IRS will make you pay taxes on the forgiven interest. You can approach your family and friends by offering collateral and by making the loan as businesslike as possible with a formal loan agreement.

Your Employer.   Ask your employer. Often employers are a good source of short-term loans.

Advances.   Ask your employer for an advance on pay. An employer might even pay bonuses early or allow you to take money from nonqualified plans.

YOU LOSE YOUR JOB AND NEED MONTHLY INCOME

Often, when we have an emergency, we do not necessarily need a lump sum, but instead, money to live off of month after month.

Reverse Mortgages.   If the emergency requires monthly income, consider a reverse mortgage if you are in your 60s and qualify. These mortgages allow you to borrow against the equity in your home and pull out funds each month instead of a lump sum.

IRAs.   If you need lifetime income, you may be able to take a monthly income from your IRAs. If you have lost your job, there are ways you can get monthly income with no penalties by following IRS rule 72(t), which we discuss in Question #28.

Income Aid Programs.   Many employers have income aid programs for employees who have lost their jobs. When you receive these loans they are taxable, but usually, if you are out of work, your tax bracket will be low anyway. You can deduct these loans from your income when you pay them back. Usually by then your income will be higher, and you may save net taxes on these programs.

Severance Plans.   You have to plan ahead, but while you are working you may want to negotiate with your employer to place funds in a severance package. Usually these plans are given to all levels of workers in lieu of raises or cash.

Split-Dollar Insurance.   If you have split-dollar insurance policies at work, you can borrow without tax consequences from these plans.

Taxes.   If you have a major loss, such as your house burning down, or all your furniture falling into a river during a moving accident (it can happen, it did to me), this can affect your taxes. Check immediately with your accountant on the best way to handle and carry losses forward.

LONG-TERM TERMINAL ILLNESSES AND CRISES

Prepayment of Insurance Death Benefits.   Although life insurance normally pays off only when you die, if you have a terminal illness, the insurance company may pay you the proceeds early, and you can get the care and medical help you need.

Clubs and Service Organizations.   If you belong to a club or service organization, it will often have short-term emergency loans for members and their families.

Selling Your Insurance Policy.   As horrific as this sounds, this is being done with increasing frequency and gives you the ability to gain income immediately. If you have a terminal illness, you can sell your policy and in return for a large percentage (usually 50 percent of the face value), you name the purchaser of the policy as your ben eficiary. As repulsive as this sounds, it is a way for many terminally ill patients to salvage some funds and make their final days more comfortable. The legality of this strategy is now being examined and there are so many scams and unsuspecting victims that I usually caution against this.

The Government.   If you have no resources left, you may have to seek government-assistance programs. For those who have worked hard all their lives, it is often embarrassing and difficult to request such help. However, especially when there are young children involved, you should at least know all your alternatives.

Religious Groups.   Religious and spiritual groups often will have aid available, especially for mothers and children. It is likely that you will be able to remain anonymous. In a true emergency, you will find a lot of support and willingness of those around you to help.

Government Relief Programs.   If your emergency is the result of a natural disaster, look at government grants. There is also disaster unemployment assistance payments.

Pawnshops.   Don't laugh. These are still around, and although their interest charges can be exorbitant, they may allow you to keep valuables that you may otherwise have to sell. If you have a good stamp collection or coin collection, consider going to a coin dealer and using these as collateral. You may want to take these measures only as a last resort.

Local Utilities.   Your local utility may be able to give you some assistance with your heating and electric bills. While this is especially true for senior citizens, utilities also frequently help anyone in need.

Small Businesses.   If you are a small business owner, you may want to consider loans against your accounts receivable, SBA loans, your suppliers, as well as your customers, or anyone who benefits if your company survives. Avoid venture capitalists, but if you have exhausted all other sources, you may be able to get some short-term financing. Small businesses have many other sources of financing available. Get information from the Small Business Administration.

28 HOW CAN I AVOID PENALTIES WHEN I NEED TO WITHDRAW MONEY FOR EMERGENCIES?

When you are planning your investments, you should plan a liquidity map. Your map should show the time frames when each investment will come due. You should map out the dates due for emergency funds, for new cars, for home purchases, for children's education and for retirement, so that your funds will come due at the appropriate time.

Build In Liquidity. Your first pool of money should be two months' worth of income in very short-term, easily accessible funds, such as money market, Treasury bills, brokerage CDs and savings accounts. This money should not be saved in noninterest-bearing checking accounts where it is commingled with everyday operating cash.

It is just as important to build liquidity into your investments as it is to have proper diversification and asset allocation.

Once you have two months' worth of income in these very short-term funds, consider another month's income in a secondary pool of funds that are stable, but also could be earning good returns for you if you do not need them. You may want to consider utility funds, asset allocation mutual funds, adjustable rate preferred funds, longer-term CDs, municipal bonds, Treasury notes (maximum maturity should be three years) or cash value in insurance policies. When you are investing, you should attempt to minimize the penalties and costs of funds that you may need in the short-term. When you work with a financial adviser or broker, one of the first things you should discuss is when your funds might be needed. Over the long run, stocks do better than nearly all other investments and are very attractive for long-term goals, but very unattractive for emergency funds. Every investment has good and bad points. When you are considering an investment, ask your adviser how much interest rates, market, inflation, credit and liquidity risks the investment has as well as the fees associated with it.

Avoid CD Penalties. By careful planning, you can change some investments that tend to be illiquid and that have selling penalties into very liquid investments. For example, buy CDs at a brokerage firm rather than at a bank. At a brokerage firm there are no penalties when you sell. There are no commissions, and your broker can shop around at many banks to find the best rate.

If you need money in an emergency, you can sell the CDs and avoid the penalties. If interest rates have gone up since you purchased the CDs, you may get less than you paid, but if interest rates have gone down, you may get more. This difference is interest rate risk, but in most cases it is less than the penalty. If the penalty is less, you can always pay the penalty instead. You can also try using broker margin accounts and borrow against your CD if the maturity date is imminent. The margin interest may be tax-deductible and you will avoid the penalties on the CDs.

Avoid IRA Penalties. Normally when you pull money out of retirement plans, if you are younger than 59½, you will have to pay a 10 percent penalty. However, even if you are under 59½, you can take money out of an IRA once a year for 60 days.

If you have lost your job, need the funds for a longer period of time and cannot pay the loan back in 60 days, you can still use your IRA. You have to follow IRS 72(t) rules and you must take payments that are substantially equal in size and on a regular basis. Also, you need to take the funds out for at least five years, or until you are 59½, whichever is longer. You have to take at least one payment each year. Under IRS rule 72(t), you can take out distribution, based on your lifetime, or joint life expectancy with your spouse.

Even if you need money in a lump sum, it may be better to borrow the money elsewhere and use monthly distributions from your IRA to pay off the loan.

Avoid Retirement Penalties. Some of your nonqualified retirement plans are actually insurance policies. You will be able to borrow the cash value. Instead of cashing in 401(k)s and retirement plans, borrow from them.

Avoid Surrender Charges on Insurance Policies. If you have insurance policies and you need money, do not cash in the policies but borrow instead.

Avoid Bond Fund Losses. Actually, I should tell you to avoid bond funds altogether. But if you are investing in short-term bond funds, these may be suitable for emergencies. But if you have your emergency funds set aside in long-term bond funds, cash out when interest rates are low and move into CDs or Treasury notes. Bond funds have no guarantees and have management fees and interest rate risk.

Avoid Mutual Fund Back-End Fees.   If the emergency is that you want to get out of mutual funds because you think the market is going to fall, instead of selling a fund with a back-end commission, just swap it into the cash fund. You have kept your money safe, have avoided the back-end penalty and have your money earning interest while you are waiting to get back into the market.

Avoid Penalties When Disabled.   If you are disabled, you can cash in retirement funds *without penalties even if you are under 59½.*

Avoid Annuity Penalties.   If you have annuities, which you should not have unless you set aside enough emergency funds, you will be assessed a 10 percent penalty from the IRS if you are under 59½ years of age and possible back-end penalties from the annuity companies. Annuities will have penalties as high as 7 to 8 percent for up to eight years. In addition, you will have large tax consequences.

If an annuity is your only asset, have the policy annuitized so that you will get monthly income and can avoid the annuity penalties. If you are over 59½ years of age and you have had the annuity for a while, then it could be a good source to tap into. When you are purchasing an annuity, if you think you may have to tap into it, consider some of the newer annuities that do not have back-end penalties. You have to pay about an extra .25 percent in fees, but if you are not sure of your future finances, it may be worth it. Many annuities will let you take out 10 percent a year plus interest without penalty.

Avoid Penalties by Staggering Maturities of Emergency Funds. You can avoid interest rate losses on bonds by staggering your bonds and fixed income investments over several maturities. Too often we think of bonds as our guaranteed emergency fund. However, if we have to liquidate and cash these bonds in, there may be large losses because of interest rate risk and possible commissions. To avoid this, always ladder your bonds' maturity. Use your own bonds and avoid bond funds.

Watch for Changes in Retirement Laws. You may even be able to pull money out of IRAs and retirement plans for college education and home purchases if Congress changes the IRA rules.

29 HOW CAN I MINIMIZE TAXES WHEN I NEED MONEY FOR AN EMERGENCY?

Think of taxes as another penalty when trying to get at your funds, and you may find it easier to find ways to avoid tax penalties. If you are selling securities that have profits, consider the tax consequences. You need to avoid taxes especially in cases of emergency so that you will have as many dollars working for you as possible. Remember, tax avoidance is legal, it is not tax evasion.

- ♦ **Sell securities with lowest tax consequences first.** When you are liquidating securities, always sell those with the highest cost basis first or those with losses, if you are trying to minimize taxes. Make sure your broker notes which securities are sold for tax purposes.
- ♦ **Bonds:** Sell bonds before stocks. Usually bonds will have the least capital gains, because your returns come from income on which you have already paid taxes.
- ♦ **Mutual funds:** Income-oriented, balanced, utility or asset allocation mutual funds will usually have the next lowest tax consequence on selling. Like bonds, most of the returns have come from dividends and income you have either been receiving or reinvesting over the years. On bond funds, it is very likely that you will even be able to show a loss, so sell these before you start selling longer-term growth funds that have a lot of appreciation and have not been taxed so much in the past.
- ♦ **Stocks:** When selling stocks, sell the ones with the losses and least profit first. However, make sure that the profit is long-term as opposed to short-term. Short-term gains are taxed at your tax bracket that could be as high as 39.6 percent for federal taxes, but long-term capital gains are taxed only at 28 percent.
- ♦ **Transfer assets to children's names:** If your emergency is related to your parents or children, then don't sell. Transfer

the securities instead. Your children and parents are likely to have a much lower tax bracket and they may pay taxes at their rate, not yours. For example, if you have a $5,000 investment that has doubled and you are in the 33 percent tax bracket and you sell, you may only net 83.5 percent of the proceeds ($10,000 minus $1,650 taxes on $5,000 profit). If your children or parents sell, they may pay no or very little taxes depending on their tax situations.

◆ **Hold off selling your home.** If you are planning on selling your home, wait until you reach 55 before you do. You will get a $125,000 exclusion on the capital gains taxes. If you need the money now and are not quite 55, you may find it very easy to get a second mortgage to tide you over.

◆ **Plan ahead with split-dollar and severance packages.** Save in split-dollar insurance plans and severance packages so taxes will not be a concern. There is no limit to these plans and your funds grow tax-deferred in either a whole life or variable life policy. You can take the funds out before you reach 59½ without penalty and taxes since the withdrawals are considered loans. Congress has gone after insurance products in the past and won, so don't rely too much on these plans.

30 SHOULD I BORROW FROM PENSION PLANS OR MY EMPLOYER?

If you can control your debt, borrowing from your employer or pension plans is a good idea. However, if you are always in debt, it can be dangerous to borrow from your employer and your retirement. You want to use these sources for true emergencies. If you are late paying back your employer, not only do you jeopardize your credit rating, but also your job.

Before you borrow from your employer, make sure your financial house is in order. If you find yourself in need of borrowing again and again, you probably should question the way you handle money before you borrow at work.

If more than 70 percent of your income is for basic necessities, evaluate your housing situation and consider that you may be living above your means. You need 10 percent for savings, and the other 20 percent can be for your discretionary income. You should not get into the habit of borrowing from pension plans or from your employer if you cannot pay the funds back with regularity and if you do not have a long-term budget that you can follow.

However, for a true emergency, borrowing from your employer's income aid program and pensions is inexpensive and you can usually borrow money for five years.

31 SHOULD I BUY MY OWN DISABILITY INSURANCE EVEN THOUGH MY EMPLOYER PROVIDES IT?

Yes, even though your employer may provide disability insurance for you, you still should consider purchasing some insurance on your own. Before you do anything, check your employer's policy to see what provisions it covers.

Your employer's plans are usually the least expensive and have several disadvantages, such as:

- ◆ Disability benefits are taxable when you receive them.
- ◆ Usually these plans are for total disabilities only and not for "own-occupation."
- ◆ Most are limited in coverage.

Consider the following advantages to owning your own policy, when applicable:

- ◆ **To pay taxes:** When your employer purchases disability insurance, the benefits will be taxable. If you have your own small disability policy, you can make up for the money you lose to taxes. For example, if your employer's insurance policy provides you with disability income of $40,000, you may have to pay $12,000 in taxes on this amount. If you purchase a $12,000 policy yourself, the $12,000 will be tax-free and can make up for the taxes on your employer's policy.
- ◆ **To get you coverage for your own occupation.** Most employers' plans and Social Security will only pay if you can't work at all. General occupation insurance is much cheaper, and your employer may often opt for this less expensive insur-

ance and leave you in trouble if you can no longer work in the job you want or for which you were trained.

For example, if you are a violinist and lose your arm, your policy might not pay since you could teach, become a janitor or do some other type of work. If you have coverage for your own occupation, you will receive benefits if you can't work at your own job.

◆ **To make up losses in income**: Your employer's policy will reduce the benefits paid to you the first year by the amount you receive from some other sources. If you are eligible to receive benefits from Social Security disability, workers' compensation or state disability plans, the amount they pay may be deducted from your employer's policy.

Assume that your employer's plan pays $40,000 but you receive $20,000 from workers' compensation, Social Security and state plans. Your employer will reduce the payments by this amount. The $20,000 you receive from your employer's plan is taxable, and you may end up with as little as $14,000 from your employer's plan. If you purchase your own plan, you will not have to worry about reductions in your policy. Check to make sure your employer's policy doesn't reduce benefits by the amount you receive from policies you purchase yourself.

◆ **To offer protection for less than total disability.** Many employers' policies only cover you for total disability. If you are partially disabled, you may not be able to collect disability, even though you are out of work, suffering and losing income. Having your own individual policy can offset this problem. If you try to work part-time to increase your income, you could lose all your benefits.

Pay for some disability yourself to make up taxes on employers, to add flexibility, to add tax-free income and to make up for loss coverage because of Social Security, workers' compensation and state disability. Make sure benefits are not limited to total disability and are for own-occupation. Also check your life insurance for provisions that allow you to take funds prematurely for terminal illness and disability.

Call Social Security at 1-800-772-1213 and request a breakdown of your current benefits and what they cover.

32 DO I NEED BOTH SHORT-TERM AND LONG-TERM DISABILITY?

If you have adequate money saved for emergencies, and have accumulated leave and good sick day provisions, you may not need short-term disability. However, in most cases, you will need long-term.

Prudential Insurance company's statistics show that if you are between the ages of 35 to 65, you have a 50 percent chance of being disabled for 90 days or more.

> According to insurance and government statistics, your chances of being disabled are two and a half times greater than dying at age 52, four times greater than dying at age 42 and six and a half times as great at 32.

You may not feel that you need long-term disability insurance because your employer and Social Security will supply some of these benefits. However, you may want to think again.

Social Security does supply disability benefits to anyone who is eligible for retirement benefits. However, Social Security does not start until six months after the disability, and you have to have a permanent disability that is expected to last for over 12 months or for life. Many Social Security benefits are not that attractive:

♦ It is difficult to qualify for these benefits, with over 40 percent of claims denied.

♦ You have to be permanently disabled for at least 12 months.

♦ The coverage and income is minimal and does not start for six months.

Although some states offer disability, like Social Security, usually the benefits are minimal, and it is difficult to qualify.

To determine whether you need short-term disability, make a list of all your short-term sources of income, interest, savings, employer's short-term plans, spousal income and so forth. These may be able to carry you through a couple of months of lost income, especially if you have attractive health insurance.

To determine if you need long-term disability, make a list of all the sources of income that you can tap into. Look at your current employer, state and Social Security benefits. If they do not cover you for long-term partial disabilities as well as total disabilities, and if you do not have sufficient resources on which to live, consider your own long-term policy. Remember, it is difficult to adapt your employer's policy to your needs. These policies are regulated by the Employee Retirement Income Security Act (ERISA), and your employer is limited by the requirement to offer similar benefits to all employees.

33　ARE LONG-TERM CARE PLANS NECESSARY?

Long-term care policies can offer much peace of mind since they pay your bills if you ever need to be admitted to a nursing home. But they can be very expensive. Even if you are healthy and you wait until you're 70, they can cost over $4,000 a year.

Look at your employer's long-term care policies. You may be able to save money if you buy a policy through your employer for your parents or yourself.

When asking, "Do I need long-term care insurance," keep in mind that about 25 percent of 65-year-olds will spend more than a year in a nursing home. For individuals with assets of less than $100,000, these policies will probably not be worth it, since they are so expensive and because the government will eventually provide Medicaid services. If your assets are over a million dollars, you should have enough income to pay for even the nicest of nursing homes, so, again, you probably don't need this insurance. Those with assets between $100,000 and $1,000,000 should probably consider such policies. If you don't purchase long-term care, you should be aware of the following regarding Medicare and Medicaid.

Medicare.　It's getting more and more difficult to qualify for Medicare. Even if you do qualify, the benefits are only for 100 days, which isn't much since the average stay in a nursing home is one year. You also need to show that you've been entitled to Social Security disability benefits for two years. You may get some relief from Medicare supplements, which take over where Medicare payments leave off.

Medicaid.　While Medicaid pays for over half the nursing home costs in the United States, you have to impoverish yourself before you can qualify. If you want to keep your estate intact and keep your assets, you may want to use long-term care policies. If you gift assets to your children and then try to apply for Medicaid, your gifts have to have been made three years before you apply and five years before gifting to a trust.

If you do purchase long-term care, purchase it when you are healthy. Many illness, like Alzheimer's disease, will disqualify you. Many insurance companies will send someone out to test your memory once you are in your 70s. When you are considering these policies, pay attention to the following areas:

◆ **Waiver of premiums:** Most policies will waive the premiums when you enter the nursing home, but check your policy anyhow.

◆ **Length of coverage:** If you have enough assets, you may want to opt for lifetime coverage with a short waiting period for $100-a-day coverage and an inflation COLA of 5 percent. A policy like this for someone who is 70 and healthy will run over $4,000 a year. You can often save $200 a year for a policy that covers you for three years instead of life.

◆ **State benefits:** Before you pay for longer coverage periods, consider the state you live in. Some states, such as California, New York, Connecticut and Indiana, allow you to keep some of your assets intact and go onto Medicaid after your long-term insurance.

◆ **Elimination periods:** For a policy that offers lifetime benefits, let's say you would pay $3,027 for a 100-day waiting period, but $3,452 for a 20-day waiting period. You can save over $400 a year by waiting 100 days for coverage instead of 20. But how much would those 80 days really cost you? Eighty days at $100 would cost you $8,000 and would take you 20 years of premiums to break even. If you are young, it is probably definitely worth opting for a longer waiting period, but if you are older, you may want to pay the extra premium for these benefits.

◆ **Inflation clause:** Often, you need and should have an inflation clause of at least 3 percent. For a lifetime policy, you might save as much as $400 a year if you give up the inflation clause. If you have real estate, or stocks that keep growing in value each year, or if you have a pension plan with a cost-of-living index, you can forgo these inflation clauses.

◆ **Qualifications:** Many individuals buy these policies assuming they can enter the nursing homes voluntarily. If you are elderly and are having a hard time making it on your own with medical problems, you might want to admit yourself to a nursing home. However, these programs do not really cover voluntary admittance. A doctor, sometimes the insurance company's doctor, must certify that you can't perform two or three important activities yourself. Be careful to read the policies closely. Some policies will just have one or two words, such as "direct" or "continual," to describe the assistance you need. Defining the terms may eliminate your inability to use a nursing home.

34 WHAT SHOULD I LOOK FOR IN INSURANCE POLICIES?

One of the biggest problems with insurance plans is that we often do not understand what they cover until it is too late. In our fear that we may not have enough coverage, we may duplicate coverage and waste money.

If you decide that you would like to change to a new policy, do not cancel your old one. Keep older policies in effect until all elimination periods and time frames for preexisting conditions under your new policy have ended.

HOW MUCH INSURANCE DO YOU NEED?

Don't use magic formulas. Only get the amount of insurance that you need. If you are single, it is unlikely that you will need any life insurance. If you are married and you and your spouse both can support yourselves, you also may not need insurance, especially if you do not plan on having children.

Don't just buy life insurance so that you can make someone rich if you die. Allocate your insurance dollars among your health, disability and life insurance needs. Usually for someone young, health and disability are more important than life insurance.

Life Insurance

When buying life insurance consider the following:

- **Time periods:** If you are buying insurance to protect your family until your mortgage is paid off or your children are through school, then you may find the best bargains are set term insurance for 20 or 25 years. Consider policies whose cost will stay the same for this period, instead of annual renewable term (ART) policies.

◆ **Long-term insurance:** If your insurance needs are longer-term, more than 20 years, consider some whole life policies. These can be very expensive and filled with many hidden fees, but they can be attractive for a part of your insurance needs, or if you need money in an emergency. At retirement, you may find that borrowing from these policies instead of surrendering them can provide you with a stream of tax-free income.

◆ **Conversion features:** It may be smart to pay a little extra for your term for the ability to convert to whole life insurance without medical exams. Although term is often the best, as you get older or your health deteriorates, you will appreciate this conversion feature.

◆ **Shop around:** Compare prices on insurance. The prices vary dramatically for the same quality and quantity of insurance. Some states, such as Massachusetts, Connecticut and New York, have Savings Bank Life Insurance. These policies can sometimes be inexpensive policies. Check with companies such as Quotesmith Corporation in Darien, Illinois, at 1-800-556-9393. They will give you free quotes on many different companies.

◆ **Check ratings:** Check the ratings of your insurance companies to make sure they are going to be around when you need them. One of the most common sources are the ratings from A.M. Best Company, usually available at your local library.

◆ **Level premium:** Level premiums lock in rates for several years, but the rates can skyrocket when it is time to renew. Make sure you know the rates ahead of time.

Disability and Health Insurance

◆ **Preexisting conditions:** Look for clauses such as "preexisting conditions." These clauses will prevent you from getting coverage on any preexisting conditions you or your family may have. For example, if you have a child with asthma, you may want to be careful before you change jobs.

◆ **Coverage**: Review your policy carefully to determine the maximum coverage and how it is calculated. See if the maximum is for each illness, cumulative for one year or for a lifetime. Some policies will have a maximum for each family member; other policies will have it for the whole family. Be careful to look at the fine print and understand exactly how the maximums work. If your family has a history of cancer or heart disease, you should be very concerned with these limits. Hospital costs can run over $4,000 a day for many severe illnesses. You may not only be wiped out financially, but may not be able to get the care you need. If your maximum coverage is low, under $500,000, consider an excess major medical policy that supplements your current policies and offers higher limits for catastrophic illnesses.

◆ **Deductibles**: Do you need to pay a new deductible for each person, each year, each illness? The ideal is a policy that has a deductible that applies to the whole family on an annual basis.

◆ **Length of stay**: Some health and disability policies severely limit the length of stay in the hospital. The easiest way to reduce an insurance company's costs is to get patients out of the hospital as soon as possible. Many insurance companies require that healthy women only stay in the hospital 24 hours after the birth of their babies. Although the American Medical Association (AMA) is fighting this, check your policy and be certain that this is a clause with which you feel comfortable. You should learn the number of days and the dollar limits per day of your policy.

For disability insurance pay attention to the following:

◆ **Waiver of premiums.** Make sure your policy waives premiums if you become disabled.

◆ **Waiting periods.** This is the amount of time you have to wait for your payments to begin once you are disabled. Check and make sure these are no more than 60 to 90 days. A policy that makes you wait a year may be useless and you may find that you'll be wiped out financially before payments begin.

◆ **Lifetime benefits.** It is usually important to have disability benefits that will protect you for long periods of time. Lifetime benefits, however, are extremely expensive and add as much as 20 percent a year to your premiums. You should probably consider benefits that will continue until you are 65 or until you qualify for Social Security retirement. If you are totally disabled, you will qualify for Social Security disability.

◆ **Inflation hedges.** Protecting from inflation can be costly, but it is also important. Having at least a 3 percent COLA is probably necessary. If you have a COLA in your pension or growth investments, you may not need it for your disability.

◆ **Residual or partial benefits.** These payments are to compensate for less than full-time income when you return to work, but can't perform your normal duties. Always read the definitions and descriptions of terms, such as own-occupation, total permanent, partial permanent and residual benefits. Compare the definition of partial disability and proportionate benefits. Make sure your policies include terms such as "noncancelable" and "guaranteed renewable."

35 IF MY SPOUSE DIES, WHAT DO I DO ABOUT BENEFITS AND INSURANCE?

If one spouse dies, it can affect the surviving spouse's health, disability and group insurance as well as retirement assets.

Health Benefits. We all know to arrange for any life insurance policies after a death, but it may be more important to ensure that disability and health benefits continue for the living spouse and family. If you are covered under your spouse's group employment health policy and your spouse dies, what do you do?

First contact your spouse's employer immediately to find out if the group policy will cover **you** for a limited period of time. You should be able to get COBRA coverage for 36 months after your spouse's death. Do this immediately. As time passes, there is more opportunity for preexisting conditions to surface. If you miss out on COBRA, you need to convert to a new policy, either through your own employer, through some organization or as an individual. Be aware that individual coverage is very expensive.

Your COBRA coverage will end if you do not pay the premiums on time, if you become eligible for Medicare or if you and your dependents become covered under another group health care plan (unless the group health care plan has a preexisting condition clause that limits your coverage). If there is no coverage, get an interim insurance policy until you can find a new plan.

Life Insurance.   Make plans now, so that your spouse knows where and how he or she can get new insurance. Leave the names of contacts or personnel department representatives that should be contacted.

After you have taken care of new insurance for yourself, then start looking for insurance proceeds on your deceased spouse. In addition to the typical sources of life insurance, you should look into other sources. If your spouse was a government worker, look into payments under the Federal Employees' Compensation Act (FECA).

Also look at your auto insurance, which frequently includes medical or accidental death benefits. Check credit card companies, for many of these automatically offer accidental death insurance. If your spouse was a veteran, contact the Veterans Administration for benefits. Make sure you keep copies of discharge papers.

Retirement Plans.   Be especially careful about whom you name as your beneficiary on your IRAs and retirement plans. Discuss your decision with your tax adviser and lawyer. If you name your spouse, he or she can continue to hold assets tax-deferred in retirement plans. If you name a revocable trust or an estate as the beneficiary, at your death your IRA will cease to exist. Get IRA *Publication 590* for more information on beneficiaries.

Survivor's Benefits.   Most importantly, do not give up your rights to your survivor's benefits. By law, you have to sign before your spouse reduces the benefits given to you. Before you give up any of these benefits, be certain you understand the consequences.

36 ◢ DO EMPLOYER'S STOCKS AND BENEFITS PACKAGES AFFECT MY WILL AND ESTATE PLANNING?

Employer stocks and benefits can affect your estate more than any other assets. You need to get good tax advice on how to protect your estate if you have large amounts of employer stock.

Stock ownership in a healthy business is one of the best possible ways to increase your wealth. If you die or become disabled and you work for a publicly traded company, you should not have to worry about the ability of your family to cash in your stocks at your death.

But if you work for a small company, as over 50 percent of Americans do, you may find it more difficult to cash in your stocks. If you own stock in a small business, especially if you are a partial owner, make sure there are provisions to buy your stock back if you become disabled or die. Be certain that the company has a stock purchase agreement or a buy-and-sell agreement.

These agreements should clearly describe what happens if you or your spouse dies or becomes disabled. If you own company stock, your heirs need to have a way to sell it back to the company. Your company should also have life insurance for the stock owners so that funds are available to buy back the stocks and to back up the buy-and-sell agreement.

Valuation of Business Assets. It is important to have the buy-and-sell so you can get some money out of the business, and for estate and tax purposes. The buy-and-sell will allow you to plan your estate taxes ahead of time. If you do not have such an agreement, the IRS will put a value on the business and overvalue it. It is better to have a price agreed upon ahead of time, so you and your partners have control. In fact, it may be your single most important consideration.

Trusts. Don't try and write trusts yourself. Get a lawyer, especially if you have any nonqualified plans or benefit packages. Trusts are complicated, but if you are a high-income employee with substantial benefits, you should consider trusts to avoid large estate taxes.

Bypass Trust. If you have an estate over $600,000, you need a bypass trust in your will. This can save thousands on taxes. Don't assume that your estate is worth less than $600,000. If you work for a good company, by the time you add in insurance, benefits packages, personal belongings and your home equity, you may be worth that amount. Bypass trusts allow you to pass up to $1,200,000 in assets without estate tax. Your lawyer or financial adviser can show you what assets are better to hold in different trusts.

Living Trusts. Talk to your lawyer about dividing your estate between two living trusts, yours and your spouse's. It doesn't save on estate taxes, but it does make life easier for the person left behind. These are one of the most oversold vehicles today, but revocable living trusts do have some good points, such as avoiding probate, adding privacy, giving you immediate access to your funds and allowing you to change or revoke them at any time.

Charitable Remainder Trusts. If you have received large amounts of stocks and options over the years from your company, you may find the tax consequences so high that your only alternative is to leave the stock in your estate and let your heirs sell it at a stepped-up-cost basis. However, if you need the income to live off of, you might want to consider charitable remainder trusts. You don't have to be a millionaire for these to work, but you should have a large amount of appreciated nonincome-producing assets such as land, property or growth stocks.

Let's look at Henry Almost-retired. He has very little savings outside his company stock option plan and some land that he bought 50 years ago. If he sells the stocks or land, his cost basis is so low, he will have to give up a large portion in taxes and he will not have enough income to live on.

For example, he paid $5,000 for the land in 1946, and it is now worth over $105,000. The average cost of his stocks is $55,000, but they are now worth over $255,000. If he were to sell the stocks and land, he would have to pay capital gains taxes of $84,000. Between the two sales he has over $277,000 and if we assume he can earn 8 percent, he will have an income of $22,080.

But, instead, if he gifted the stocks and land to a charity, and placed it in a charitable remainder trust, the charity would have $360,000 of assets. When the charity sells the assets, there are no capital gains. If the charity earns 8 percent, it can give Henry an income of $28,800. Not only does Henry receive a higher income, he has avoided the capital gains. He can have the income for 20 years or until his or his beneficiaries' deaths. Robert Lionette, a consultant on charitable gift giving, says the best part is that "In addition to supporting a charity if he doesn't need the income from the trust, it can also be used to purchase additional life insurance to pay estate taxes."

If Henry does not extend the income for a long time or take the whole amount of income, he will also get a tax deduction that he can use now. The IRS calculates the deduction based on your age, the amount you gift and the rate of return you expect the trust to pay. If he takes less income from the trust, his tax deductions will be higher.

Get professional advice and be careful, because once you set these trusts up, they can't be undone.

Guardianship. When you are planning for your employee benefits, you also must consider your children, especially if they are underage. Make sure you know all the medical, educational and financial benefits from your employer, as well as from Social Security. Be careful to appoint a guardian who will not only love and care for your children but who also has experience managing money. Consider some spendthrift trusts and other trusts to help protect your children.

You may not want to name your children as beneficiaries on insurance and employee retirement accounts since they may not be able to collect the benefits directly. Have the funds directed to trusts for the children. When you plan for your children, you can have a single trust that will pool the funds and provide for all the children based on their individual needs. This trust will terminate when the last child reaches the age of majority.

If you feel one child may need more money or more funds, these trusts can work out well. If you do not use a trust, you need separate guardianship appointments for each child who is a minor. The problem with this arrangement is that one child may need more money than the others because of age or special circumstances. If they all share equally with separate guardianship, it may be difficult to shift funds from one child to another.

Your children are too important to leave to chance, so get a good lawyer and financial planner to help you decide on the best arrangements.

Large Pensions. Be especially careful of leaving large amounts in pensions. When we are alive, it is very attractive to postpone distributions for as long as possible to avoid current income taxes. But if we pass away, it can create many estate tax problems. Estate taxes are very high on many of these assets, since there is no stepped-up cost basis for retirement assets. If you have large pension assets, it is worth hiring a tax adviser to assess the merits of various distribution strategies.

37 HOW MUCH SUPPLEMENTAL GROUP LIFE INSURANCE COVERAGE DO I NEED?

Group life insurance sounds like a great deal, especially when your employer pays, but be careful. While the first $50,000 paid by your employer is tax-free, any amount of insurance over that is included in your taxable income. You should take the first $50,000, but you should compare the cost of supplemental insurance and estimate the taxes on additional employer-paid coverage. Before you sign up for additional group insurance, calculate the amount of life insurance you need.

If you decide you need additional insurance, you should compare the costs of supplemental insurance through your employer versus a term policy elsewhere. If you are young, healthy and do not smoke, you may find that your employer's plan is likely to be more costly. Most group plans offered by employers are attractive for older workers and smokers, if the plans are based on a flat rate.

38 WHAT SHOULD I DO IF I AM ILL OR DISABLED?

- ◆ **Contact list.** Make an important person contact list that lets your friends and family know what to do and who to contact.
- ◆ **Insurance companies.** Notify all your insurance companies immediately, from health care to life insurance, and check the waiver of premiums. This is a standard feature on most disability policies. If you have a terminal illness, you may be able to tap into your life insurance proceeds.
- ◆ **Investments.** You need to think seriously about increasing your safety and minimizing your risks with investments. Call your broker and have any automatic reinvestment plans stopped. Start an orderly, systematic approach to converting funds to emergency cash. As opportunities appear to move out of positions, do so. Have your broker put in safeguards on any stocks. Place "stop-loss" orders under the price, so if they fall, you will get out before your profits erode or you face

large losses. Sell "calls" on your stocks to generate extra income and minimize downside risk (We'll talk more about this in Chapter 7).

◆ **Stop reinvestment programs** on stocks and mutual funds.

◆ **Stop retirement contributions.** If you can't tap easily into your retirement plans, then stop contributing as soon as you know the severity of your illness or disability.

◆ **Stop payroll deductions.** You may need to change your payroll deductions such as the amounts you are paying to credit cards and loans, and money going to savings and retirement plans.

◆ **Creditors.** Contact your mortgage company and any other creditors and negotiate a loan schedule that will allow you to postpone payments.

◆ **Social Security.** If a physician certifies that you can't work for 12 months or more or that you are expected to die, you may qualify for Social Security benefits.

◆ **State disability plans.** Look at your pay stub and see if there are deductions for state disability.

◆ **Worker's compensation.** If you are hurt at work, notify your employer and check out worker's compensation. Look into the allowances or reimbursements that are paid to the handicapped under the Employment Opportunities for Handicapped Individuals Act.

◆ **Taxes.** Get tax advice. You will find that most of your benefits from workers' compensation, Federal Employees' Compensation Act(FECA), compensatory damages, disability insurance proceeds in which you paid the premiums for, reimbursements for medical care and compensation for permanent loss of a body part are usually not taxable. However, there are always small glitches that can trigger tax consequences.

39 WHAT AM I ENTITLED TO UNDER WORKER'S COMPENSATION?

If you become ill or sick because of work, you may qualify for worker's compensation. The most important thing to remember is that not all companies offer the same benefits. Think of worker's compensation as a benefit when you are comparing job alternatives.

Worker's compensation laws were created to protect workers who become ill or disabled because of work-related issues. You do not have to prove your employer was at fault, only that you were hurt as a result of your job. You may qualify for medical expense reimbursements, rehabilitation services, lost income and survivors benefits. These benefits have maximums and they will change from state to state. Do not assume that you automatically are covered under worker's compensation. In some states your employer can elect not to participate and you will have to sue for damages. If you are a federal government employee you are covered under the Federal Worker's Compensation Act. Some workers, such as stevedores, longshoremen and ship repairers fall under their own laws, as well as railroad employees and seamen aboard ships.

Some workers are excluded because of their occupation, such as agricultural, domestic or casual employees. If you work for a small employer, you may find that there also is no worker's compensation. With all these different plans, how do you know what you will get?

Your disability or illness may be classified under worker's compensation as temporary total, meaning that although you may recover, you are completely disabled for a period of time, or permanent-total, or temporary-partial. Worker's compensation disability payments usually last for a limited amount of time, such as ten years. The amount you receive is based on your income. For example, if you are permanently disabled, you will get 66⅔ percent of your average weekly wage based on the preceding 13 weeks. Even though that sounds like you might be taking a large hit in income, since most of this income is tax-free, you may net an amount close to your previous income.

There is one catch, though. If your worker's compensation is reduced because of Social Security or Railroad Retirement benefits, then those benefits will be taxable. Once you return to work, any worker's compensation you receive is taxable.

CHAPTER 5

Planning for Retirement

 **40** HOW DO I KNOW WHICH TYPE OF
PENSION PLAN I HAVE?

When we look at retirement plans, the easiest way to identify them
is by **who contributes** the money. If your employer contributes the
money, your risks and responsibilities are much different than those
plans in which you contribute.

We can also look at plans by **who manages** and invests the
assets. When you manage and invest the money, the plans are called
"segregated" and "self-directed." When your employer directs the
assets, they are "managed" and "pooled."

Think of four different recipes for your retirement. The ingredients are the amount of contributions and the investment talent.

RECIPE #1. DEFINED-BENEFIT PLAN

Recipe #1 is quite simple. There are no surprises. Your employer puts
the dollars into a pooled account, manages your money and makes
a promise to pay you a set amount of retirement income. You know
exactly what you will get. As you can see, this is a very simple
concept. The only ingredient is the promise your employer makes to
you.

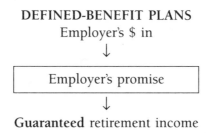

DEFINED-BENEFIT PLANS
Employer's $ in
↓

| Employer's promise |

↓
Guaranteed retirement income

RECIPE #2. POOLED DEFINED-CONTRIBUTION PLAN

Recipe #2 has some surprises. The contributions are defined, but you are not sure what will come out. Your employer pools the ingredients—the dollars and the investment management—but makes no promises as to how much you will get in retirement. There can be a lot of surprises depending on your employer's talent for investing. Defined contribution plans can include money purchase, profit-sharing, stock bonus, ESOP, 457 and cash balance plans.

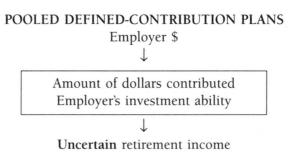

POOLED DEFINED-CONTRIBUTION PLANS
Employer $
↓

| Amount of dollars contributed |
| Employer's investment ability |

↓
Uncertain retirement income

RECIPE #3. SEGREGATED DEFINED-CONTRIBUTION PLAN

Now you are the cook. Your employer contributes the ingredients, but you are the one who has to mix them properly. Your employer puts a defined amount of dollars into a segregated or separate account for you. To avoid the fiduciary liability involved in managing your money, he or she turns those funds over to you and you are responsible for the investment's management. Sometimes your employer may select broad categories of investments for you, such as mutual fund families (typical with 401(k) matching plans), but you have to select from among those options. Or your employer could contribute the funds into segregated accounts in which you have complete control, such as segregated profit-sharing, money purchase and Simplified Employee Pension plans (SEPs). There can be lots of surprises. Not only do you have to rely on your employer for the amount of the contribution, but you have to count on your own investment talents.

SEGREGATED DEFINED-CONTRIBUTION PLANS
Employer $

Amount contributed Employer's ability to pick good funds Your investment abilities.

↓
A **surprise!** or a very **uncertain** retirement income

RECIPE #4. EMPLOYEE SEGREGATED ACCOUNTS

Now you are the person supplying the ingredients. You have to put up the "dough." You put the dollars in and you handle the investments. You could go hungry if you do not do a good job. You really are almost entirely responsible for your own future. Your employer may have a little input, as with 401(k)s in which he or she selects the broad categories of investments, but you are now really the one in control. Your employer may even contribute some money into the plan, such as the matching portion of a 401(k) or the SEP portion of a SARSEP, but you still will need to make contributions. These plans include 401(k)s, SARSEPs, IRAs and 403(b)s.

EMPLOYEE SEGREGATED ACCOUNTS
Your $ in
↓

> Your investment talent
> Your contributions
> Tax savings

↓

A **big surprise** or a **very uncertain** retirement income

It is extremely important to monitor funds that your employer controls and even more important to monitor funds that you control yourself. When your employer invests the funds for you, you must be sure the funds are diversified; that you are receiving statements showing the gains, losses and values of the account; and that the account is following retirement guidelines. In employee-funded plans such as 401(k)s and 403(b)s, your employer may select the broad funds, but you are in control of the investments to a great degree. In SARSEPs, SEP-IRAs, segregated, self-directed plans and IRAs, you are in complete control. With plans you control and invest, you cannot stop with just monitoring the accounts. Your retirement planning gets much more complicated, and you must do more work.

401(k)s

The most popular employee-funded plans today are 401(k)s. Both you and your employer can contribute to these plans, and both you and your employer, to some degree, control the investments. Your employer may pick the companies and the broad categories of mutual funds that you can invest in. It is then up to you to select among those alternatives.

If you participate in a 401(k), you must be given at least three broadly diversified investments to select. Typically, this means a money market fund, a diversified stock fund and a bond fund. You must be given the opportunity to move your funds frequently enough to protect you from volatile markets. Your employer is still usually responsible for selecting the families of funds and the investment professionals that you are forced to work with. Therefore, your employer is not relieved of all fiduciary responsibilities and can be held liable for losses resulting from rash and thoughtless selection of fund groups or managers. However, you are the person primarily responsible for selecting the funds, determining your risk level and monitoring your performance.

In addition to knowing what type of plan you have, you should also know:

◆ The name, address and phone number of the plan fiduciary.

◆ Information on how you can handle exchanges, purchases and specified limitations and restrictions to your investments.

◆ When you can transact trades. If your plan is an employer stock fund, the stock must trade in sufficient frequency and volume to enable you to buy and sell it.

◆ The past performance and rates of return of the different investment options that you are given.

◆ Your employer's fiduciaries and agents. Make sure your employer has no conflict of interest when selecting the institution, people or investment alternatives used. If your employer gains any benefit, such as discounted commissions on personal accounts or lines of credit on loans, then you have recourse for losses in those situations.

41 IS A DEFINED-BENEFIT PLAN SAFER THAN A DEFINED-CONTRIBUTION PLAN?

In most instances defined-benefit plans are safer than defined-contribution plans. Since defined-benefit plans guarantee you specified retirement benefits for life, you don't have to worry about the investment performance. The risk of poor investment performance rests with the employer, not with you. If there is a loss or shortfall in performance, the employer has to make up for the loss by contributing more to the plan.

Most of these plans are guaranteed by the Pension Benefit Guaranty Corporation (PBGC), a corporation in the U.S. Department of Labor. Your employer pays premiums to insure that if the company fails and terminates the plan, your retirement assets will be protected. A word of warning, however: Some defined-benefit plans are not covered by insurance, such as government plans, plans that cover owners only and plans for professional service companies with less than 25 active participants. You don't have to worry about the solvency if your employer is the government, but if you work for a small professional service company, such as a lawyer's, doctor's or dentist's office, accounting or architectural firm, make sure the plan is solvent, fully funded and managed responsibly.

In the past many large employers offered defined-benefit plans. But today, many businesses are eliminating these plans because of the large expenses, liability and commitment required on the part of the employer. Instead, **employers are shifting the risks to you, the employee,** and no longer guaranteeing any specified retirement benefits. They are reverting to plans in which employers and/or employees contribute, but do not guarantee any specified return. Your income will depend a lot on your employer's or your experience and talent at picking stocks.

DEFINED-CONTRIBUTION PLANS

If your employer contributes to a plan for you, but your retirement depends on how much is contributed and how well the assets perform, then your plan is a defined-contribution plan.

> Defined-Benefit plan:
>   Employer \$ in → guaranteed retirement → out
> Defined-Contribution plan:
>   Employer \$ in → uncertain retirement → out

While defined-contribution plans are riskier than defined-benefit plans because poor performance and losses in investments will affect your retirement income, they may actually offer you higher retirement income if the investments perform well. Ultimately, your retirement income will be determined by the contributions that your employer makes as well as the income, gains and losses on these plans, so you should monitor these plans carefully.

How much does your employer contribute for you?

If you have a money purchase plan, your employer is required to make a contribution each year. The amounts can range from almost nothing to 25 percent of compensation. These percentages can be found in the plan documents and cannot change from year to year.

With profit-sharing plans, the contribution can change depending on the profit of the company. The percent can range from zero to 15 percent (with some variances for age-weighted plans). However, even though the contributions are discretionary and can fluctuate with the company's profits, IRS regulations require that there must be some regularity and the contributions must be substantial, in order for the plan to be tax-qualified.

42 HOW CAN I PUT MY MONEY INTO A 401(k), SARSEP OR 403(b) AND STILL MAKE ENDS MEET?

Whenever you are given the opportunity to save in retirement plans, you should take it. Retirement plans are simply a way for you to save without paying taxes on your earnings until you pull the money out. In addition, you get a tax deduction. If your plan has a matching agreement, then your employer will help by putting money into the plan, too.

Many workers refuse to contribute at all to these plans, and almost 23 million eligible employees do not participate in 401(k)s. And, of the over 72 million participants in 401(k)s, many contribute only minimal amounts. We come up with many excuses not to participate. Here are a few of them.

> Excuse #1: 401(k)s, 403(b)s and SARSEPs are difficult to understand.

Actually these retirement plans are just savings plans with some bells and whistles. The unique feature of these plans over a bank savings account is that you get a tax deduction when you put the money in and the money grows year after year without any tax consequences. Unlike savings accounts, you can't just pull your money out whenever you want.

There isn't much difference between 401(k)s, SARSEPs and 403(b)s. The 401(k)s are pretax saving accounts for companies with more than 25 employees. SARSEPs are similar to 401(k)s except they are for smaller companies with less than 25 employees. The 403(b)s are pretax savings accounts for public schools, colleges and tax-exempt employers such as hospitals, churches and charitable institutions. In 1995, you could save up to $9,240 in 401(k)s and SARSEPs and up to $9,500 in 403(b)s.

Excuse #2: We might need the money someday.

If you are afraid to save in these plans because you may need the money someday, you should be aware that many plans allow you to borrow your retirement funds. Check with your employer about the restrictions and limitations on borrowing. Although you will have to pay taxes on these funds when you pull your money out (if you are under age 59½, you may have a 10 percent penalty), 401(k)s are very flexible. You can borrow for an emergency, education or home purchases. Currently, 81 percent of these plans allow you to borrow for such reasons. Often, you can take funds out without penalties if you become disabled.

If you change jobs, you do have to worry about the portion that your employer contributed. In some companies, if you quit or leave before five years, you may not be fully vested and therefore aren't entitled to your employer's contributions. You can always take all of yours.

Excuse #3: We can't afford to save.

If you think that you cannot afford the loss in cash flow, have the taxes coming out of your paycheck reduced. Simply go to your employer and ask to increase the number of withholdings. If you contribute to a retirement plan, your take-home pay will be less, but your total wealth will increase. Tax deductions and tax-deferred compounding are the best reasons to save in retirement accounts instead of saving in individual accounts. Tax-deferred compounding is more important than most workers think.

For example, a couple in the 30 percent tax bracket who saved $2,000 outside their retirement accounts over the past 6 years would see their savings grow to over $15,308 at a 10 percent pretax and 7 percent after-tax rate. In 41 more years, it would be worth $459,264. Not bad for $12,000 saved. But if they had saved in their tax-deferred retirement accounts, it would be worth almost $1,073,273, because they were able to earn the 10 percent of income tax-deferred.

Many times we don't participate because we cannot afford to save. The fact is, we cannot afford not to save. The reason your employer is probably offering a 401(k) or SARSEP is because you are no longer offered other, more attractive pension plans, such as defined-benefit or defined-contribution plans. You can no longer count on the government and Social Security to support your retirement. The 401(k)s, SARSEPs and 403(b)s are some of the best ways to do that. As we showed previously, you increase your real income when you save in these plans.

43 HOW MUCH SHOULD I CONTRIBUTE TO A MATCHING PLAN?

You should contribute the maximum amount. If your employer is willing to give you free money, take it. If you don't, you are throwing money away. Aside from saving for emergency funds, 401(k)s are truly the best saving vehicles available to most workers. As we saw in Question #9, if you do not match your employer's contributions, you will be throwing thousands of dollars away, even if you are in lower tax brackets. You will be giving up the possibility of doubling and tripling your money in one year.

Always contribute to your 401(k) before any other savings if your employer matches. The maximum contribution for 1995 was $9,240. Usually this number is indexed for inflation, but for 1995 there was no increase from 1994. The income that you can base your contribution on has been reduced for all retirement plans. Currently, you can only base your retirement contribution on $150,000. This is down from the previous amount of $236,000.

You should always save at least 10 percent of your income, but you may have a hard time doing that. If your employer matches dollar for dollar, it will give you a good opportunity to meet your goals and you only need to save 5 percent.

44 HOW DO SARSEPs AND SEPs BENEFIT ME?

If you work for a small company, you may find that sometimes you do not get the benefits larger companies offer. However, if your company has a SARSEP, in many ways you may find it better than large company plans. These plans, designed for small companies with less than 25 employees and for self-employed individuals, can save some of the dramatically increasing administrative costs of 401(k)s and other plans. Because the contributions are made directly to the employee's accounts and the employee immediately gets to control the investments, the normal administrative and reporting requirements (Form 5500) are generally not applicable with SEPs.

As employers shift from employer-funded plans to employee-funded plans, they are no longer so concerned about negotiating the best rates for the employees. Since funds come out of the employee's pocket, employers often pass on the hidden costs of the plans to employees by reducing benefits. SARSEPs, however, if managed properly, have minimal or no administrative fees. Most brokerage firms and banks handle these accounts for as little as $35 per participant, per year. There are fees associated with commissions for the investments, but unless you trade a lot, these can be kept to a minimum.

SARSEPs and SEPs offer almost all the same advantages as 401(k)s. There are a couple of differences that, for many workers, enhance the opportunities of SARSEPs over 401(k)s. Once your employer makes the contribution on your behalf, you are 100 percent vested. That means if you leave, the funds are all yours. It also means your employer has no control over your account, and regular IRA rules govern it. You have more responsibility than with 40l(k)s since no one is even selecting the broad range of funds for you to choose from. SARSEPs let you select and manage any investment you want, unlike 401(k)s, which restrict you to several mutual funds.

You also have less government oversight and less avenues of recourse if something goes wrong. You are truly on your own. Although your company will not have to file IRS and Department of Labor reports, your employer must provide you with a copy of the completed SEP agreement form and a yearly statement showing any contributions made on your behalf to your SEP. Additionally, you must be provided with general information on SEPs.

If you run a small business yourself, or have any self-employment income, consider Keogh plans (profit-sharing and money purchase plans for small businesses) and SARSEPs. You can contribute up to 20 percent of your income or $30,000 annually, whichever is less, into money purchase Keogh plans, and $22,500 into SEPs and profit-sharing Keogh plans.

WHAT DO YOU NEED TO KNOW
ABOUT YOUR SARSEPS?

- ◆ Think of SARSEPs as two accounts. The SAR portion is made up of your contributions, and the SEP portion is made up of your employer's. You can also add an IRA to it and make it a SEP-IRA.

- ◆ Know how much your employer is contributing on your behalf. SEPs and profit-sharing plans are flexible and the annual contributions can range from zero to 15 percent of your compensation. If your company is experiencing a weak cash position, you may see your contributions fluctuate. The maximum amount that both you and your employer can put into a SARSEP is $30,000. The amount you can put into the SAR portion is $9,240.

- ◆ Know your responsibilities. You are now the one responsible for the investment performance. Your employer has basically eliminated much of his or her fiduciary liability by transferring control to you, so you should understand and invest your funds properly.

- ◆ Know your employer's responsibilities. Your employer is still responsible for losses resulting from fraud or prohibited transactions, and for limitations on investment alternatives.

- ◆ Know the type of investment options you have and the expenses and fees related to these investments. With 401(k)s you have several mutual funds to select from, but with SARSEPs, your options are almost unlimited. If you are knowledgeable about investing, you may do much better than with the limited choices of 401(k)s and 403(b)s. If you have never handled investments before, get some professional help. Look at the investment strategies in Chapter 6.

45 IS MY COMPANY PENALIZING ME BY SEPARATING MY FUNDS FROM ITS FUNDS?

Segregation or separating your funds from your employer's can make your pension safer or riskier. It depends on you. Frequently, retirement plans expose your employer to liability because of employer mismanagement and lack of financial experience. To reduce fiduciary liability, companies give the employees the right to determine their own investment by segregating or separating each employee's account.

You, as an employee, can benefit from segregated accounts because you have more control over the assets. You have what is known as a self-directed account. If you have experience and the time to manage your own finances, these accounts can be preferable. However, they increase the need for you to become more knowledgeable about investments. If you are uncomfortable with investing, consider a conservative portfolio, such as those described in Chapter 6.

SELECTING YOUR INVESTMENTS

When you are responsible for your own retirement, you should follow some basic investment rules:

1. Diversify your funds into several categories so that you do not expose yourself to inordinate amounts of risk.
2. Remember that opportunity risk in forsaking higher-returning investments is just as much a risk to your future as market risk, or interest rate risk. To protect from inflation, have a portfolio that is invested in stock funds and tangible assets as well as bonds and CDs.
3. Stagger or ladder your investments over several maturity dates to minimize interest rate risk.
4. Work with the plan's adviser in selecting an appropriate asset allocation for your age, risk tolerance and current economic conditions. Lean more to growth investments if you are young and to shorter-term income investments as you approach retirement.
5. Stay with investments you understand.
6. Monitor your investments quarterly.
7. Have the broker or banker give you annual reports comparing the returns for your funds versus the returns for the market indexes.
8. If you have a high-risk tolerance and are young, consider adding international investments to your portfolio.

9. Take your responsibility seriously. Mismanaging retirement accounts can be the most costly and damaging financial mistake you can make.

10. Avoid investing more than 5 percent in any one investment.

46 ARE DEFERRED-COMPENSATION PLANS TOO RISKY TO OPT FOR?

In a deferred-compensation plan, your employer actually defers pay for you to be used at a later date, usually retirement. But deferred-compensation plans can be a lot riskier than other plans. If your company is sued, you could lose your entire deferred package. Deferred-compensation plans can be either funded or unfunded. If funded, an annuity is usually purchased as the funding mechanism. If unfunded, you basically have a promise from your employer, a promise that is unsecured and not backed by much more than your employer's word.

There are big pluses to these plans, however. You often are allowed to contribute as much as you want to these plans, tax-deferred. They are a good alternative to taxable raises. Also, your employer can discriminate and tailor the plan to you. The same plan doesn't have to be given to everyone. Your company does not receive any tax deduction for these until you are finally paid, but it is still worthwhile for it to utilize these plans, especially if the corporation wants to reward you and has a low tax liability.

47 MY EMPLOYER HAS SO MANY DIFFERENT PLANS FOR ME. WHAT ARE THE PROS AND CONS OF EACH?

There are so many variations of qualified and nonqualified plans that employers offer that there is almost no way to keep track of all of them. Most of them apply to highly paid executives and will not apply to all workers. Each company can have so many unique aspects, it is often beneficial to check with your employer. Many of these plans you will have no control over and will not be able to join. However, it is important that you know about them, since you may want to negotiate some of the nonqualified packages in lieu of raises or bonuses. Usually, most nonqualified plans revolve around insurance of some type to avoid much of the tax consequences of savings. Many employees and employers revert to nonqualified plans in which they do not have to abide by all the same vesting and participation rules. Qualified plans offer tax advantages, but they must meet rigid IRS rules that don't allow employers to discriminate or to give benefits to one employee without giving to all or to an entire class.

Most of these plans have the advantage of allowing you to save without paying taxes on the current income earned. They offer you some negotiating power with your employer. They also allow you to save much greater amounts than you ever could save otherwise. Many of them do not appear on your pay stub at all, so they save you current income taxes.

The disadvantages are that many of these plans are vulnerable to lawsuits and whims of management. Most of these plans will be entirely taxable when you withdraw the funds, unless you borrow from the insurance portions. None of these plans allows for rollovers when you retire or change jobs, so you could have more complicated tax problems.

Look in the glossary for more detailed definitions of thrift plans, supplemental executive retirement plans and COLAs.

48 CAN MY EMPLOYER REDUCE THE CONTRIBUTION TO MY RETIREMENT PLAN BY INTEGRATING IT WITH SOCIAL SECURITY?

In order to reduce the contributions for employees, employers can integrate retirement plans with Social Security. This simply means that your employer's contribution for you can be based on your income after Social Security is taken out. For example, if your income is $20,000, instead of basing your contribution on $20,000, it is based on $18,470. This means you will get a smaller contribution. If your employer was contributing 10 percent, your share will be $1,847 versus $2,000.

At first glance it seems unfair, but in many cases this method is used to balance off the reduced retirement funds now allowed for higher-income employers.

If you had two job offers, with the same income and the same pension plan, but one pension plan is integrated with Social Security and the other is not, choose the nonintegrated plan. There are many subtle variations of pension plans and benefits, so carefully check out all the details and get as much information as possible on all the benefits that are offered.

Even though a couple of hundred dollars does not seem like much, it can build up dramatically in a tax-deferred account and make a big difference to your retirement security.

49 WHY DO WOMEN HAVE TO SAVE MORE THAN MEN?

Historically, women live longer than men. That means there is more risk that they will outlive their retirement assets and fall into poverty later in life. Since women's salaries are as little as two thirds of men's, it is even more important for women to make better financial decisions and imperative to make every dollar count.

While it is assumed that women historically haven't seemed interested in money management, women are often concerned with the goals that money provides: children's education, security, less stress, a comfortable retirement and their parents' care. To achieve these goals, women must learn to manage money more effectively. The Department of Labor recently decided to provide women with a better understanding of workplace and financial decisions. It has begun an educational program designed to make women aware of retirement needs.

Just as importantly, women who don't work and remain home to provide for their families also need to participate in and understand workplace decisions. Homemakers are more vulnerable to a spouse's bad decisions. Often, because of a simple lack of understanding about finances, women aren't equipped to protect their families from financial ruin. Often they turn that responsibility over to their spouses.

Many women who face the dreaded "D"s—divorce, death and disability—are often left with little or no assets and frequently enter the workforce at minimum wages. In fact, according to Prudential Securities' *Women and Investing*, over 73 percent of people who live below the poverty level are women with an average Social Security payment of less than $600 a month.

◆ If you are married make sure you understand your spouse's benefits, as well as your own benefits.

- ◆ Have an emergency plan. Know where you can get your money quickly. Check the borrowing potential of 401(k)s.
- ◆ Women don't save enough. Only 25 percent consider saving important, according to a study conducted by Prudential Securities and *Working Woman Magazine* in 1995. When women do invest, over 70 percent tend to remain with what they consider the safest investments such as CDs and money market accounts. Be sure to follow the savings guidelines I've referred to in other sections of this book.
- ◆ Make a list of exactly what income your family will be able to tap into in case of death or disability. Evaluate all Social Security, worker's compensation and employee benefits.
  - ◆ If you or your spouse has the ability to choose among several job alternatives, consider those that offer the best benefits and insurance packages, even if the wages are slightly lower.
  - ◆ If you can't support yourself or your family without your spouse's income, purchase some additional employer's group term insurance on your spouse's life.
- ◆ If you or your spouse own your own business or are in a partnership, make sure that there are proper buy-and-sell agreements in place so that business partners can buy you out of the business at a fair price.
- ◆ Get good disability policies.
- ◆ When your spouse retires, make sure you review carefully the survivor benefits, and do not waive your rights to these benefits unless you are absolutely sure you can survive without them.
- ◆ Consider naming spouses as beneficiaries on IRAs and pension plans instead of your estate. That way, assets can avoid probate, go directly to the spouse and often maintain their tax-deferred status.
- ◆ Have wills and estate plans, even if you do not feel you have a large estate. Titling property correctly can often avoid estate taxes and a lot of hassle. For example, if property is titled joint with rights of survivorship, it will pass to your survivor directly rather than going through the will. Be careful especially on how you title your home and business assets.
- ◆ If you are taking time out of your career to raise a family, make sure you keep your work skills current.

◆ Even if you don't work, get a spousal IRA and have the maximum contributed to your account, not to your spouse's. Individuals often assume that if they are contributing the maximum $2,250 allowed for a couple with a nonworking spouse, that the entire $2,000 must go to the working spouse and only $250 to the nonworking spouse. This is not true. In most situations you want to have the $2,000 go to the nonworking spouse so that for estate planning purposes there will be some division of property. You can divide the $2,250 up in any way, as long as neither one gets more than $2,000. You both can get $1,125, or one year the husband can get $2,000 and the wife $250 and then the next year flip-flop it.

◆ If you are nervous about investing, attend seminars, take community college classes or contact The National Center for Women and Retirement Research, which holds seminars across the country. For free information, you can call The National Center for Women and Retirement Research at 1-800-426-7386 for information on its own financial-planning seminars, or Money Matters for Women or Prudential Securities 1-800-321-2623 or 1-800-432-0068, which have set up a series of seminars with *Working Women Magazine.*

50 CAN I STILL CONTRIBUTE TO AN IRA IF I HAVE A PENSION PLAN?

If you have money to invest, in addition to what you are saving through your employer's retirement plans, you should consider IRAs. Make sure you have three months of emergency money set aside, but after that, "think" IRA.

One of the most common misconceptions that workers make is to think if they have a retirement plan, they cannot contribute to an IRA. Everyone with earned income can contribute to an IRA, although sometimes you may lose part of your deduction. It's true that if your income is above certain levels, you might not qualify for the deduction. Then you need an IRA more because you can use the tax deferral and the additional retirement savings.

If you do not have a pension, there are no income levels to worry about, you can contribute no matter how much you earn and your IRA will be tax-deductible as well as tax-deferred.

1. Anyone who is not covered by other pension plans qualifies for the full deduction up to $2,000 or 100 percent of income, whichever is less.
2. Anyone who is covered by a pension plan but who falls below the following adjusted gross income is allowed the full deduction: under $40,000 if filing jointly; under $25,000 if filing singly.
3. Partial deductions are also allowed for some individuals even if they are covered by other pension plans. Those qualifying for the partial deduction must have adjusted gross incomes of: between $40,000–$50,000 joint; between $25,000–$35,000 single.

   The deduction phases out by 20 percent for each thousand dollars above $40,000 for joint and $25,000 for single. For example, if you earn $30,000 and are single, you are allowed only a $1,000 deduction. See the chart below.

Joint Income	Single Income	Deduction Allowed
$40,000	$25,000	$2,000
41,000	26,000	1,800
42,000	27,000	1,600
43,000	28,000	1,400
44,000	29,000	1,200
45,000	30,000	1,000
46,000	31,000	800
47,000	32,000	600
48,000	33,000	400
49,000	34,000	200
50,000	35,000	0

4. Couples filing jointly and earning $50,000 and more or those filing singly earning $35,000 and more cannot take a deduction for IRAs if they have pension plans. You can contribute but you can't deduct.

Where To Invest Your IRA. The first and most costly misconception is that you can invest IRA dollars only in CDs and in money markets. In fact, these often are the least attractive alternatives for young investors who need to prepare for many future years of inflation.

Investing in CDs and money markets may give investors the safest investments when considering default. However, CDs and money markets average 5 to 10 percent lower than the average high-quality mutual fund. Concentrate on achieving higher yields is crucial in IRAs and pension plans, where such rates can make a dramatic difference. For example, if you were to average an 8 percent return on your money over 40 years with the maximum annual contribution of $4,000 for a working couple, you would net approximately $1,119,124! If you were to lock into longer-term yields and average 12 percent, you would net closer to $3,436,570, a $2.3 million difference. This would mean you would have income of $36,380 a month for 20 years rather than $7,563 a month. Those amounts should alleviate anyone's fear of inflation and insecure retirement.

When To Contribute.   A second costly misconception is assuming that it doesn't matter when you contribute to your IRAs. It does matter. Delaying contributions can be very costly. If each year, for the next 30 years, you were to delay a $4,000 contribution (allowed for a working couple) from January 1st until April 15th of the following year, it will cost you over $80,000 at an assumed 10 percent rate of return. At higher rates it will cost even more.

Effects of Inflation.   It is true that regular contributions to an IRA can make you a millionaire. But that may be misleading. If rates are high enough to allow you to accumulate large sums in your IRA, most likely inflation also will be high and those dollars will be worth much less.

If inflation were to average around 10 percent annually, as it did in the 1970s, over the next 35 years, one million dollars could be worth as little as $35,000 in today's dollars. If inflation looks like it is increasing, consider some natural resource funds for part of your IRA.

Coordinate Your IRA with Other Investments.   If your 401(k) has limited funds to select from, your IRA can be a good opportunity to complement those funds and fill in the gaps of your portfolio. You must coordinate your IRA carefully with your other investments. Place your riskiest investments in your regular account and your higher-yielding, income-oriented investments in your IRA.

There are two reasons for this. First, if you have a loss in your regular account, you can write it off on your taxes and the government will absorb part of your losses. Second, higher-yielding income investments have high tax consequences, so you want to shelter them as much as possible.

Funding Your IRAs.   You do not have to contribute to your IRA before you can claim it on your tax returns and file your return. If your IRA leads to a tax refund, you can use the refund for part of your IRA contribution. The law presently requires only that you fund your IRA before April 15th of the following year, so if you can file early and get your refund back before the 15th, you can use it for part of your IRA. If it does not come in time, it is probably worth borrowing money for your contribution from other sources (you can even borrow from your 401(k)).

Change Your Withholdings.   You do not have to wait for your tax refund to experience the tax savings. If you wish to receive your tax savings each month, change your withholding to reflect the IRA investments, which will result in reduced taxes all year. You can roll the monthly savings into the following year's IRA. If you will be tempted to spend the extra dollars, this concept doesn't work well.

IRA and Liquidity.   Everyone always assumes that IRAs are so illiquid that they are useless. That is not true. Although there are penalties if you withdraw before age 59½, you may still find, if you qualify for the tax deduction and if you can hold the funds for seven to ten years, that you will still benefit from IRAs. If you do not qualify for the deductions, you will have to hold your IRAs longer to break even. Should you need the IRA dollars in an emergency, you can withdraw the funds with no penalty if you return them within 60 days. If you lose your job, you can do so without a penalty if you withdraw the funds for at least a five-year period or until you are 59½, or over your lifetime, if you take the distribution in equal payments over that time.

Managed Versus Self-Directed.   Another misunderstanding is that IRAs are managed by a bank or financial institution. This is not necessarily true. In fact, there are two types of IRAs, managed and self-directed. Managed funds are just what their name implies.

Banks, insurance companies, mutual funds and other institutions manage and invest your funds, usually in CDs and money market funds. However, you also can have a self-directed IRA in which you choose the investments. Your investments can range from the safest government securities to riskier options. You can secure almost any type of investment, except collectibles. You can even purchase U.S. gold eagle coins.

Tax Sheltering. Only 40 percent of those eligible to open IRAs actually do, believing that they can invest money more profitably elsewhere. But that is unlikely. IRAs offer a chance to participate in returns unlikely to happen anywhere else. You can strive for lower returns to meet your goals, because you do not need to worry about the immediate tax burden. If you need a 10 percent return to meet your goals, you only need to achieve about 12 percent in your IRA, since you have to pay taxes on that money when you pull it out at retirement. But if you save outside your IRA, you need to earn at least 15 percent.

Cutoff Ages. The oldest you can be and still contribute to an IRA is age 70½. However, if you are still working, a $2,000 IRA contribution may be made into your spouse's IRA, if your spouse is under the cutoff age.

Annuities. Don't use annuities for IRAs. They are already tax-deferred. They have higher fees than mutual funds, and they have their own penalties if you withdraw the funds early. In fact, you could be paying up to 18 percent in penalties (10 percent for IRS penalty and 8 percent for annuity penalty) if you invest for a short period of time and are under 59½ when you withdraw funds from an annuity IRA. Don't use municipal bonds since they are already tax-free. Usually you do not want to place your Treasuries in IRAs either, since they are state tax-free.

Number of IRAs. Often, investors believe they can have only one IRA. Actually you can have as many as you want, provided that you do not exceed the annual contribution limitations. Rather than have a large number of IRAs at several institutions, the most convenient way to save is to have just one self-directed IRA that allows you to diversify investments from many different firms. This also gives you the convenience of having all your administration and record keeping done by one trustee.

Buying and Selling in Your IRA.   Another dangerous misconception is that you cannot buy and sell in an IRA. Just as with any investment portfolio, at some point investments may sour, or others may become more attractive. In an IRA, as with any other account, you can buy and sell your securities and investments as frequently as prudence dictates. Find investments, however, that you can move without commissions or fees, such as switching within mutual fund families.

Transfers and Rollovers.   You can transfer your IRA as many times as you like from one custodian to another, and you can roll it over once a year. The difference between the two is that a rollover means you take receipt of the cash or securities from one IRA and deposit it back into an IRA within 60 days. With transfer, you do not come in contact with the funds. They are moved directly from one trustee to another. Your bank or broker will handle the transfers for you. You should only use a rollover if you need the money for a short period of time.

Contributing a Little at a Time.   You do not have to contribute your whole contribution at one time. As a matter of fact, one of the most popular ways to contribute is through monthly payroll deductions from your employer. You can have the deductions go to both you and your spouse's IRAs. This is especially attractive if you have a hard time saving.

Fund Your 401(k) First.   Because you can borrow more easily from a 401(k), invest the maximum your employer allows before you invest in IRAs. Especially if your 401(k) has a matching provision, it is worth your while to contribute to the maximum.

Nondeductible IRAs.   If you have nondeductible IRAs and deductible IRAs, make sure you keep good records and file Form 8606 with your tax return. You do not have to pay taxes on the nondeductible IRA contributions when you withdraw funds. A one-page list, noting the date, the amount and the deductible portion is, all you need.

CHAPTER 6

Investing Retirement Funds

51 DOES AGE AFFECT MY PENSION OPTIONS AND THE INVESTMENTS I SHOULD USE?

The younger you are, the more you need growth investments, such as small company stocks (small-cap), midsized company stocks (midcap), sector funds and international stocks. As you get older, you can shift to balanced, income-oriented utility and timing funds. However, no matter how old you are, you should be aware that what appears to be a safe income investment can often be more dangerous than a growth stock.

If you are older, want peace of mind and short-term safety, consider investments that give you cash flow and guarantees, such as bonds, CDs, money market funds and government mortgages. Don't use bond mutual funds, even government bond funds. They eliminate the best feature of bonds—the guarantees—and have lots of high, hidden fees.

If you are investing long-term, be careful with bonds. Bonds are especially vulnerable to interest rate and inflation risks and have never performed as well over the long run as stocks. They offer no growth and no participation in strong economies.

One of the saddest experiences of my career was meeting a 67-year-old widow in 1984. In the 1970s, she had taken $10,000 from her husband's insurance proceeds and purchased what she thought was the safest investment, a U.S. Treasury bond. As interest rates increased, her bond kept losing value. When I told her the bond was only worth $6,800, she kept saying over and over, "But this is a guaranteed U.S. government bond." Unfortunately, any fixed-income investment, even a government bond, doesn't guarantee all your money back if you cash in early.

If you were given $10,000, how would you invest it? Depending on the investments, yields, amount of time and risk, the outcomes can be dramatically different. Compare several possible $10,000 investment alternatives and assume the following returns:

	CDs 5%	Bonds 8%	Blue Chips 10%	Aggressive Funds 12%
30 years	$54,271	$100,620	$174,490	$299,599
35 years	71,944	147,853	281,024	527,996
45 years	95,773	217,245	452,592	930,509

If Ali Young-and-single invests $1,000 in her IRA for ten years starting at age 19, invests in an aggressive growth fund at 12 percent, her $10,000 will grow to over a million dollars by age 65.

Kathy and Chris Just-starting are in their 20s. They invested a $10,000 wedding gift in their retirement plan CDs. It will grow to almost $100,000 and generate an income of $4,788 a year when they retire in 45 years. If, instead, they had invested in a small-cap index fund, then they risk losing money from time to time, but also have the potential of earning almost a million dollars and $111,000 in retirement income. They could leave an estate to their son, Chris Jr. that's ten times larger and an income that's over 20 times larger.

Betty and John Thirtyish invest their $10,000 gift for growth. Since there's a possibility they might need some of the money for their two girls' education, they split their $10,000 equally between an aggressive fund and blue chip index funds. They have 35 years to save, so, if all goes well, they will retire with almost $400,000.

Bob and Mary Fortyish aren't quite so lucky. They had a son in college and could not take the same risks as younger investors. They split their $10,000 between government bonds, blue chip index funds and aggressive funds. With only 25 years to save, compounding and time do not work so well for them. Still, their $10,000 may grow to $86,320 and generate $7,700 a year in before-tax income.

Will and Jane Empty-nesters are in their midfifties, and with only 15 years until retirement, they want more security. They strive for a 9.4 percent yield, with the bulk of their portfolio in blue chip funds and the remainder in government bonds. Their $10,000 will grow to $38,482, if tax-sheltered.

Henry Almost-retired's $10,000 grew to only $13,000 in five years, since his investments in government notes and CDs earned only 4 percent.

As you can see, the same $10,000, in some instances, amounts to very little, such as Henry's $13,000, or it can grow to a million dollars. The difference in the yields that good growth funds offer over bonds and CDs can mean the difference between a comfortable future or poverty. Historically, nothing has done as well as diversified stock portfolios, so if you are young, you should strive for higher, long-term and more growth-oriented investments.

Too many numbers spinning around? Think about it in a different way. If you invested in growth, picture yourself traveling through the Grand Canyon and playing golf in retirement. If you invested in CDs, picture yourself playing miniature golf and seeing the Grand Canyon on *National Geographic* specials.

We are living longer and need to be sure we have enough income to last 20 to 30 years into retirement. A woman who reaches her 50s free of major medical problems can expect to live into her late 80s, even 90s, in many cases. A healthy man who reaches retirement can expect to live to his early 80s. One of the greatest risks we currently face is the possibility of outliving our investments, so it's important to focus on growth.

When you are young, invest in young companies and young countries. It is when countries, companies and even individuals are very young that the greatest growth will occur, as well as the greatest risks and uncertainties. When you see a young child, you can't be sure of his or her potential, intellectual strength, morals and personality. There can be hidden medical, emotional or personality problems. But as the child grows, it becomes safer to make assumptions about the future. The growth becomes less explosive and more predictable. By the time early adulthood is reached, it is even safer to make assumptions. However, by then it is probably too late to share in most of the excitement and potential. The same is true for companies and countries. As they mature, we learn more and more about the risks associated with them, but there is also less and less oppor-tunities to share in the potential, exciting growth periods, and the above-average returns. The risks are high, so it's important to diver-sify and purchase several different aggressive small-cap and emerging market funds. No one fund will lead you to all the best companies.

52 HOW RISKY ARE GUARANTEED INSURANCE CONTRACTS (GICs)?

Most workers are given the opportunity, quarterly, to select and real-locate their retirement options. There are often so many choices that 60 percent of the time, confused workers select what they believe is their safest alternative, guaranteed insurance contracts (GICs).

With GICs, participants are guaranteed the full amount of their principal plus a fixed return, regardless of changes in interest rates. GICs are appropriate for those investors who have little or no short-term risk tolerance and for workers retiring in a few years. However, for many, GICs can be a poor choice and riskier than most employees think.

- The word *guaranteed* is deceiving. Guarantees are only as good as the companies backing them. Several insurance con-tracts have failed in the past, so it is important to make sure GICs are sponsored by high-quality companies. Check the Standard & Poor's or A.M. Best's credit ratings.
- If you cash out early, GICs, like any fixed-income investment, will have no guarantees and you may have a loss or penalty. "Guaranteed" means that you get your money back, but only if you hold it until maturity.
- GICs have hidden costs and fees paid to the insurance companies for assuming the interest rate risk associated with the underlying mortgages and bonds. The fees may be as high as 2 to 3 percent going in and 2 to 5 percent if you cash out early.
- Like all fixed-income investments, GICs have opportunity costs. Once you lock in the interest rate, even if the rates in-crease, you will still earn the lower rate. One solution is to constantly stagger the maturities so a portion of the GICs comes due each year.

◆ Lastly, in the past, guaranteed or income investments have never performed as well as stocks or equity investments.

53 HOW OFTEN SHOULD I MAKE CHANGES IN MY 401(K) OR RETIREMENT FUNDS?

Most 401(k)s allow participants to move their funds at least four times a year and some allow unlimited moves in order to give the employee more control and reduce the employer's fiduciary liability. In IRAs, SEPs and some other segregated retirement accounts, you can move as much as you want among different investments.

Moving funds around (known as "timing the market") can improve returns, especially if you have a crystal ball and can be out of the market before it falls. Marty Zweig, a famous timer, notes that if you were out of the market during the ten worst days from 1980 to 1989, you would have done 9 percent better than investors who didn't move investments. If you were out during the worst 40 days, your returns were twice those of the market.

Tempted to try timing the market? Timing takes a lot of work and many hours of researching economic indicators and complicated technical analysis. Fidelity Magellan is one of the best-performing funds, and yet over 60 percent of those who invested in it lost money because they kept moving in and out. When we see the market falling, there is a tendency to sell out. Unfortunately, most investors sell when the market is already down and buy back when the market is high.

If you do decide to time the market, consider some successful automatic strategies such as value cost averaging, interest rate guides and stop-losses.

Value Cost Averaging. Instead of trying to guess when to move in and out of the market, value cost averaging gives you a strategy to increase the value of your account by a certain amount each month. For example, if you want your account to "**grow**" by $500, start by investing $500 the first month. If it grows to $600, you invest only $400 the second month, thereby reducing the amount that you invested when the market is high. The account would now be worth $1,000, increasing by $500 a month. If the account fell to $800 the next month, you would invest $700, investing more when the market is low. You will be buying more when the market is low and falling and buying less or selling when the market is high.

Interest Rates.   If you decide to take advantage of economic changes, then watch interest rates, the best indicator for timing the market. The market tends to perform the very best when interests rates are falling and the worst when interest rates are increasing. For every 1/4 point anticipated increase in interest rates, decrease your position in stocks and mutual funds by 3 to 5 percent. If interest rates increase 5 percent, you could be 80 percent out of the market. When rates seem to have leveled out and appear to start falling, move back into bonds and stocks.

Stop-Losses.   Another approach that not only will help you move your funds but also protect you from large losses is to use "stop-losses." These are orders to sell stocks if they start to fall. Once the stock hits your target price, it is sent to the exchange and sold. It does not guarantee you that you will get out at your price, but it does work well as a strategy to get you out of the market if there are large falls. For example, if you paid $25 for a stock and it is now up to $50, you may want to protect your profit by putting a stop-loss under it at $45. If the stock falls, your order will go to the exchange and will be sold at the current market price.

Stock value	$50
stocks falls	↓
stop-loss of	$45 → goes to market
and sold out at	$44.50.

This is an easy automatic way to move in and out of the market.

Buy and Hold.   There are just as many arguments and statistics that defend buying good investments and holding as there are for timing or moving in and out of the market. According to American Capital Mutual funds, if you missed out on the one best day a year for the past ten years, your returns were 12 percent, 3 percent lower than the market average of 14.5 percent. If you were out of the market for the 20 best days, your return would have dropped to as low as 9 percent.

Most workers are busy at their jobs, and trying to shift with every new economic wind or economic move is time-consuming and often not as rewarding as you might think. Over the long haul, timing has only added 2 percent to the success of most portfolios. Buy and hold portfolios offer most of us a much better chance of doing well than timing and missing the few best days each year.

The market will go up, maybe not this year or next, but it will go up. It will also go down and has fallen more than 10 percent, 104 times over the last 94 years. Yet every time the market has fallen, it has returned to higher levels. With all its ups and downs, a dollar invested 60 years ago has grown to over $800. So for most investors, the solution is to buy and hold a good portion or amount of your portfolio.

54 ◆ HOW DO TAXES AFFECT MY INVESTMENT STRATEGIES?

Taxes can eat up a third of your profits, or more. Remember how a dollar invested in the stock market grew to $800? However, that $800 can dwindle to $20.71 or just a 4.56 percent return after taxes and inflation. Taxes can erode most of our returns and reduce a 10 percent return to as little as 6 percent.

The best strategy for dealing with taxes is to place investments with the highest tax consequences into retirement accounts and keep those investments with minimal tax consequences in individual accounts. Tax-sheltered accounts are ideal for "covered call" programs, income-oriented investments, mutual fund switching programs and conservative trading. Investments with long-term capital gains or growth investments that you can hold for many years are more suitable for nonretirement accounts. Place very aggressive investments with the potential to incur losses outside retirement accounts. Short-term cash and emergency funds should also be held outside pension and retirement accounts, so there are no taxes if they have to be withdrawn.

Even if Congress reduces the capital gains tax, allowing you time to trade more, it is still important to utilize your retirement accounts for the majority of your trading. For example, if you invested $10,000 at 12 percent in retirement funds, in 20 years you would earn as much as **three times more** than you would if you had traded stocks each year outside your pension. If you are looking for ways to improve your returns, avoiding taxes is best. Save smart by saving in tax-deferred accounts as much as possible.

55 WHAT ARE THE BEST INVESTMENTS FOR MY RETIREMENT FUNDS?

For the long run, there are few that will argue that stocks are the best place to invest. According to Ibbotson Associates, between 1926 and 1994, a dollar invested in a portfolio of S&P stocks grew to over $800 (or a 10.2 percent return), 30-year bonds grew to $28 (a return of 5.02 percent) and Treasury bills grew to only $11.73 (3.7 percent). The same dollar invested in small-cap, aggressive funds grew to over $2,757.15 (a 12.36 percent return).

For most investors, mutual funds and index trusts are usually better than individual stocks, since individual stocks do not have the diversification needed to protect from the risks related to a specific stock.

Many retirement plans such as 401(k)s offer you a limited amount of mutual funds. If you are young, growth-oriented funds are usually the best, but for older employees, more balanced funds may be better. If your plan is self-directed, such as with SARSEPs and IRAs, you will have unlimited choices.

Here's a description of some of the more common and more attractive options.

Index or Broadly Diversified Equity Funds.   Most 401(k)s and retirement funds include a market index fund. This is a fund that mimics the market as much as possible. The Standard & Poor's index or an index on what is called "the broad market" has historically outperformed almost 80 percent of mutual funds and makes an attractive core holding for most retirement plans.

When you are considering indexes, Standard & Poor's offers the most safety and the best returns. In the past, the Standard & Poor's index has done better than the Dow Jones Industrial Average (DJIA), or the Dow. From October 1926 to October 1989, the DJIA grew to $119,022, the Dow to $168,627 and the S&P grew to $179,696. The broader and more diversified market indexes reduced the risk and increased the long-term performance.

Broadly Diversified Funds. If you are not offered an index fund or trust, look for a broadly diversified stock fund. Diversification increases safety. Sixty percent of the movement in a stock is related to the market. Only 20 percent is related to the industry and only 20 percent to the stocks themselves. Therefore, select broadly diversified funds to reduce risk and the need to constantly reevaluate sectors and stocks.

Value and Growth Funds. You also may want to invest a small percentage in both a value fund and a growth fund. Value funds have performed better in the past 20 years than most growth funds. They select stocks that have fallen out of favor and are facing turnarounds and restructuring. When the market falls, these stocks tend to fall less than those stocks with large run-ups.

When the market does well, growth funds are likely to have the highest returns. Aim Aggressive, Janus Mercury, Pimco Opportunity or Govett Small Company Fund, to name just a few, see returns in the high 20s, 30s and even 40 percent when the market does well. They are too risky for your entire account, but including a small portion can increase overall returns dramatically.

Having a little of both types of funds and an index trust can give you a diversified, balanced portfolio. This approach strives for more consistency. Whenever you opt for more consistent and safer returns, you give up a little extra yield, but for most retirement accounts, it's a good strategy. If you are very young, you may want to consider a more aggressive account.

If you want average returns (the market has averaged over 10 percent historically), stay with good long-term diversified funds and index trusts. By buying the whole market or market indexes, you will probably see your money double every seven years.

56 WHAT ARE THE BEST INVESTMENT STRATEGIES TO INCREASE THE RETURNS ON MY RETIREMENT FUNDS?

When planning for retirement, your strategies will depend on your individual situation, the economy, your age and your goals. If you want returns in line with the market, consider broad market indexes and broadly diversified mutual funds. But if you want to outperform the market, consider some successful strategies such as the value cost averaging strategies we discussed in Question #53 and the Dow Dividend Strategies (DDSs). If you want to increase the safety of your account, consider covered call programs, asset allocation programs, dollar cost averaging programs and guaranteeing strategies.

Increasing Your Returns.   The Dow Dividend Theory, a strategy made popular by Michael O'Higgins in his book *Beating the Dow*, has historically achieved higher returns than investing in the Dow itself. DDS is a strategy of investing in the ten highest-yielding Dow Jones Industrial Average stocks (DJIA).* From 1972 to 1994, this strategy has experienced returns of more than 15.4 percent versus 11.5 percent for all 30 Dow stocks. These returns require that you reinvest the dividends each year, and you reallocate your invested dollars at the beginning of each year in the stocks that are then the ten highest-yielding.

Would you rather earn even higher returns, possibly as high as 20 percent? Consider, then, a little riskier strategy of investing in the five lowest-cost of the ten highest-yielding Dow stocks. First, you select the ten highest-yielding stocks in the DJIA and then determine the five lowest-priced stocks of these ten. The five lowest-cost stocks averaged a return of almost 20 percent compared with the 11.5 percent for purchasing the 30 Dow industrial stocks and a 15.4 percent for the ten highest-yielding Dow stocks.

If you invested $10,000 21 years ago in the five lowest-cost, your initial investment grew to over $450,000. This compares with approximately $200,000 for the ten highest-yielding Dow stocks and $98,350 for the DJIA portfolio. This strategy outperformed the ten highest-yielding Dow stocks 71 percent of the time. In 19 of the past 21 years, it has had a positive performance. However, in 1990, when the Dow stocks such as IBM took big hits, this strategy had the greatest fall off, down 15.8 percent. However, in 1991 it recovered, and had a 62.5 percent return.

Past performance is not a guarantee of future performance; however, if you have several strategies that you use consistently, they tend to create a sense of discipline that is the best and most successful way to approach the market. **Concentrate on sectors** and

---

* The Dow Jones Industrial Average is the property of Dow Jones, Inc.

asset allocation instead of individual stocks. A 1991 study by Gary Brinson, Brian Singer and Gilbert Beebower for the *Financial Analysts Journal* showed the elements that went into creating successful portfolios. For overall portfolio performance, stock selection plays only a minor role (less than 6 percent) in increasing a portfolio's success. Good portfolio performance depends almost entirely on asset allocation (91.5 percent) or balancing your account in the appropriate sectors. Timing, trading or switching accounts for less than 2 percent of a portfolio's overall success. So the trick is not in choosing the hottest stocks, but in how you allocate your money among different types of investments.

57 I'M A BABY BOOMER AND I HAVEN'T BEEN ABLE TO SAVE. WHAT CAN I DO TO CATCH UP AND RETIRE COMFORTABLY?

Today we can expect to live four years longer than workers 25 years ago. This means we need to save more for our retirement. Baby boomers have been poor savers, saving as little as zero to 3 percent. Although they contribute to retirement plans, they often increase debt faster than savings and end up with negative savings. Typically, baby boomers have as little as 2 to 3 percent of the money needed to retire by the time they hit their 40s, although they probably need almost 25 percent. The amount you need to save depends on your after-tax returns, your planned retirement date and how much you have in savings now. Look at the following chart for an idea of how much you should have in savings. We rounded the numbers to make them easier to work with.

At an anticipated 8% return	At an anticipated 10% return
5% at age 25	2% at age 25
9% at age 30	4% at age 30
15% at age 40	10% at age 40
32% at age 50	25% at age 50
46% at age 55	40% at age 55
100% at age 65	100% at age 65

If you haven't saved 35 percent of your needed retirement assets by age 45, and 45 percent by age 55, then you have to move fast. You are forced to play the "catch-up game."

Here are a few tips to get you started:

1. Get serious. Make a financial plan and determine your goals and the possible alternatives available to you.
2. Control all risks and unforeseen events that can disrupt and destroy your savings by getting adequate health, disability and long-term care insurance for your parents.
3. Save as much as possible. If you are in your early 40s and have 25 years to save, you need to save 10 percent of your income at 10 percent to retire with the same income you have today. If you are in your 50s you may need to save 15 to 25 percent.
4. Try for higher-than-average returns. You don't have time doing most of the work now. The higher the returns, the smaller amount you need to save. If you earn 12 percent instead of 10 percent, you would need to save only 7 percent of your income. Conversely, if you earn less on your savings, you will have to save much more.
5. Save in tax-sheltered investments.
6. Start today.
7. Evaluate your current job's retirement packages before changing jobs. It can take as long as five years before you are vested in a pension plan. Once you reach your 40s and 50s, it can be costly to move and change jobs. Seniority is also a major factor in stock option plans and deferred-compensation plans.
8. Don't count on inheritances. With parents living longer, any inheritance money may be spent, and estate taxes are likely to increase and take even more inheritance dollars.
9. Plan adequately for emergencies. Evaluate likely home and car repairs and save for them immediately, so you do not incur debt.
10. Every time you plan a large purchase, realize that it will reduce your retirement income.
11. Concentrate on growth. If you invested $10,000 in CDs 45 years ago, you could have income of $5,000 a year. Instead, if you averaged 12 percent in growth funds, your income could be $130,000, even if you shifted to 8 percent bonds in retirement.

58 HOW MUCH INCOME DO I NEED TO RETIRE COMFORTABLY?

How much income you need depends on your definition of comfortable. Most financial planners pick numbers such as 50 percent of preretirement income. The U.S. Department of Labor says we need 70 percent. Sometimes you need even more income in retirement than you did when you were working, especially if you plan on traveling extensively, or have large medical bills. Consider the following:

◆ *Look at your likely tax situation.* Plan on tax increases since they are more likely than decreases. President Clinton dramatically increased the amount of Social Security that is taxed from 50 percent to 85 percent. Your taxes will depend on the sources of your income, such as tax-free bonds or tax-deferred pension plans.

◆ *What kind of retirement are you planning?* Will it be quiet, at home, with minimal entertainment? If so, you may want to assume your spending will decrease when you retire, but be realistic. Even simple hobbies, such as gardening, can be more expensive than most of us assume. You still will probably need all the same household expenditures, and possibly even more, since you might need to run the heat or air-conditioning all day.

◆ *Add in expenses for traveling, leisuretime activities, boating or golfing and any expensive hobbies.*

◆ *Evaluate your home's cost and value.* Is there sufficient equity to allow you to pull funds out through a reverse mortgage, if necessary? Check with your local government to determine if you will be able to get an exemption on your real estate taxes. Evaluate future repairs that will be needed, furniture and cars that will have to be replaced and normal maintenance costs that will occur. If you are renting, consider possible rent increases.

◆ *Do you plan on moving?* Don't forget that moving costs can be as much as $10,000 to $20,000 and that that money will come out of your savings. Carefully check all the hidden costs of moving, and the taxes in the state where you plan to relocate. See if both your present and future states will be taxing your pensions. Even if you move to another state, your previous state may still tax the pensions you accumulated while working in that state. Since you accumulated those funds on a tax-deferred basis, when you retire the state feels it has a right to tax those funds. This can be one of your worst nightmares if you do not plan carefully. (Be especially careful if you are moving from New York to Florida.)

Calculate taxes for any capital gains on the sale of your home, especially if you move into a less-expensive home or an apartment. Even though you are allowed to roll over the proceeds of your current home to another and are also allowed a one-time exclusion of $125,000 if you are over 55, you still may end up owing taxes if your current home has appreciated greatly.

◆ *Do you have children that will still depend on you for some support?* Most of us assume that our children will be independent when we retire, but marriages are being postponed longer and children may move back home. Many can't get good-paying jobs, or any jobs at all. You might not only end up supporting your children but your grandchildren, as more and more families split up.

◆ *Do you want to help educate your grandchildren?* College is becoming financially prohibitive for most middle-income families, and assistance is only available for the poor. If your children earn over $60,000, you may find that they are not able to get any assistance for their children's education. Yet they also may not have the current $15,000 to $25,000 annual costs for college—costs that may be inflated several years from now.

◆ *What is your family's health history?* Health costs may be a minimal burden when you are working, but you may find them to be the greatest burden in your retirement years. Do you feel it is important to have the peace of mind associated with long-term nursing care insurance? If so, plan on expensive insurance costs. Will you be able to accept your dependence on government assistance for long-term care or are you adamant about remaining in your home through your retirement? These are all factors that will determine the cost of your health care program.

◆ *Will you be residing in a high cost-of-living area?*

The list can go on indefinitely. The best way to calculate your needed retirement income is to work from your current budget, and determine those expenses that will likely decrease or increase. Since most of us do not keep good budgets, using a percentage such as 70 percent of your current income is an easier approach.

59 WHAT CAN I EXPECT FROM SOCIAL SECURITY AND MY PENSIONS?

Only 46 percent of employees have pensions, and even those who do can expect to receive less than 20 percent of their retirement income. As more and more companies shift to less costly plans, you may not even be able to count on this percentage.

Don't count too much on Social Security, either. It was never intended to be the lone source of retirement income. It was to be a supplement. In the past, you could count on receiving 50 percent of your retirement income from Social Security, but by the turn of the century, it may provide less than 20 percent of the income needed to live on. The Social Security administration claims the sources of income for current retirees are 26 percent from savings, 17 percent from part-time work, 16 percent from pensions, 3 percent from charity and 38 percent from Social Security. If you work full-time, you can assume that you will receive roughly 25 percent of your pre-retirement income if you are retiring before the year 2000. If you are retiring after the year 2000, plan on 20 percent.

MONTHLY SOCIAL SECURITY PAYMENTS
Your earnings in 1994

Your age in 1995	$20,000	$30,000	$40,000	$50,000	$60,000 and above
45	$775	$1,039	$1,178	$1,302	$1,418
55	770	1,033	1,163	1,253	1,325
65	761	1,014	1,111	1,749	1,798

To get a more accurate estimate of your own individual benefits, call Social Security at 1-800-772-1213.

You will not only receive less from Social Security, it is likely to be taxed much more. Under the new laws, the amount of Social

Security that can be taxed is 85 percent. What will the tax be in 5, 10, 15 or 20 years from now?

- ◆ **Check your benefits every three years.** If you wait too long, you may not have accurate information, and Social Security is not required to correct errors over three years, though they almost always do.
- ◆ **Check with your human resources department** and get some figures on your expected pension benefits, ESOPs, deferred compensation, split-dollar insurance and other retirement plans.
- ◆ **Look at the figures for your IRA** distributions from the Individual Retirement Table in Appendix A.
- ◆ **Estimate your potential income from the** investments you have today. Estimate what you expect your average return is and refer to the Future Value Table in Appendix E.
- ◆ **Estimate** your future savings and any other future income from royalties or inheritances.

60 HOW MUCH DO I HAVE TO SAVE FOR MY RETIREMENT NEST EGG?

If you have 40 years left until retirement, you may only need to save approximately 7 percent of your income each year to have 75 percent of your preretirement income when you retire. If you have only 20 years left, you need to save over 10 percent a year. In order to know how much you have to save, you first need to know how much income you need, and how much you will be receiving from pensions, Social Security and other sources.

CALCULATING HOW MUCH YOU HAVE TO SAVE

1. Calculate your shortfall. Subtract the income you are likely to have from the income you will need. Refer to Question #58.
2. Take the shortfall and divide that amount by the interest you expect to receive.

i.e., capital needed $= \dfrac{\text{income short fall}}{\text{anticipated yield}}$

This is the additional savings you will need when you retire. For example, if you need another $24,000 and can earn 12 percent, then divide

$$\frac{\$24,000}{12\%} = \$200,000$$

3. Include inflation by using the table in Appendix E.
4. Calculate how much you have to save each month to reach your goal by using the table in Appendix B. For example, if in step #3 you find you need $300,000 in 20 years and you can earn 12 percent, the table indicates that you need to save approximately $1 for every $1,000 you need or $300 a month.

61 WHAT ARE THE MOST IMPORTANT THINGS I NEED TO KNOW ABOUT RETIREMENT SAVINGS?

The most important thing you need to understand about retirement assets is that since they are long-term, you need investments that will perform the best over the long run. It is also crucial that you use retirement funds to the maximum and that you save as much as you can.

The secret to a comfortable retirement is: Save 10 percent, earn 10 percent, invest no more than 10 percent in any one investment.

If you can save 10 percent of your income for 25 years at 10 percent, you will have the same income in retirement as your current income. The longer you have to save, the less you need to save and the lower your returns can be. If you can save for 31 years, you will only need to save 5 percent of your income to retire with the same income you have today.

You not only have to worry about current and future taxes but also inflation and the impact it has on distributions from future retirement funds. If you invested in government securities, which just barely outperform inflation, you would be in pretty bad shape after inflation and taxes. As the famous Ibbotson chart shows, $1 invested in Treasury bills or comparable money markets and CDs grew to $11.73. However, after taxes and inflation, it was only worth 49 cents. You actually lost over half your money to taxes and inflation if you invested in short-term Treasury bills.

CHAPTER 7

Protecting
Your Pension

62 HOW SAFE IS SOCIAL SECURITY?

In many ways Social Security is a lot safer than many of us assume.
It has some risks, but not the risks we usually think of. When Social
Security was created, there were 42 workers paying into the system
for every person receiving benefits. By the year 2035, there will be
only 1.9 workers supporting each recipient. This means that in addition to supporting themselves and their families, every worker will
also have to pay half the support for a retiree. Theoretically, there are
only a few solutions: We need less retirees, more workers, higher
taxes or stronger growth in "real wages" (or wages minus inflation).
The best solution is real wage growth and more productivity. If real
wages grow by 1.7 percent, the Social Security trust will stay intact.
However, if real wage growth does not improve soon, we could see
a system that will require massive tax increases in order to survive.
There are other risks involved with Social Security however, risks
that have nothing to do with its solvency. These risks include:

♦ **Errors in your Social Security calculations.** If there are errors
   that you can't resolve easily with the Social Security administration, you can ask for a copy of the factsheet called "The
   Appeals Process."

◆ **Increased taxes.** Social Security recipients pay taxes on what is called "combined income," which is your adjusted gross income plus nontaxable interest (from municipal bonds) plus one half of your Social Security benefits. You will have to pay taxes on 50 percent of your benefits if your combined income is between $25,000 to $34,000 for singles and $32,000 to $44,000 for couples. You pay on 85 percent if your income is over $34,000 for a single person and over $44,000 for a joint return.

◆ **Needs or "Means" testing** is becoming a likely possibility. The government made a promise to pay Social Security benefits based on work experience, not financial need, and there is a danger that this promise may be broken.

◆ **Opportunity Costs.** Every dollar that goes to Social Security is one dollar less that you could be investing and probably earning much higher returns on. Employers will pay an average of $6,000 a year for 40 years or over $240,000 into Social Security for each employee. However, if you save the $6,000 yourself every year for the next 40 years, at just 5 percent, it would be worth over $761,040. If you invested it in the stock market that has averaged over 10 percent the past 40 years, your $6,000 would grow to over $2,921,110. We would all be wealthy if the government could invest our retirement funds wisely.

◆ **Retirement Age.** In the past, you could retire at age 65 with full benefits. If you were born after 1960, you now have to wait until you are 67 to retire with full benefits. There is a risk, if Social Security runs out of funds, that it will postpone the age even further.

◆ **COLAs** or cost of living adjustments have kept current retirees ahead of inflation. These COLAs were extremely important during the 1970s when inflation was growing at double-digit numbers. Inflation can raise its ugly head again, and when it does Social Security COLAs may not be there to protect us.

Don't rely too heavily on Social Security for retirement for it is unlikely to continue paying even 20 percent of your preretirement income after the year 2000.

63 HOW SAFE IS MY PENSION PLAN?

All across the United States, businesses are failing. If the economy goes into a recession, even more will fail. Such failures may jeopardize workers' jobs and jeopardize their retirement benefits, as well. The risks to retirement savings are not just limited to business failures but also include risks from mismanagement, misunderstanding of benefits, poor investment performance, and lawsuits against you and your company.

Let's take a look at a few of the ways your pension fund could be jeopardized, and how you can protect yourself and minimize your risks.

Underfunding. Underfunding occurs when employers delay contributions. Starting in 1995, employers have to notify employees if pension plans are less than 90 percent funded. Large firms such as CSX, USAir, Westinghouse, General Motors, Woolworth's and over 1,000 more have plans that are less than 90 percent funded. There are also 4,000 smaller companies that are not fully funded. Four million workers have plans that could run into problems if their companies go bankrupt. While most of these companies are insured by the Pension Benefit Guaranty Corporation, it's only for $30,886 per participant per year. Business failures can be devastating to pensions if employees don't take steps to protect themselves.

Dorothy worked 42 years for the same, small, family-owned company. She survived two bouts of cancer and a painful divorce. She was looking forward to her retirement and was planning to travel extensively. But her retirement dreams evaporated when the economy turned and her employer's business failed. Dorothy, at age 67, was faced with an almost worthless retirement plan.

Solution: If your pension plan is in your employer's company stock, consider selling some stock and diversifying as soon as your plan permits. Even if you work for a financially strong and healthy company, it is important to diversify your retirement assets. If you can't liquidate your company stocks (there are time frames and restrictions on most of these plans), attempt to save as much as possible in IRAs and other alternatives.

Poorly Performing Retirement Plans. John had a thriving law practice. However, he lacked financial experience and purchased large amounts of penny stocks. The stocks plummeted and caused large losses in the firm's pension plan. In fact, he did so poorly that over the last three years, he lost over 60 percent of the value of his and his employees' retirement account.

Solution: Whether you or your employer are managing your retirement assets, be sure your retirement fund investments are balanced and diversified. Review your statements or the 5500C tax forms that show the gains, losses and value of the account. If your employer is managing the funds poorly, ask if you can have your funds "segregated" out and take control yourself. You may need to seek legal help, but it's hard to sue your own employer.

Municipal Plans. Many municipal workers assume that their pension plans are safe, yet municipal pensions can also be underfunded. Even if the plans are completely funded, there is no guarantee that your retirement is safe. Municipal workers who participated in Orange County's 457 plan may be facing the possibility of losing some of their retirement benefits because of losses associated with risky investments known as derivatives. Since assets in a 457 plan are technically nonqualified and belong to the employer and not the participants, they are subject to the employer's general creditors.

Solution: Stay informed about who is investing your funds and understand the investments and risks associated with such plans.

Nonqualified Plans. Barbara owned a small accounting firm. Her firm was sued and she not only lost her business but her SARSEP, which was not protected under ERISA. Most qualified pension plans are protected from lawsuits, but check before you assume yours is. Many states are extending asset protection to IRAs and SARSEPs, so eventually you may find that most of your retirement assets are safe from attachment, but there are still many nonqualified plans that have only limited protection.

Solution: Check whether your state protects the assets of IRAs and SARSEPs from attachment by creditors. If not, get active in state political groups that are seeking such protection. If your plans are not qualified, discuss with your employer the possibility of qualified versus nonqualified plans. If you find your pension assets are exposed, you might want to consider liability insurance for yourself.

HOW SAFE IS YOUR PLAN?

Fortunately, the government has increased its scrutiny of pension plans and increased its vigilance in reviewing IRS Form 5500, the form your employer has to file with the IRS and the Department of Labor to show investment performance and compliance with retirement rules. Moreover, stricter rules on bonding and insurance have made pension plans much safer. But despite increased government vigilance, there are still risks associated with poor management, lack of portfolio diversification and a weak economy, which can result in business failures or smaller contributions to your plans. Constantly monitor and investigate the solvency and alternative retirement plans available to you.

64 WHAT DO I NEED TO LOOK FOR IN MY RETIREMENT PLAN DOCUMENTS?

One of the best ways to protect your retirement assets is to learn as much as possible about your plans. Most of the information you will need is in your pension plan documents.

In addition to monitoring the contributions and investment performance, you should also be familiar with the summary plan description, the benefit statement, the summary annual report and the notice of interested parties. What can these documents tell you and what do you need to look for?

- ◆ **Summary Plan Description (SPD):** Your employer is required to give you a summary of the plan. The SPD must describe all the provisions and the employee's rights under the plan. Make sure you read and understand the contribution amounts and the rules laid out in the plan document. You should understand the types of investments that the plan can contain. If your plan deviates from the investments outlined in the summary, your employer may be held liable for some of the losses. For example, if the plan did not allow for investments such as options, derivatives, partnerships, aggressive stocks or junk bonds, your employer could be responsible if the plan suffers losses because of investments in these products. You may want to report any violations to the Department of Labor.

◆ **Benefit Statement:** Most employers will issue this statement at least annually. The benefit statement tells you all the benefits that you have and the amounts accrued to you individually. Most of the benefits will be quantified, so this is one of your most important documents. It is also the easiest to read and the only one containing your personal information and benefits.

◆ **Summary Annual Report:** Be sure you receive a Summary Annual Report (SAR) each year. The SAR is a summary of the information contained in the 5500 Form that your employer is required to file with the IRS and the Department of Labor. The annual report should be given to you within nine months after the end of the plan year. You will be able to see how the investments are performing as well as the contributions to the plan.

◆ **The Notice to Interested Parties:** This notice is given to you when your employer files for a determination letter from the IRS. It lists the appropriate parties or federal agencies in the event of an inquiry or a problem.

65 HOW CAN I MONITOR MY PENSION PERFORMANCE AND MAKE SURE MY EMPLOYER IS PROPERLY INVESTING MY PENSION MONEY?

Your employer must follow rigid rules if he or she is managing the assets for you. Many companies have been sued in recent years because they did not follow these rules. What you want to look for are the following:

◆ Is your employer following the prudent person standard?
◆ Is there any conflict of interest or prohibited transactions?
◆ Are the assets diversified? No more than 10 percent should be in any one investment other than short-term government securities and your company stock.
◆ Are the assets appropriate for the plan's stated goals and risk tolerance?
◆ Are they liquid enough to fund distributions and loans?

Prudent Person Standard.   When investing, employers and fiduciaries must take care in selecting proper investments. These investments must be evaluated in light of the plan's goals, the age of the participants, the risk of lost opportunity for gain as well as the risk of losses. The investments must be diversified and must take into consideration the need for liquidity. Leaving all the funds in CDs, for example, would be in violation of the prudent person standard and diversification rules. A pension in Massachusetts was fined several years ago for having the entire pension invested in CDs. Although the employer thought that the safety of the CDs justified the lack of diversification, the court ruled that pension plans, because of their long-term nature, had to follow the ERISA rules for diversification. Your employer should have a written investment policy statement to satisfy the statutory requirements of the plan, which defines the boundaries in which the fiduciaries can invest.

Prohibited Transactions. Employers are required to ensure that the fiduciaries of the plan act solely in the interest of the plan participants and their beneficiaries. This means your employer has to always select investments, managers, individuals and institutions that he or she believes will act in the best interests of the employees instead of in the personal interests of the employer. For example, if a bank promised your employer an attractive personal line of credit if the pension plan were moved there, by accepting this proposal your employer would be in violation of his or her fiduciary responsibilities.

If you suspect fraud, mismanagement, conflict of interest, underfunding or violations of any pension rules, call the Department of Labor or the IRS. In many cases fiduciaries will have to make up losses if the losses resulted from violations of retirement rules.

Diversification and Balance. In most cases your employer should not have more than 10 percent of the assets in any one investment category except government securities and company stock, and no more than 5 percent in any one individual stock. Your employer should also have a balance between inflation hedges, growth and income investments.

Liquidity. Your retirement funds should have enough liquid or short-term investment to pay funds in case of employee retirements and emergencies. If there is not enough cash flow, investments may have to be liquidated at losses to meet distribution needs.

Monitor Your Investments

1. Each quarter write down the value of your total account.
2. Use color codes—they are visual and help you spot trouble quickly:
   - ◆ If the account decreases in value, write your amount in red.
   - ◆ If the account increases in value, write in black.

   Don't worry if there are several red months in a row. If you hear that the market is down and all investments are doing poorly, you can assume that your account is going through the normal ups and downs of the market. If, however, your account is constantly in the red and you know that the markets are doing well, you must take action.
3. Calculate your returns.
4. Compare your returns to inflation. If your returns are not beating the inflation rate, underline in red. Your real rate of return or the true measurement of your increase in wealth is determined by calculating your returns and subtracting out inflation. Use at least 3 or 4 percent if you are making assumptions about inflation.
5. Compare your returns to your goals or your ideal returns. Place a red arrow pointing down (↓) if you keep falling short of your goal.
6. Compare your returns with those of the market. Your account statement will usually be broken down according to categories, such as bond funds, stock funds, international funds, fixed income, money markets and so forth. If your funds did not do so well as the indexes or the funds your are comparing them with, then place a red minus sign (-) beside them. If they did better, put a plus sign (+). If your worksheet ends up with lots of losses when the market is doing well, then you are making the wrong investments. If your employer is managing the assets, discuss the possibility of segregating your account and managing it yourself.

If your returns are not matching the indexes or other funds, consider switching your investments.

If your returns are not keeping up with inflation, look at your asset allocation or your mix of investments. Shift more to inflation hedges, such as real estate investment trusts, natural resource funds and growth mutual funds.

If your goals are not being met, make sure you have realistic assumptions before you strive for higher returns.

66 WHAT ARE MY EMPLOYER'S RESPONSIBILITIES AND WHAT ARE MINE?

Your employer's responsibilities and yours differ, depending on the type of plan you have.

Self-Directed Plans.   If you have a self-directed plan such as an IRA or SEP, then you are in the driver's seat.

◆ Your employer's responsibilities may include making some contributions and plan administration.
◆ Your responsibilities are to make contributions and to manage the investments. If you have any self-directed retirement plans, it is especially important that you read Chapter 6 and make sure that you are doing all the right things when it comes to investing, such as asset allocation, investing in growth, avoiding losses and so forth.

Self-Directed SARSEPs

◆ Your employer is responsible for contributing funds to the SEP portion for you if you are at least 21 years old, have worked during at least three of the preceding five years and earned over $400 this year. This is nice for part-time workers who are usually excluded under most other plans. If you are part-time, you should see that you are not unfairly excluded from any retirement plans. With SEPs, when you are over age 70½, unlike most other plans, your employer can still contribute for you, and you may be able to contribute on a pretax dollar basis.
◆ You are responsible for contributions to the SAR portion and for the management of the funds. The maximum that can be contributed to SARSEP is $9,240 for 1995. This limit can be increased annually to reflect inflation.

Segregated Profit-Sharing Plans

- ◆ Your employer's responsibilities are contributing the money, making sure the plan is amended for any changes in the laws, reporting to the Labor Department, supplying plan documents, administration and finding trustees.
- ◆ Your responsibilities are to manage the investments, monitor investment performance and determine the asset allocation and investments. These funds are probably the largest and most important pool of money that you will ever have to manage so you must have a strategy and blueprint of where you want to be in 5, 10, 20, 30 and 40 years from now. If you are busy and are not willing to take courses and read constantly, then you should consider working with a financial planner, a fee-based financial adviser or a trusted broker. Pick these people carefully. Check out their experience and sit with them several times before you turn over your financial future to them.

403(b), 401(k)

- ◆ Your employer's responsibilities are selecting the families of funds and broad categories of investments, handling all the paperwork, and the IRS and Department of Labor reporting. Typically, your employer has to offer at least three funds: a money market fund, an equity fund and an income fund. Many will also include guaranteed insurance contracts (GICs), employer stocks and a variety of other mutual funds.
- ◆ Your responsibilities are naming your beneficiary, determining how much you want to contribute and selecting the right mix or allocation of funds. You do not have so much responsibility as someone with a completely self-directed account, but you have a lot more responsibility than with retirement plans in which your employer manages the assets. If you incur losses because you picked the wrong mix of funds, or over-weighted in risky funds or because of poor market conditions, then you are entirely responsible for investment losses. If you have investment losses as a result of the failure of your employer to assume his or her fiduciary responsibility by selecting appropriate funds, removing conflict of interest, offering

enough selections and giving you the opportunity to switch your funds in a timely manner, then your employer may be held liable for some of the losses.

Pooled Money Purchase and Profit-Sharing Plans. If your employer pools your portion of funds with other employees into one large account, it is called a "pooled" account.

+ Your employer's responsibilities are to contribute the money, to invest and manage the money; to do all reporting, paperwork, administration and trustee work; to handle all amendments; and to abide by prudent person rules.
+ Your responsibilities are to monitor the performance, review your benefits statement and the value of your account, compare your account's growth to indexes and other benchmarks and to seek legal help if the plan experiences losses for several years. If your employer is a lousy investment picker, it is not only your employer that will suffer, but you.

Defined-Benefit Plan

+ Your employer's responsibilities are contributing the money, investing the money, making sure you get the retirement income promised you, absorbing all the losses and handling all the paperwork amendments and IRS reporting.
+ Your responsibilities are making sure your employer is bonded, monitoring the funding of the plan and making sure the plan is not underfunded, naming and updating your beneficiaries and making sure you understand your benefits and how they are calculated.

With defined-benefit plans, almost all the responsibilities and risks rest with your employer, which is why these plans are being discontinued.

67 CAN THE ECONOMY HURT MY PENSION?

One of the most important factors in your ability to retire will be the performance of your investments, and your investment performance is closely tied to the economy. The growth of the economy can be a major determinant of how well your account does over the long run. When you are investing your retirement money, you will have risks associated with rising interest rates (interest rate risk), with price increases (inflation risk), with companies going out of business (credit risk), with the stock market falling (market risk), with missed opportunities from being too conservative (opportunity risk) and risks associated with natural disasters and political changes (event risk).

One of the greatest risks to our retirement is inflation. For example, those investing in a 5 percent savings account in 1982 with inflation at 12 percent actually were 7 cents poorer for every dollar they saved. This means that the account lost purchasing power, and if you went shopping at the end of the year instead of the beginning of the year, your money bought you 7 percent less food, clothing, houses or anything else. You would have been better off purchasing an oriental rug, a house, stamps or any other collectible, instead of saving. Unfortunately, inflation is often a hidden, subtle risk that most investors aren't unaware of. During periods of high inflation, normally "hard assets" such as real estate, commodities, collectibles and antiques tend to perform even better than financial assets. During low inflation, financial assets tend to do better. Stock funds, stocks, variable annuities and bonds thrive and outperform hard assets when inflation is low.

- ◆ **Interest rate risk.** When interest rates increase, you lose some of the principal value on every fixed investment you own. Those who purchased U.S. Treasury bonds or other long-term debt obligations in the 1970s became aware of interest rate risk during the 1980s. Not only were they disappointed with their low yields, averaging around 7 to 8 percent compared to 14 to 16 percent offered in 1981 and 1982, respectively, but if they tried to sell their bonds, they may have lost as much as 40 percent of the value.
- ◆ **Market risk.** Everyone is afraid of market risk. They remember all too well what happened in the 1920s and the 1970s, 1987 and 1994. The market does fall, but it has come back stronger and has reached new highs. There are many ways to minimize this risk, and over the long run, it's one of the lesser risks. You can minimize market risk by guaranteeing invest-

ment strategies, using stop-losses and covered call programs, and balancing your portfolio. As scary as the stock market is, it offers one of the best opportunities to outperform inflation and to achieve your long-term financial goals.

◆ **Credit risk**, or risk of default, is a risk that most investors are often overly concerned about. The default rate on high-quality AA or AAA municipal bonds is as low as 1/10,000 or 1 percent. Although corporate bonds have a higher default rate, if you stay with high-quality companies and put less than 5 percent of your money into any one bond, there is often no reason to stay away from corporate bonds.

◆ **Event risk** occurs when there is an earthquake, a revolution, an epidemic, a natural disaster, a political upheaval, a great new invention or a war. It can also occur when an assassination attempt is made on a president, a pope or any national leaders or when derivatives cause the financial market to face increased danger. Because these risks are unpredictable, they are difficult to protect against.

◆ **Opportunity risk.** The economy offers new opportunities every day. However, fear often dominates our investment strategies and prevents us from taking advantage of these opportunities. An overly conservative portfolio can sometimes be as detrimental as an overly risky one. Make sure you are taking calculated risks toward maintaining a healthy portfolio.

68 WHAT CAN I DO TO PROTECT MY RETIREMENT EARNINGS FROM LOSSES?

There are some basic strategies that can guarantee your principal and minimize your losses such as stop-losses, covered calls, dollar cost averaging, as well as hedging strategies.

SAFETY STRATEGY #1: GUARANTEEING YOUR PRINCIPAL

If you know you should be in the market, but are afraid to take the leap, there are ways that you can guarantee all your money back when your retire. It's basically just a math trick, but the peace of mind it gives is immeasurable, and often allows us to participate in more growth-oriented investments.

In order to guarantee your investments, you simply match up the riskier stock portion with a guaranteed portion. This only works if you do not pull the funds out early. Let's say you have $10,000 and you want to be sure that in ten years you will have all your money back. If you get a 7 percent zero coupon bond for $5,000, you know it will mature in ten years for the face value of $10,000. If you invest the remaining $5,000 in the stock market and you were to lose every penny, you would still have all your money back. It is extremely unlikely, no matter how bad the stock market is, that you would lose every penny, but let's say it fell 50 percent. You would still have $12,500 at the end of ten years. In the past, the most the stock market was ever down over ten years (from 1929 to 1938) was less than a percent, so you can be fairly certain you would have all your money back plus an attractive return.

If you are only concerned about getting all your money back, look at the "Guaranteeing Your Principal" strategy. If you are concerned with earning at least a minimal return or better than a savings account, look at the "Guaranteeing a Minimal Return" strategy.

Guaranteeing Your Principal

1. Call your broker or banker, refer to your retirement documents or do a little research yourself to find out what U.S. Treasury zero coupon bonds, GICs, GNMAs, CDs or other guaranteed investments are yielding.
2. Look at the Saving for Future Goals Table in Appendix C. Determine what you have to put aside today in a guaranteed investment to get your entire principal back. For example, if you have $10,000 to invest for ten years and you found you can get 10 percent, go to the table and look down the 10 percent column until you come to the ten-year row. You will find that you need $386 for each thousand dollars you want in ten years. If you want $10,000, you need to invest $3,860 at the guaranteed rate.

   Where do you invest the rest of the money? Since your risk tolerance showed that you needed to only be assured of having the $10,000 returned, you should consider investing the rest in stock mutual funds. If you were lucky enough to get a mutual fund that averaged 12 percent over the next ten years, and there are many that have, your stock portion will grow to $19,070, for a total value in ten years of $29,070. That is $13,000 more than if you left it in a savings account.

Example #1 - Zero at 10%, Mutual Fund at 12%	
Guaranteed Zero Coupon Bond at 10%	Growth Mutual Fund at 12%
Invested = $3,860	$ 6,140
Value in 10 years = $10,000	$19,070
Total Value =	$29,070

Compare this to the $16,288 your $10,000 would have earned in a 5 percent Treasury, money market or savings account. It's almost a $13,000 difference!

SAFETY STRATEGY #2: GUARANTEEING A MINIMAL RETURN

Let's assume that you want to guarantee that you have as much as you would have in a savings account. You want to have your $10,000 guaranteed to give you a specific amount or $16,000, the same a savings account at 5 percent would give you. You have to put more aside in the guaranteed zero if you want this much peace of mind and you would have to multiply the amount in Appendix C by 16 or the number of thousands you want.

STRATEGY #3: PREPACKAGED GUARANTEES

There are many prepackaged zero and stock trusts offered by many brokerage firms. Each brokerage firm names these trusts differently. Prudential Securities calls them GETs, PaineWebber calls them Pathfinders and Merrill Lynch, MITs. While each varies slightly, they are typically zero coupon bonds matched to a mutual fund or stock index. Zero coupon bonds and stock trusts offer the nervous novice investor an opportunity to guarantee his or her principal and yet invest in the stock market. These trusts employ the same concepts as the "Guaranteeing Your Principal" strategy.

Packaged Guaranteed Government/Equity Trusts

Pros:

- ◆ Cannot lose principal if you hold them to maturity;
- ◆ Allow you to participate in the stock market with minimum worry;
- ◆ Can be cheaper and safer than participating in the market through most mutual funds;
- ◆ Stocks offer inflation hedges to offset the typical risk of guaranteed bonds;
- ◆ Usually have 7- to 15-year life;
- ◆ Even if the stock market falls to zero, you would have your money back when you retire.

Cons:

- ◆ If you invested in stock funds and if you hold them over a 15- to 20-year period, greater returns are almost certain;
- ◆ Although you never see them, there are hidden fees in these trusts, sometimes as high as 4 percent;
- ◆ Zeros in and of themselves are not terrific investments since they have more interest rate risk than any other type of bonds;
- ◆ Zeros have taxable interest in most cases, so keep these in your retirement accounts;
- ◆ If you are looking for above-average returns, not just guarantees, then these trusts are not for you.

STRATEGY #4: ASSET ALLOCATION

You can add safety to your portfolio if you allocate your funds among several different types of investments, such as stocks, cash and bonds. In the past, when the stock market went up, the bond market went down. If you had a portfolio with stocks and bonds, you could usually balance off the risks of one market against the other. However, since the 1980s, the stock and bond markets have tended to move together, so the same theory of having a balanced stock and bond portfolio has not worked. In 1994 this theory was especially disproven when everything fell: the dollar, the stock market, the bond market and even the international markets. However, in general it is a good idea to have some investments in many different sectors, and to take advantage of higher-yielding investments as well as conservative investments.

SAFETY STRATEGY #5: DOLLAR COST AVERAGING

Dollar cost averaging is one of the most popular theories in investing. It requires that each month you save and invest a little at a time. This is done automatically with some retirement plans such as 401(k)s by contributing a fixed amount each month. By averaging into the market instead of investing your money all at one time, you tend to buy less shares when stock prices are high and more when prices are low. There are some legitimate arguments against this theory, showing you could do better by investing lump sums. Even if you invested on the day before the market crash in October, 1987, you would have more today than the person who held off and invested the money in equal portions over the past five years. However, for most investors, dollar cost averaging is a safer discipline.

STRATEGY #6: STOP YOUR LOSSES
WITH "STOP-LOSSES"

As I mentioned in Question #53, a stop-loss order is simply an order you give your broker that instructs him or her to sell your stock if it falls to a certain price. Your stop-sell order is placed on the books, good until canceled, at a price below where the stock trades. If the stock falls, then your order goes to the exchange and becomes a market order. Your stock can be sold for less than your stop-loss order if the market is falling. Sometimes the stock can come right back up and you will regret selling, but many times this is a very attractive way to build in safety. In October, 1987, when the market fell 90 points on Friday, and then over 500 points the following Monday, I was commuting every week between Puerto Rico, where my husband was the commander of a navy squadron, and Washington, where my clients were. I needed a stress-free way of handling my accounts, so I relied very heavily on an asset allocation program and on stop-losses. After the market crash, I realized that the best thing I could have done for my clients was to remove myself emotionally from volatile times and have an automatic system in place. Instead of my trying to second-guess the market, my stop-losses took over and sold us out on Friday. If I had been in the office, I am not sure I would have had the courage to do that, and I certainly would not have had the time.

SAFETY STRATEGY #7: WATCH OVERWEIGHTING

Evaluate your weighting in different investments each month, and see if it is in line with your goals. During the 1980s, the market was doing so well that many stock positions became overweighted. You may have only wanted 60 percent in stocks, but suddenly because the stocks had done so well, you had over 80 percent and thus were "overweighted" in stocks. When you end up with a larger percentage in one investment than you want, consider shifting some of your funds to other investments.

STRATEGY #8: HEDGING WITH INSURANCE OPTIONS

If you are nervous about the market, you can buy an insurance policy, or in the financial world what is called a "put option." This put gives you the right to "put" or sell a stock at a predetermined price. Like all insurance policies, you have to pay a premium for the insurance. And like all insurance policies, if the disaster never occurs, you have wasted your money.

STRATEGY #9: COVERED CALLS

You can also sell a "call" to generate extra income and to protect you if the market falls. You are basically selling someone the right to "call" your stock away from you if it goes up in price. This cuts off your upside potential, but if the market falls, you just collected extra money that reduces your downside risk.

STRATEGY #10: WATCH BETAS

Watch your betas if you want to increase your safety. Betas are simply a measurement of how your stock or mutual fund moves in line with the market. If the beta is greater than one, then your stock will move up and down faster than the market. If the beta is less than one, then your stock will move less than the market. If the beta is one, your stock will move in-line with the market. If you want to make your portfolio safer, when the market looks shaky, switch to low-beta stocks and funds. A good strategy is to move out funds as they gain in profit, from high-beta funds to lower-beta funds in the same family. When the market falls, move back into high-beta stocks and funds.

69 IF MY PENSION LOSES MONEY OR IS NOT FUNDED PROPERLY, WHAT CAN I DO?

If you manage your own retirement funds, there is usually little you can do. But if your employer is managing your funds, you may have some recourse. If the losses are a result of normal market risk, your employer is not responsible. But if your employer acted imprudently or participated in prohibited actions, you may be able to sue for losses.

- ◆ If you are nervous about your plan, write the U.S. Department of Labor. It is better to write and keep copies of all your correspondences.
- ◆ Keep good records and each year make sure you get the amount of contribution that you are supposed to. Ask to see the Form 5500c and the statement of benefits each year.

◆ If you think the interest rate has been miscalculated, contact the Academy of Actuaries and get a local number for an actuary.

◆ If your employer will not cooperate with you, write to the American Association of Retired Persons, Worker Equity, 601 E. St. N.W., Washington D.C. 20049, or Pension Rights Center, 918 16th Street, N.W., Suite 704, Washington, D.C. 20006. They can give you a list of lawyers who are knowledgeable in this field.

CHAPTER 8

Profiting from Your Employee Benefits

70 HOW DO I READ MY BENEFITS STATEMENT?

One of the most important places to begin understanding your employee benefits is your benefits statement. If you work for a large company, you will receive a benefits booklet. If you work for a smaller company, you may have to ask your employer for a statement. While it may only be a few pages and not a formal document, it should be complete enough to allow you to understand your benefits.

Make sure you keep your benefits statement with all your other important insurance papers and wills. This is an important outline of what your family and you are entitled to in emergencies.

Many workers never even look at these booklets and assume that the information is general, but it isn't. It is personal information that relates to you only. Look in these statements for information on your disability, life and health insurance.

You will find more general information in your summary plan descriptions called SPDs. Your benefits statement is only a fraction of the information that is available about your benefits. Your SPDs will provide even more information, but even the SPDs do not give you all the information you need. You may have to look for additional information in plan documents, trust agreements, insurance contracts and medical booklets. If you want or need any additional information, your benefits department should be able to help you.

Over the years as things change, it is important to have a running balance of your benefits. Start by going through your benefits book and highlighting or underlining all the important elements.

- **Make sure you are getting the proper credit for your work** and the additional credits and contributions to your pension that you are entitled to. Get proper credit for overtime.
- **If you are in a multiemployer plan, make sure that your hours from each employer are included.** The more unique aspects about your job, the more overtime hours, the more flexibility, the more employers involved, the more job changes and the more benefits and perks, the more likely you are to have errors.
- **Benefit statements** should give you dollar amounts of retirement and insurance benefits. You will frequently get a separate breakdown for flexible savings plans after you sign up for them.
- **Look for your various benefits.** If your company has more than 25 employees, it is likely you will have several medical options such as PPOs, HMOs and indemnity plans. If you work for a small company, you may only have a notation of who your insurance provider is and a brief description of the company and phone number. This section will tell you who pays for the benefits and how much. It will also describe the coverage, such as hospital and surgical coverage. If your company has a flexible spending account, it will usually be described. There is generally no dollar amount shown, however, because you'll receive a quarterly statement. Look to see if Social Security and worker's compensation will be used to reduce disability payments. This section will also show you the amount of insurance that your employer is paying for you. Often you will find listed accidental death policies, travel accident policies and any other insurance plans that you have signed up for as well as information on Social Security and additional insurance coverage information.
- **Retirement section.** Look in this section to see when you are vested or entitled to 100 percent of your retirement assets. If you work for a large company, you will see estimates of the income you will receive at retirement from your employer's plans and from Social Security. If you work for a small

employer, you may have to do the calculations yourself. Your contributions will usually be shown separately. Contributions to any employee contribution plans such as 401(k)s will be shown as current value. There are usually no projections of future income for these accounts since no one knows what the actual returns will be.

◆ **Descriptions of fringe benefits and cafeteria plans** may or may not be included. Usually nonqualified plans, expense accounts, frequent-flier mileage and other perks are not shown in these booklets and you have to search for their value in the summary documents and other plan documents.

◆ **Check to make sure your Social Security number, your date of hire and your birth date are correct.** Your retirement benefits are calculated frequently based on your age and date of hire.

71 WHAT BENEFITS ARE OFFERED AND HOW CAN I EVALUATE THEM?

Evaluating benefits is probably the most important part of understanding your net pay. Sometimes it is difficult to quantify benefits and often you have to make sure that you are participating in them. You also have to consider their tax implications. Know your marginal tax bracket and make sure you take the taxes off the top when you are evaluating them. Fill in the benefits worksheet in Question #1 and review the tax consequences of benefits in Question #77.

There are three different types of benefits you should consider. First, there is your employer's tax-free benefits to you. These you can list as they appear on the statement. Second, there are taxable employer benefits. List the after-tax benefit of these. And lastly, there are benefits that you can participate in yourself. Some of these will save you taxes, such as 401(k) plans, and others will be less expensive to buy through your employer. You will want to note the tax savings aspects to these benefits.

72 ARE HMOs AND PPOs ALWAYS THE BEST WAYS TO GO?

Health Maintenance Organizations (HMOs) became popular in the 1980s when companies were looking for ways to reduce the cost of medical insurance. They promise a lot, but do they deliver? The popularity of HMOs is growing dramatically. But there is some question as to whether they are the best alternative or just the least expensive one.

Employers are shifting from higher-cost indemnity plans to managed care. The reason companies are moving so quickly to HMOs is the cost factor. According to Prudential Insurance, 53 percent of companies with over 500 employees offer HMOs. Forty percent offer Preferred Provider Organizations (PPOs).

We know why companies are moving to HMOs, but why are employees moving so quickly? Last year 27 percent of eligible employees selected HMOs and 25 percent selected PPOs.

Each HMO is different and you should evaluate yours by asking other members how satisfied they are. Visit the HMO and see if you can talk briefly with the staff. Sit in the waiting room and watch how patients are being treated. Then evaluate the benefits, deductibles and copayments.

Costs.　Price is becoming the main attraction for most workers, especially since deductibles and copayments for HMOs are almost negligible. Employers and the government, who are the biggest buyers of HMO services, keep pressure on rates. The cost of health care, including HMOs, was increasing for several years. In 1992, the cost increased almost 10 percent for the average worker, in 1993 almost 8 percent and in 1994 over 5 percent. Yet in 1995 we saw a first-ever decrease in the costs of HMOs. Do these reduced costs mean you will get less quality? If the reason costs are down is because of improved efficiency and productivity, these are pluses for you as the consumer. But if the prices are down because of cutbacks in hospital stays, services and specialists, then HMOs may not be the best alternatives.

HMOs are known for the quality of their preventative care. Most of the commercial insurers and the "blues" only provide coverage for illness or injury. Before you opt for HMOs or even PPOs consider the following:

   ◆ **Relationships with staff.** It may be important to you to use your own physician, especially if you are older, have a history of illness and have maintained a close personal relationship with your own doctor. If such a relationship is important, then HMOs are probably not for you.

- **Convenience.** Location can be important also. If the HMO is inaccessible and difficult to get to, you may postpone needed appointments.
- **Hospitals.** Make sure the HMO has a relationship with the hospitals in which you feel comfortable. You usually will have no choice of hospitals.
- **Deductibles and copayments.** When you research the costs of HMOs versus the alternatives, you must also consider that with HMOs you usually pay no deductibles or copayments.
- **Specialists and serious illness.** Although HMOs do a good job of preventative medicine such as cholesterol screening, mammograms and pap smears, still not many studies are conducted that analyze their treatment of serious illnesses or the availability of specialists.
- **Limited care.** In order to keep costs down and profits up, most HMOs may limit the quality of care instead of seeking the best and most extensive care for participants. HMOs are competitive businesses who not only need to charge less to attract new clients, but also must earn money to attract investment capital and support their stock prices.
- **PPOs.** Preferred Provider Organizations are like traditional indemnity plans, but members get more coverage at lower cost if they choose health care providers that are affiliated with or approved by the plan. PPOs are the "in-between" solution. PPOs try to negate the bad qualities of HMOs, namely the limited choice of physicians and hospitals. A PPO is made up of various hospitals and physicians in an area. You get to select which physician you want. If it is not one of the preferred providers, you will receive only 80 percent coverage.
- **Indemnity plans.** These plans are usually the best coverage, but you also pay the highest deductible and copayments. Since they are the most expensive to companies, their demise is imminent.
- **Medical Savings Accounts (MSAs).** In addition to HMOs, PPOs and indemnity plans, many companies offer a variation of all three, called medical savings accounts. MSAs tradeoff higher deductibles for much lower insurance premiums and rebate the premium savings to the employee to cover the deductible. The idea is to make each individual a more conscientious health care shopper.

These plans are gaining in popularity and some state governments have changed their tax codes to give tax advantages to these plans. The federal government is likely to do the same. These plans cut costs, but if they also cut care, they may not be so attractive.

73 WHOSE HEALTH CARE PACKAGE SHOULD I PARTICIPATE IN, MINE OR MY SPOUSE'S?

One of the easiest ways to throw money away is to duplicate the benefits of your spouse. If both you and your spouse are employed, you should compare your policies. If you are both paying insurance premiums, you may be throwing money away. In most cases, the only advantage of having two policies is that the second policy will usually cover your deductible and copayments, but even this practice is changing. In addition, the costs of these policies is almost always more expensive than their deductibles.

Typically, if John and Mary work for different companies and both have insurance, their individual policies will cover them. But who pays for their dependents? Most states have rules that will determine what policy pays, usually either by gender or birth date. The policy for the spouse with the earliest birth date will be the policy that pays, under the birthday rule. Both parents shouldn't carry dependent coverage if only one policy will pay.

Since only one policy will usually cover, consider dropping one policy. If your employer is paying for the plan, you may want to negotiate for other employee benefits. Even if you work for a small company, the ability to select among different benefits is becoming more popular. Cafeteria plans in which you can take a specified amount of employer dollars and spread it among several different benefits make it more attractive for dual income families to select the programs that benefit them most. Employers will usually give you a credit if you drop your coverage, as much as $85 a month for family plans and $60 for individual plans. If you drop out completely, over three quarters of large employers will also pay you a refund as long as you are covered by your spouse's plan.

In addition you may find that you no longer can "coordinate" your benefits. In the past you could submit the bills to your spouse's medical plan if they were not covered by yours. You would end up with 100 percent of your expenses covered. But most employers are adding provisions that allow you coverage only up to the maximum that either plan would allow. If your employer is paying for your benefits, you may be required to drop benefits for your spouse, if your spouse is covered under another plan.

74 WHAT TYPE OF EDUCATIONAL ASSISTANCE CAN I EXPECT FROM MY EMPLOYER?

Whether your employer offers financial aid for outside college courses or in-house training programs, some of the most important benefits you can receive are educational benefits. Some of these benefits will be taxable and some will be tax-free.

For many years the IRS allowed employees to receive up to $5,250 of educational assistance on a tax-free basis. The laws fluctuated, denying the tax advantages for a while, but reinstating them in 1994. You can again exclude up to $5,250 of educational assistance if it is for education that allows you to maintain or improve skills required in your current job. A computer programmer taking an art course may not qualify unless he or she can show it improves his or her graphic skills. The exclusion applies for undergraduate and graduate-level classes, even if you are not seeking a degree.

If your employer included educational benefits on your tax return for the second half of 1992 and you paid tax on it, you should be entitled to a refund. Get a Form W-2c (Statement of Corrected Income and Tax Amounts) from your employer and file Form 1040x (Amended U.S.Individual Income Tax Return). Also ask your employer for refunds on Social Security and Medicare taxes since these were based on the income that included these benefits.

Deductible Education Courses. Even though your employer may not pay for education, often if you are taking courses to keep current on your job, some of them may be tax-deductible as miscellaneous business expenses. These expenses can only be deducted if they maintain or improve skills that are required in your trade or business or if the courses are required to retain your present job. If the education courses are to meet the minimum educational requirements for your position, you can't deduct them, nor can you deduct them if they are to further your career and enhance your chances of promotion.

In-House Education and Training.   If employers offer in-house training, take it. In many instances, these programs actually increase income more quickly than outside educational courses. Motorola, one of the nation's leaders for in-house training, spends more than 3.6 percent on each employee for training. After employees have completed these programs, they are almost immediately rewarded with pay increases. At Corning, once you have passed a two-year program with approximately one day a week in training and become a Celcor specialist, you receive hourly pay raises of 20 percent.

Companies see the relationship between education and company growth more clearly with in-house training than they do with outside college courses. Many are abandoning outside educational assistance in favor of these courses, offering on-location training through teleconferencing and video workshops.

Such classes can be more valuable to you than college classes. Do not ignore or bypass these programs. In many ways, your rewards are much higher, since you may be able to use company time to advance your career.

75 CAN MY EMPLOYER HELP WITH ADOPTIONS?

Although couples have been adopting forever, the new baby boomer group has a lot of clout at the workplace and is pressuring companies to provide adoption benefits comparable to maternity benefits. Leave is also being granted to adopting parents, similar to leave for natural childbirth parents. Federally mandated leave is being extended to cover adoptions also.

In addition, many companies now offer resource and referral programs that offer advice on adoptions, help to minimize legal costs and provide counseling assistance.

If your company offers cafeteria plans, you may have the opportunity to select an adoption credit as one of the benefits.

76 MY EMPLOYER OFFERS A CAFETERIA PLAN.
HOW DO I KNOW WHICH PACKAGES TO SELECT?

No, these are not lunch programs. These are plans that offer a variety of benefits that the employee can select. Since you have the ability to review the list and select the ones most appropriate to you, these plans are called cafeteria plans. The menu can include insurance, dental plans, extended vacation, educational benefits and child care benefits. Some offer on-site child care or vouchers, waivers and credits for child care. Your employer gives you a specified amount of dollars and you can then pick the benefits you want.

The flexibility that these plans offer makes them attractive for the many different phases in workers lives. If you or your spouse has such a plan, it allows you to pick and choose the benefits most attractive to your situation. You can fill in the gaps in the coverage that you need. Make sure you do not duplicate coverage with your spouse. Coordinate the benefits that both of your companies offer.

These plans are increasing in numbers as employers try to find ways to satisfy the different needs of workers but stay within the guidelines of IRS rules. Even if you do not have a cafeteria plan yet, you may soon. Over 25 percent of companies with 1,000 or more employers currently offer these plans.

77 WHAT ARE THE TAX CONSEQUENCES OF MY DIFFERENT PERKS AND BENEFITS?

In order to understand the true value of your benefits you have to know the tax consequences. This is especially important when you are negotiating for raises with your employer and trying to reduce your taxes.

- **Awards.** If your awards are for suggestions, they are included in your income. If you receive qualified plan awards based on your length of service, amounts under $1,600 are tax-free.

INSURANCE

- **Disability insurance** premiums are not taxable. However, disability benefits are taxable if your employer pays. If you pay, they are tax-free.
- **Group life** is taxable if over $50,000.
- **Whole life or permanent life insurance** premiums are included in your income and subject to taxation. However, the

proceeds are free of income tax, and if you do not own the policies you can avoid estate taxes.

◆ **Group medical and dental insurance.** In general the premiums paid by your employer are tax-free. The benefits are generally tax-free to you. There is an exception for discriminatory self-insured medical reimbursement plans.

◆ **Group property and liability insurance.** The benefits are generally tax-free, but the premiums your employer contributes represent taxable income.

SERVICES

◆ **Group legal expense plans.** There are no taxes on your employer's contributions.

◆ **Wellness programs.** Medical screening programs are tax-free, but some wellness programs or lifestyle management programs are actually taxable to employees. The use of athletic facilities located on premises is tax-free.

◆ **Dependent care assistance** provided by employers is tax-free up to $5,000 for couples filing jointly, and $2,500 for married couples filing separately. This assistance may, however, be taxable to highly compensated employees unless special rules are met.

◆ **Discounts** on merchandise and services are tax-free. These are especially important benefits to those working in low-paying retail and service jobs.

◆ **Vacations and holidays** are usually included in compensation and taxed as such.

◆ **Educational assistance** is tax-free on the first $5,200 of benefits, if the plan is nondiscriminatory.

◆ **Moving reimbursements** are reported as taxable income.

◆ **Gifts** are usually tax-free if the gifts are small or inconsequential.

◆ **Frequent-flier miles** are taxable income to the employee if the flight on which miles were earned was paid for by an employer, and the miles converted to personal use. If your employer uses the miles, the cost of the previous tickets are reduced by the value of the miles, so it is a no-win situation.

If the IRS audits you, it will value these miles at the maximum. The best way to avoid paying too much on taxes is to find out the lowest possible cost of the flights that you used the mileage for and keep that in your records. You can use that value as the taxable income portion.

◆ **Financial planning services** are usually included as taxable income, but you may be able to claim a deduction on your taxes for that portion that is related to investments and tax strategies.

◆ **Parking** is a benefit that can be offered to higher-paid employees on a discriminatory basis and not be taxable.

◆ **Transportation, tokens and travel reimbursements** less than $15 a month are tax-free.

◆ **Company cars** follow complicated tax implications. Depending on the amount of time for personal use, these benefits may have minimal tax consequences.

◆ **Subsidized eating facilities.** The value of meals served to employees may be tax-free if they are furnished for the employer's benefit. Any meals that your employer supplies when you work overtime or attend meetings is usually tax-free.

When you are negotiating raises with your employer, you may want to consider some of the benefits listed previously instead of cash. As we saw in Question #14, benefits may be more feasible in many situations.

78 CAN TAKING SABBATICALS AND LEAVES OF ABSENCE HURT MY FUTURE RETIREMENT AND SENIORITY?

There are many arguments in favor of leaves of absence and sabbaticals. Many studies show sabbaticals enrich our lives, reinvigorate the workplace, lead to increased education and travel and provide time to step back, reevaluate and bring creative ideas to the workplace. They can add dimension and emotional strength and help create strong families, but they can also jeopardize career advancement and raises.

When we discuss the difference in the pay scales for women and men, most assume that the difference is a result of gender. However, many new studies, including a study conducted for the *Journal of Labor Economics* by June O'Neil and Simon Placjheck, found that women in 1987 spent only 70 percent of their potential work years in the workplace versus 90 percent for men. They theorize this limited amount of time is probably one of the major impediments to higher pay and seniority. Retirement income also depends very heavily on the amount of income you earn and the number of years you work. Leaves of absence and sabbaticals often reduce income and the number of years worked.

Extra income and getting ahead can be costly to both men and women and may require giving up valuable time for young children, education, elderly parents, travel or whatever. Sometimes the extra income can be costly in terms of nonquantifiable values and time. Many psychologists present strong arguments in favor of leaves of absence not only for workers and families but also for employers. As a mother who took off time when her children were young, I can't imagine how extra dollars in retirement would make me want to give up those years. Every person has to determine for themselves how important these gaps in their career are. Frequently, gaps for education can actually increase your potential, your ability to advance and your income.

Before trying to evaluate the pros and cons of leaves or sabbaticals you may want to review Questions #5 and #6.

79 HOW DOES FLEXTIME WORK?

Flexible hours or flextime is anything that deviates from the traditional nine-to-five work schedule and may include job sharing and part-time work. Flexible hours simply let you adapt your work schedule to your lifestyle. It may mean coming in early so you can leave in time to be home for your children. It may mean cutting back to 30 work hours and skipping lunches and breaks, or it may mean four ten-hour days each week. Flextime allows workers to care for children as well as elderly parents, reduce work-related expenses, improve the emotional stability of families and reduce stress.

Many employers are eager to offer employees flexible hours since these programs usually do not add any costs to the employer. As employers are forced to cut down on more traditional benefits, flextime benefits provide an attractive alternative and often reduce turnover, absenteeism and instead help to recruit employees. Sixty-six percent of large companies have flexible work schedules, including job sharing and part-time work.

But as with every job alternative, there are negatives to consider. Flex workers may not put in enough hours to qualify for many retirement and health care benefits. But if a spouse has attractive benefits packages, this may not be an important issue.

How Do You Get Your Employer To Accept Flextime?

1. Offer examples to your employer on how and why flextime succeeds. Explain how it attracts new workers, retains you and other workers when family needs affect your job and increases loyalty. Johnson & Johnson saw a dramatic reduction in their turnover after they instituted flextime.
2. Show that you are able to complete your work just as efficiently as you would during a normal workday.
3. Quantify the benefits to your employer by demonstrating the lack of cost and increase in worker productivity flextime produces.

80 ARE THERE ANY DRAWBACKS ATTACHED TO MY EMPLOYER-PROVIDED PERKS?

Some of the most important drawbacks of perks are the hidden tax consequences and the loss of privacy.

Tax consequences. There can be many hidden taxes on some perks. For example, frequent-flier mileage may not be so free as you think, since you have to pay taxes on whatever the value of the flight is that you exchange the mileage for.

Many service industries tend to offer no-additional-cost services or discounted services. Airlines may give tickets to their employees, or telephone companies may give a discount on phone services. Retailers usually offer their employees discounts to compensate for the poor pay. These benefits are usually tax-free, but there are limitations on the amounts that can be discounted, and if the discount is greater than the gross profit, there may be some tax consequences.

Loans received at a discounted rate of interest may have taxes. Usually higher-paid employees will not be able to receive perks without tax consequences, unless the perks are offered to all employees on a nondiscriminatory basis. Free trips your employer gives you can be very expensive, since they are often taxable for any portion not related to business, especially amounts paid for spouses.

Privacy. Employers are offering more perks, yet many of them are really to improve the bottom line and make the workplace more productive. What are labeled as wellness programs are usually packaged with monitoring programs that threaten your privacy. Employers want to know which habits are the riskiest. If you work for large companies, your daily health habits are probably being monitored for surveys in many lifestyle programs. Employees hesitate to participate for fear this information may hinder future promotions within the company. Many companies evaluate the risks of various physical and mental problems and reward nonsmokers and employees with good health habits. Are these surveys a drawback for employees? In general, probably not. However, if this information is used to force lifestyle or wellness programs in order to improve the bottom line, you may feel your freedoms are being restricted and your privacy invaded. The more your employer knows about your personal life, the more you may have to pay up. If you drink and are in a car accident, for example, your employer may charge you a $1,000 deductible for medical coverage.

Many employee-assistance programs are designed to improve productivity, minimize absenteeism and help employees with problems that result in poor performance. These programs offer assistance for marital problems, alcohol abuse, drug abuse, legal and financial problems.

Overall, employer-provided perks are usually a mixed blessing, so study them carefully before accepting them.

CHAPTER 9

Making Job Transitions

81 I'VE LOST MY JOB. NOW WHAT?

It happens to the best of us. According to the Department of Labor, at any given point there is an average of 12 percent of Americans with jobs in transition.

When you lose your job, there are several factors you need to consider, in addition to worrying about getting a new job. You should also consider viable ways of "hanging on" with your old employer, continuing insurance coverage, protecting your retirement benefits, making sure you get all the benefits and disbursements you are entitled to and negotiating severance packages.

- **Hanging on.** If you have any unique skills such as computer, engineering or marketing skills, or expertise in a specialized area that your employer will sorely miss, you may want to hang on, through networking, temporary assignments, contracting back, consulting, acting as a supplier or reducing your hours.
- **Networking.** Networking, or staying in touch with your fellow employees and employers, is still the number one way to not only get a new job, but to linger on in your old job. Often, if the economy improves, and you keep in touch, you may be first in line to come back. Keep the personnel depart-

ment informed of any education and additional training that might make you suitable for another position.

◆ **Contracting back.** Many companies are willing to contract back some laid-off workers, for they can avoid high compensation packages without worrying about IRS discrimination rules. Contracting back allows for many tax-deductible, self-employed work expenses and often after-tax pay is only slightly diminished.

◆ **Become a supplier.** If you have been supplying a specific service or product for your employer, you may want to consider acting as a supplier to your former company and other companies.

◆ **Consulting.** Packaging yourself as a consultant allows you to present yourself to potential employers on a less threatening basis and gives you opportunities to receive exposure at many different companies. Working on specific tasks for a period of time and seeing them come to a conclusion offers a lot of satisfaction. Those in the military, those who have held many different positions within a large company, as well as those who have worked for small companies in which they had to "wear many hats" are particularly suitable for task-oriented consulting projects. You need to network, belong to many professional organizations and keep marketing yourself as any self-employed person or small business must do.

◆ **Reducing hours.** Many times you may find that you can work part-time or reduce your hours when your employer can't afford you full-time. Compare your part-time income to unemployment compensation. Part-time work can keep you informed and knowledgeable about what is going on in the company and make it easier for you to look for other jobs in the interim, but there are seldom any health benefits.

◆ **Temporary assignments.** Although temporary jobs account for just a little over 2 percent of all jobs, they are increasing at double digit rates. By the year 2000, government officials predict there will be 3.5 million temps. Your current employer is probably hiring temps to replace a lot of the displaced workers and it may be less expensive to hire you back as a temp than someone else who needs to be trained. Taking temporary work, while sometimes lacking in benefits and retirement packages, can be a stepping-stone into many new jobs. Temps are often hired full-time. If your goal is to get a full-time job, make sure your temporary service representative knows this so you are placed in appropriate positions. Use these temporary assignments to network, to meet personnel and human resource people and other employees, to explore different companies and impress many possible employers. Many of the larger temp agencies, such as Manpower, Olsten and Career Works, may offer you some employee insurance benefits. Some temporary companies specialize in professional positions, and others specialize in converting temporary jobs to full-time, such as Interim Management Corporation (IMCOR). To find the company that specializes in your particular field, contact the National Association of Temporary Services in Alexandria, Virginia, 703-549-6287.

Be careful with temporary assignments. Staying in a temporary position for too long can diminish your ability to gain seniority, pension funds and health care benefits.

WHERE TO GET HELP

◆ **Outplacement services.** At your old workplace, negotiate outplacement services, possibly office space, telephone and computer accessibility, secretarial help, resume preparation or whatever you need to help you get a new job. These services may have information on recruiting, government retraining programs, as well as other job leads. If you work for a small company or don't have these services available, seek the help of employment specialists and career counselors. If you are young and just a few years out of college, go back to your college career counselors. Even if you are many years out of school, this could be a good source to tap into.

◆ **Employment agencies.** You might find a job on your own, but it might also be nice to have someone work along with you. Some agencies will not cost you anything, since the new employer may pay. The National Association of Personnel

Service in Alexandria, Virginia, 703-684-0180, has a list of agencies all over the country and categorizes them by occupation as well as geographic territory.

◆ **Professional groups.** Stay involved with professional associations and clubs. You not only may need their support and friendship, but also their contacts. Attend job fairs, and read business and trade journals. Stay informed of changes not only in your company, but in the industry, in your profession, in the economy and in your community. Losing a job can be one of the most traumatic experiences in your life. In fact, psychologists consider loss of a job as destructive to one's ego and self-image as divorce. Next to the death of a loved one, it is the most draining of emotional experiences. Don't underestimate the physiological strain you are going through. Seek help from those who have experience in this area. Many companies will offer staff and support groups as well as outplacement services.

In the middle of this emotional drama, life will become more complicated. You have to look for a job and at the same time manage dozens of critical financial issues posed by your departure. Check on (1) credits for sick leave, (2) vacation time, (3) early retirement options, (4) the status of your disability insurance, (5) flexible savings plan balances, (6) health care extension programs, (7) long-term care coverage and (8) life insurance coverage. Also evaluate job placement programs and retirement plan conversions. All of these workplace decisions are crucial. While some can be postponed for a time, most need immediate attention.

You still have a job of marketing and selling yourself and you have to treat it like any other job, including working regular hours and establishing a routine. Set aside a room in your house to send out resumes, do research and follow up on leads. Make getting a good job the most rewarding job of your life.

82 HOW CAN I PREPARE IF I THINK I MIGHT BE LOSING MY JOB?

If you think that you may be losing your job, now is the time to plan. You should start negotiating severance packages, building up your resume, networking and calling headhunters and employment agencies. You also need to put your financial house in order: Refinance your home, clear up any debt, establish credit and redirect savings.

- ◆ **Negotiate a severance package with your employer.** Your employer can start saving up to 20 percent of your salary in a severance package for you, years ahead of time. If you do lose your job, the funds from these plans are distributed without taxes. It might be a good idea to opt for these plans instead of raises. Not only will they keep your current taxes low, but they make your future a lot more secure.
- ◆ **Start networking inside and outside your company and join associations and clubs.**
- ◆ **Call any headhunters you met in the past.** Even though they are only responsible for between 5 to 15 percent of job placements, as soon as you think there is a possibility of a layoff, call them. It gives you more credibility to look while you have a job. Subscribe to the *National Business Employment Weekly.* Use your local library to research job opportunities across the country. *The Kennedy Publications' Directory of Executive Recruiters* has names of headhunters that might be interested in you. These listings are geared to those with incomes over $100,000.
- ◆ **Contact old employers.** If you ever had casual conversations with other employers about jobs, call them for lunch and see what possibilities are available.
- ◆ **Get your financial house in order.**
  - ◆ Refinance your home. If interest rates are low and you have money tied up in your home, get a home equity line of credit before your lose your job. When you don't have a job, it is difficult to get anyone to give you credit.
  - ◆ Establish credit. While you are still working, take out bank and credit union loans. Pay them back quickly to establish credit. Get additional no-fee and low-fee credit cards.
  - ◆ Get out of debt now before your paychecks stop coming.
  - ◆ Stop spending and start saving. Make a budget and spend only what you anticipate you will get from unemployment compensation.
  - ◆ Reallocate savings from pension plans to individual accounts. Stop saving in places that are hard to tap into, such

as IRAs. Save in 401(k)s instead of IRAs, since you can borrow more easily from them. Stop saving in annuities and in any volatile mutual funds, use more stable and liquid funds, and start increasing your emergency funds from two months of income to four.

83　I'VE BEEN OFFERED AN EARLY RETIREMENT PACKAGE. SHOULD I TAKE IT?

As a way to cut expenses and as an alternative to firing, many large companies, such as AT&T, NYNEX, IBM and Sears are offering early retirement packages. These packages will change from company to company, but there are some basics you can look for.

- **Do you have a choice?** You can spend weeks or months trying to analyze the pros and cons of these packages, but sometimes there really is no choice. If not, review Questions #81 and #82.
- **Do you want to work?** Before you even consider the financial aspects, decide if you really want to continue working for this company. Do you see this as an opportunity to pull back and take life a little slower or look for more interesting and financially sound companies? Do you have a good possibility of getting a new job?
- **Longevity makes a big difference in retirement income.** Each additional year you work increases your retirement income. The earlier you start drawing on it, the smaller it will be forever. See Question #95 for some examples of how longevity benefits you.
- **Lump sums.** Many early retirees dip into lump sums in an attempt to supplement income until Social Security and other pension benefits kick in. However, if you dip into your principal, your income will be less for the rest of your life. Instead, you need to invest these funds and live off only the income. You will need to keep these funds safe if you are living within a tight budget. Consider government Treasuries or a package of high-quality corporate bonds and utilities. Also consider some stable utilities and income-oriented balanced mutual funds. You should never consider living off your

principal unless you are very wealthy or very old. But if you absolutely have to live off the principal, consider an annuity or government mortgages such as GNMAs, Fannie Maes and Freddie Macs (see the glossary for full descriptions). They pay out a portion of principal monthly, as well as interest and therefore act as self-annuities.

◆ **Determine your retirement income.** Make a balance sheet of all sources of income. If you have a lump sum payment from your employer or savings, only add in the income you can generate. For example, if you get a $100,000 lump sum and can earn 7 percent, then just include the $7,000 annual income. See Question #59.

◆ **Savings.** Will you be able to keep money set aside for emergencies? If not, every time you deplete your lump sum or savings it will reduce your future income. If you need money for moving, cars, home repairs and so forth, make sure you do not include these expeditures in the savings pool you are using to calculate your retirement income.

◆ **Assess your financial situation.** Know your true budget and make sure you can live on the retirement income mentioned previously. Know when your home mortgage will be paid off. If you do not get insurance as part of your severance package, make sure you calculate the cost.

If you can get a new job immediately, or if you have enough income and are looking forward to retirement, you are a prime candidate for an early retirement.

84 WHAT ARE THE WARNING SIGNALS FOR A CUTBACK?

With so many cutbacks occurring lately, you need to be alert to the warning signals. If you see the layoffs coming, you may be able to move in time. Consider the following:

◆ **Executives or "insiders" selling company stock** is one of the first clues that there may be trouble on the horizon. Check insider selling by calling your broker, looking at the annual reports or reading business newpapers.

◆ **Top executive turnover** could be a warning signal that senior executives are looking for better jobs or a restructuring is going on that may find its way down to your level.

◆ **Corporate profits** should be closely monitored. If a company loses money year after year, you can be sure cutbacks are in order.

◆ **A weak economy** may affect your company if it is interest rate–sensitive, such as a utility or phone company, or if it is a consumer-oriented company such as housing or auto suppliers. Watch economic data on housing starts, consumer spending and consumer confidence closely, as well as interest rates.

◆ **Weak stock prices** occur for many reasons, but if your company's stock is falling when the market is good, then some analysts may have special knowledge about the company. You might want to locate a Value Line, Standard & Poor's or brokerage firm's reports on your company.

◆ **Falling sales** are also a clue. Look around your company. Are sales falling? Is the company hiring? Are orders being shipped on time? Is inventory starting to back up? Are there frequent lawsuits and complaints? Is the company getting a lot of bad press? Look at your division in relation to the rest of the company. Is it pulling its weight? Is it adding to the profit margin?

◆ **Your value to the bottom line.** Have you been passed over for a promotion lately? Are your responsibilities being cut back? Do you notice others getting more attractive assignments? If so, start acting soon. Either make yourself more valuable to your employer or start looking for a new job.

85 HOW CAN I MAKE MYSELF MORE VALUABLE TO MY EMPLOYER?

Every day you work, you have to realize that your employer expects you to do something of worth, something that will make the business more profitable. Employers are looking for employees who do not create conflict, who help the workplace run smoother and who contribute something to the bottom line. If you want to keep your job, the chances are much greater that you will do so if you can prove to your employer that you are valuable, and that every day you become more valuable.

There are no guarantees. No matter how valuable and skilled you are, you may still be caught in an economic downturn. But by working hard to make yourself a valued employee, you will be more valuable to new employers and get better references and referrals from your current employer. It hardly ever hurts to do an honest day's work with enthusiasm and talent.

- **Personal skills list.** First make a list of all the benefits you have to offer your employer. Talk to your employer about your tasks, about those things that are most important to him or her. Then get to work on eliminating the negatives and strengthening those skills that your employer values.
- **Show enthusiasm.** As workers pass the 30-year mark, they become more and more disenchanted with their jobs. Many just have not accomplished what they had planned. Others are burnt out or just bored. Exercise and participate in community groups, workplace activities, investment clubs and softball leagues. You need to be multidimensional, instead of placing your whole sense of self-worth or esteem in one job. Try to enjoy work and show a genuine interest in being there. The best workers are usually those who love their jobs.
- **Education.** Make sure you have the educational skills and training that are important to your employer. Education you gain from experiences, from on-the-job training, from college courses and from life should all be part of your resume. When you talk to your employer, make sure he or she understands how you have educated yourself and made yourself a more knowledgeable and effective employee. Make notes each day of accomplishments, goals achieved, learning experiences and bits of information that you can relay to your superiors.
- **Cross-Train.** One of the best ways to make yourself valuable to your employer is to cross-train. Take advantage of any opportunities to learn several jobs and job functions. If you can fill in and cover for several different individuals, you become invaluable in the day-to-day running of the business and less vulnerable to cutbacks. Employees who can wear many hats or employees who offer unique talents are those most likely to survive layoffs.

◆ **Don't impair yourself.** In a competitive workplace, employers want those who are focused and in control of their lives. With increasing amounts of drug-screening tests and with the need to reduce absenteeism and create a more reliable workforce, employers will eventually have no choice but to weed out the weak and those with addictions. Absenteeism is not the only problem that employers have to worry about. They are also concerned about workplace accidents and liability of employees under the influence of drugs and alcohol.

◆ **Look for new challenges.** Keep looking for more challenges, for more variety in your job. Be creative. If you start off in a clerical position, take advantage of in-house managerial training courses. Make sure you keep accurate records of your accomplishments. Show that you are willing and capable of assuming more responsibilities. If you are performing tasks that are typically those of a manager, make sure your employers are aware of it. Look around at jobs in your company that you may feel are rewarding, take courses that are enriching and improve your communications, managerial and job skills so that you will qualify for those ideal jobs.

◆ **Show leadership.** In large corporations, if you find that you are the person that your peers turn to for advice instead of your manager or supervisor, make sure you keep records of your actions. Even minor incidents of helping out when needed should go into your work diary. The more leadership talents you display, the more valuable you become to your employer and coworkers.

86 WHAT CAN I DO TO PROTECT MY JOB AND MAKE IT MORE SECURE?

In order to protect your job, you must add to the bottom line and the profit margin, minimize costs and keep your total "price tag" within a range your employer can afford. You must be willing to take performance bonuses in lieu of pay, negotiate benefits, consider deferred compensation plans, take lateral positions and move in several career paths and, finally, you must be the person who is difficult and costly to replace.

◆ **Decrease your costs to your employer.** Fifty-year-olds have an increasing likelihood these days of losing a job, so they must be the most aggressive in making themselves more valuable. The fact is, the older you get, the more expensive and costly it is for your employer to keep you. You need to prove that being over 50 can be an advantage and that the additional experience and productivity you bring to the company is worth the cost. Your "price tag" may be a reason for your potential termination. Negotiate with your employer. Be willing to consider deferred compensation plans, lateral moves, split-dollar insurance and noncash benefits as alternatives to more expensive benefits.

◆ **Increase your productivity.** Be willing to make yourself more viable with increased training, and learn how to do your job better so that you are more productive and add more to the bottom line. Set goals for yourself and improve on them every day.

◆ **Accept performance pay in lieu of raises.** Negotiate performance pay plans, bonuses and stock options, and incentive plans that are directly tied to your performance in lieu of cash, so your employer knows the company is getting what it pays for.

◆ **Keep costs down.** Avoid unnecessary expenses. Don't abuse your expense account or the use of the company car. Make sure your employer knows that you have cut back on expenses. Keep track of the real costs of retaining you as an employee. Be willing to give up some perks that may be costly to your employer but not important to you. If you have a working spouse, consider giving up some medical and health care benefits or some travel allowances.

◆ **Gatekeeper.** Make yourself the gatekeeper, the person everyone has to come to for information. Learn all the right people to contact and where all the necessary information is. Become a resource center that fellow employees and your boss feel they can't work without.

◆ **Adapt.** Keep current on all the new technology and skills. Yesterday, typing skills were in demand; today computer skills are in great demand; tomorrow it could be a whole new range of talents. Make sure your employer sees that you have drive, determination, energy and a willingness to do what it takes to keep that job.

- **Profitable products.** Don't assume that because you are a top producer or a rising star, your job is secure. Always evaluate what your bring to the company. Even if you bring in large revenue, it may be of minimal benefit to the company if your costs are high. Even if you are selling large volumes, if the sales are in low profit areas, you may still be vulnerable to cuts.

- **Small company versus larger company.** Often we assume that large company jobs are more secure than those in small companies. However, if you look at the trend the last couple of years, the Fortune 500 companies have been laying off workers, but the small to midsized businesses have been hiring and adding jobs. Government records show the majority of growth in this country is with companies of less than 50 employees. Large companies lay people off when times get tough. Automation in large companies makes it easier to eliminate and replace workers with machines. Although small companies fail more frequently, they may provide more secure jobs to skilled employees.

- **Meet with the boss.** Network and stay in touch with management. Use company meetings, lunches and social events to keep in touch with those people who control your job or who can give you information on how you are viewed at the company. Have regular meetings with your supervisor and review the increased profits or sales that you have brought in. If you cannot quantify your value, discuss other ways in which you can directly or indirectly influence the bottom line. Talk about the negatives that you do not bring, such as personality problems, absenteeism or sloppy work. Look around at what makes you a better worker than someone who is incompetent, and try to define what it is that makes you more successful in your job. In the business world, almost everything reverts to profits, especially when a company is having a hard time with the economy and competition. Always show how you enhance the profit picture for the company.

- **Critical jobs.** Find out what jobs and people are the most important and critical in your company. If you can't get one of those jobs yourself, try and work for someone who is critical and has the ability to keep you hired.

87 ▶ HOW DO I GO AFTER A PROMOTION?

For many, promotions demonstrate a person's measure of success. For others, a promotion offers a new challenge, makes their lives more interesting and leads to the career path of their choice. For still others, advancing in the workplace is important, but not crucial. You may have a job that required years of training, such as an engineer, teacher or doctor, and have no desire to move to another level. Instead, you may be better off with a raise.

- ♦ **Know the job you want.** Before you ask for a promotion, be sure you know as much as possible about the job you would like. Get a copy of the job description from human resources. Know all the duties and responsibilities, and make sure you are qualified to perform all of those activities. When you talk to your supervisor about the promotion, let him or her know exactly what the job entails and why you feel you can perform it well.

- ♦ **Performance reviews.** Make sure you have reread all your performance reviews before the meeting. Highlight those points or comments that emphasize the strengths and qualifications that you have to fill the new position. Quantify your arguments as much as possible. Discuss time you have saved, money you have saved, dollars you have brought into the company and how you have added to the profit margins of your division or department. Show your supervisor how you will be able to do an even better job at the next level.

- ♦ **Specific jobs.** Make sure you and your employer are aware of the skills required in your current job. If the next level requires a degree or further education that you do not have, stress the education that comes from experience and your job.

- ♦ **Lateral positions.** Be willing to take lateral positions to increase your knowledge in other departments and other parts of the company. Be willing to learn about different divisions and operations. This is especially important if you have your goals set on much higher positions, in which a broad, generalists' view of the whole company is needed.

- ♦ **Network.** Schedule regular meetings every few months to review your performance so that you are sure you are accomplishing what your employer wants.

◆ **Job interview.** Pretend you are going after a new job, treat this as a job interview and resell yourself each time. Too often opportunities to discuss your resume and accomplishments never really appear. You need to find time to remind your employer of the reasons he or she hired you in the first place. Don't assume anything. Make sure your employer knows what you have accomplished. Share your achievements regularly.

◆ **Future promotions:** Prepare immediately for future promotions. Know where you want to be one year, five years and ten years from now. Whether you did or didn't get the promotion, negotiate for another performance review in six months. Learn now what skills, education and job requirements are needed for that next level.

88 WHAT CAN I DO IF I THINK I AM BEING TERMINATED BECAUSE OF MY AGE?

Age discrimination is a lot more common than you may think. Businesses learn how to cloak it in many different disguises, but underneath these excuses is a pragmatic desire to cut costs by cutting older employees who are entitled to large pension contributions and high salaries. As companies cut back, those who are over 50 are the most vulnerable because of the expense of their benefits packages.

If you suspect you have been terminated because of your age:

◆ Contact your state and federal agencies immediately. Age discrimination is just as much of a crime as discrimination based on color, creed or sex. The problem is that it is more difficult to prove.

◆ Contact a lawyer.

◆ Try to discover if there are any other employees in your company who are in their 50s and 60s and who have been terminated.

◆ Discuss your concerns with the human resources department.

◆ Become active in employee groups and make sure you document as much as possible similar situations to yours.

◆ If you feel that your age and pension packages may be a concern to your employer, discuss this with him or her early.

Knowing that you are aware of possible discrimination may make your employer think twice.

◆ Do not go it alone. One individual trying to pursue action is unlikely to be sufficient to build a case against your employer. Try and join in class-action suits with other employees who have been terminated.

◆ Document everything. Keep a work diary and keep close track of performance reviews, raises and accomplishments so that you can prove your termination was a result of age, not poor job skills.

◆ Be able to compare your job skills to other, younger employees who have been retained.

89 HOW DO I PROTECT MY BENEFITS PACKAGES WHEN CHANGING JOBS?

According to the Department of Labor, 12 percent of U.S. employees leave their jobs each year. This means there are not only a lot of jobs in transition but a lot of benefits packages that need to be transferred. Employers often make mistakes in calculating benefit packages for terminated employees, and frequently employees themselves handle such benefits improperly, costing thousands of dollars in taxes and lost funds.

Consider the following:

◆ **Check benefits when leaving union positions.** Even if you are staying within the same company, you need to check your benefits when changing from a union position to a management position. Union credits are often lost or forgotten when you change jobs. Make sure you keep track of the formulas and benefits under each contract. Contact the human resources department and find out who handles these accounts, since you may find one person in charge of union benefits and another in charge of nonunion benefits. You should make sure they coordinate their records on your packages.

◆ **Leaves of absence.** If you take leave, make sure your previous time and benefits are included.

◆ **Actuaries.** Call an actuary to check your benefits. He or she will charge around $100 an hour, but will usually review most plans in an hour or two.

◆ **Interest rate assumptions.** Make sure your ex-employer uses the correct interest rates when calculating your lump sum distribution.

◆ **Check insurance on funds.** If you are terminating or leaving a large company for a small company, be careful about the management of your retirement plans. Most large companies will have plans that are guaranteed by the Pension Guarantee Corp., but small companies tend to have plans that do not require insurance.

◆ **Compare different plans when moving.** The unfortunate fact is that large companies are laying off top management or middle management. These are the higher-paid employees whose wages have a great impact on the bottom line. Most of these terminated employees are finding lower-paying service jobs in small businesses. Small businesses usually offer fewer benefits packages and often have 401(k) plans, SEPs or employee contribution plans instead of the more attractive, defined-benefit plans. Not only is the responsibility for contributing shifted from the employer to the employee in these plans, but also the responsibility for managing and selecting investments. See Question #90 and Chapter 6 if you find yourself managing your own money.

◆ **Transferring retirement funds.** If you are not good at managing money, you may want to transfer your money to your new retirement plan instead of an IRA rollover. Although an IRA gives you more options, having more options may not be smart if you do not know how to use them.

◆ **Poor credit.** If you have poor credit, you should keep your funds in your employer's retirement plan rather than an IRA rollover account. In many states, IRAs are not protected from creditors while qualified plans are. If you have any past history of poor credit, are involved in a lawsuit, have children that are bad drivers or are vulnerable to lawsuits for any of a number of reasons, then you may not want to move your funds to IRAs. Many states, however, are starting to extend the same protection to IRAs as to 401(k) and qualified plans.

Check with your local bank or broker to find out if your state offers such protection.

◆ **Borrowing.** If you may need to borrow money, stick with your employer's plan. You can only borrow from IRAs for 60 days, whereas you can borrow from many employee plans for five years.

90 WHAT DO I DO WITH MY RETIREMENT FUNDS WHEN I CHANGE JOBS?

One of the big decisions you will have to face is what to do with your retirement funds. You will usually have six options:

1. Take a lump sum distribution.
2. Take a rollover distribution.
3. Transfer funds to a conduit IRA rollover.
4. Transfer funds to your individual IRA.
5. Leave your funds with you old employer.
6. Transfer the funds to your new employer's plan.

Lump Sum. Usually the worst thing you can do is to take a lump sum, yet most young workers have a tendency to do so. They will usually have to pay a 10 percent IRS penalty, ordinary income taxes, give up future tax deferral of the funds and deplete their savings pool. Often they will end up with less than 50 percent of the value of their funds.

At one time, taking the lump sum and not rolling it over was not quite so bad. You could pay taxes as if you had received the funds over a ten-year period. Now, for most, you can only use five-year averaging, only once in your lifetime and only after you reach age 59½. There are some exceptions to this rule if you have reached age 50 by 1986. The Tax Reform Act of 1986 changes the rules on lump sum distributions, and today, in order to avoid large tax consequences, you must roll over any pretax-fund distributions to your IRA within 60 days to a new employer's plan or to a conduit IRA.

Rollover. Since 1992, there is a 20 percent withholding tax on distributions that are eligible for rollover, but not transferred directly from qualified plans to IRAs or a new employer's plan. What does this mean to you? When you are changing jobs, make sure you do not take the funds from one plan and deposit them yourself. Instead have the funds "transferred" directly to the new plan or IRA.

The new law erodes the 60-day grace period allowed for rolling over distributions or making a decision on five- or ten-year income averaging (if eligible). All distribution checks received by employees must reflect a 20 percent reduction to their plan balances, unless the distribution is directly transferred to an eligible plan.

IRA Conduit and Individual IRAs.   If funds are coming out of a qualified pension plan, you should consider transferring them directly to a rollover IRA or conduit IRA, instead of to your individual IRA. If you commingle these funds with your old IRAs, you will not be able to take these new funds and move them to a new employer's plan at a later date. In addition, when you finally retire and take your distributions, you will not qualify for five- or ten-year averaging, which is allowed on qualified retirement plans but not IRAs. You can still have all the same investment options with IRA rollovers as with regular IRAs, and the only problem is that you will have two accounts instead of one.

Your Old Employer and Your New Employer.   You may want to leave funds with your current employer if, after you review the money manager's performance and the mutual fund performance, you find your old plan is better than your new employer's plan. In addition, keeping the money in the old fund usually gives you more options. If your old plan has five mutual funds and your new one has five mutual funds, you can keep both plans and have a wider selection of funds.

If neither employer's plan has been able to perform as well as your own investments, then consider transferring the funds to the IRA rollover discussed previously. If you have less than $3,500, you may have to take the funds anyhow.

Most of the time the best solution is to move it to your own conduit IRA rollover account. You will get more options on investments and you will be able to exert complete control over the selection of investments unlike retirement plans such as 401(k)s where your selections are usually limited to a number of funds. If you need a lump sum to carry you through, borrow from the plans instead, or if you need monthly income, roll over to an IRA and take monthly income under IRS rule t(72).

Never Handle Funds Yourself. Even if you need the money, do not take possession of qualified plan funds. Have them moved directly to your IRA rollover or IRA. Once they are in the IRA you can take them out for 60 days without the 20 percent withholding that only applies to qualified plans and not IRAs.

91 WHAT DO I NEED TO KNOW ABOUT COBRA?

Under federal law, the Consolidated Omnibus Budget Reconciliation Act of 1985, known as COBRA, entitles you and your dependents to certain coverage and rights. Specifically, you have the right to temporarily continue group health care coverage under your old employer's plan if you are terminated or lose your job. Unfortunately, you have to pay for the coverage, and it can be very expensive. Still, it may give you better rates than individual policies that probably require new medical exams.

When Can I Get COBRA? The coverage must be provided if you lose your job, even if you are fired (though not for misconduct), laid off or when your hours are reduced so that you become ineligible for coverage. If you die, your spouse and dependents are protected from losing coverage right away. Also, when your children no longer meet eligibility requirements after they graduate from school, you are allowed to continue coverage for 36 months. If you become entitled to Medicare, normally your spouse would lose coverage from your employer, but under COBRA, your spouse can continue. Even if your company goes into Chapter 11, you may still be able to continue with coverage.

What Is the Coverage? If you purchase "continued coverage," called COBRA, it will be identical to the coverage lost. You submit all your claims the same as you did in the past. If your old employer changes companies, then it carries you over under the new plan also.

When Does COBRA Start and How Long Does It Last? COBRA starts the day you lose coverage and it lasts for various times depending on the reasons for the termination of your original coverage. You get 18 months coverage if you are laid off or lose your job for any reason other than misconduct, or your hours have been reduced so that you no longer qualify for your employer's coverage. If you become disabled, your coverage must continue for 29 months. If your dependents lose coverage because of your death, marital separation or divorce, they can get coverage for 36 months.

When Do Your Children Lose COBRA Coverage?   If you have children that graduate from college, in most cases they immediately lose their eligibility. Typically, many policies will cover dependents until they reach age 23, if they are full-time students. You will usually have to submit proof to your insurance company that your children are still in school after they turn 21. When children graduate from college, it is such a happy time for parents that they often forget how important it is to verify coverage. When your children graduate, you can continue COBRA for 36 months or get an interim health insurance policy that is good for six months. A lot of these policies are offered without physicals. Hopefully, after six months, your child will have a job and coverage. If not, these gaps in insurance should be taken seriously.

92 IS IT WORTH GIVING UP A DEFINED-BENEFIT PLAN FOR A HIGHER SALARY?

Most likely you will have a hard time finding a better pension plan than a defined benefit. Before you decide to give up these plans in favor of a higher salary, take a look at your benefits statement. It should give you a projected retirement income from your defined-benefit plan.

For a true comparison:

◆ Compare the salaries of both jobs. You will be taxed on the higher income, so use the after-tax value of the higher income.
◆ Compare the future value of your defined-benefit plan to the future value of your new plan. If your new plan is not a defined benefit, it will have few, if any guarantees, and it is often difficult to make projections. Ask your prospective employer what returns the plan has earned the last ten years. If you will be getting a segregated plan, look at your past

investment records. Use the Retirement Table in Appendix A to estimate the income you will receive from these plans.

Even if your new employer's plan comes out ahead, remember your risks are less with defined benefit because it gives you guarantees. Your employer assumes all the investment risks. These are normally the easiest and safest plans.

However, you can't assume that you will always be better off with a defined-benefit plan. If the investments do well, you may have an even better retirement with a defined-contribution plan. Your retirement income will be determined by the contributions that your employer makes, as well as the income, gains and losses on these plans. If your plan has losses, you may face a bleak retirement. But if the assets do well, you may have an extremely rewarding retirement.

93 HOW CAN I COMPARE RETIREMENT PACKAGES?

Retirement packages vary not only by type but by the amounts your employer contributes and the kinds of income that you are guaranteed. We looked at the different types of plans as well as their advantages and disadvantages in Chapter 5. However, when you are comparing plans, you should start by looking carefully at what your employer is actually giving you. Is the company just giving you an opportunity to save for yourself, or is your employer actually saving for you?

If it applies, compare the value of defined-benefit plans over defined-contributions as we did in Question #92. Also, compare the amount that each employer is willing to contribute to these plans. Compare the various features of each plan, such as vesting, integration, the history of returns, the different investment options they allow, the borrowing power and the ability to make employee contributions.

To give you an example, let's assume you are evaluating two jobs, both equal in almost all aspects, with similar hours, commuting time and most benefits.

Job #1 pays $27,500 and you will participate in a profit-sharing plan that is usually funded to the maximum each year.

Job #2 pays $30,000 and has a 401(k) plan in which your employer matches 50 cents for every dollar up to 3 percent of your salary. Which job do you take? It sounds like job #2 is the better job, it pays more and has an attractive pension. But it's not that simple. Let's take a closer look. We find that since the first employer actually contributes the maximum 15 percent contribution to your profit-sharing plan, you really earn an additional $4,125. Even though you don't see it in your paycheck, the first job really nets over $31,625.

The second job also has a pension plan, in which the employer matches every dollar you put in with 50 cents. However, the employer matching program is only for contributions you make up to 3 percent of your salary. If you contribute 3 percent or $900, your employer will add $450 to the plan for you. The second job totals $30,450.

Which job has a better bottom line? Now it looks like the first job, especially if you want to save for retirement and are not in need of more immediate cash flow. If you have high daily expenses and need as much cash flow as possible, then the second job may still be the better alternative.

When comparing retirement plans, some will offer you a guaranteed income for life, while others will only offer to contribute to a plan for you, and others will just allow you to contribute your own money. You will have to be able to evaluate what the worth of the lifetime income is compared to the contributions made on your behalf.

94 IF I CHANGE JOBS AND I AM NOT VESTED IN MY PENSION PLAN, DOES THAT MEAN I'LL LOSE MY RETIREMENT FUNDS?

The law requires that a qualified plan have a schedule under which a participant earns an ownership interest in employer-provided contributions based on his or her years of service with the employer. Any amounts you contribute yourself are immediately vested or owned by you.

Different plans have different vesting schedules. You will have to look in your benefits package to find out what your vesting schedule is.

Changing jobs can have a big impact on your future retirement. If you change jobs before you are vested, you will be leaving behind money that was set aside for you. Not only can you hurt yourself by switching jobs too frequently and moving before you are vested, but you can also hurt your family and heirs.

Kathy is a widow whose husband unwittingly left her without any income when he died. He was a bricklayer, and when times got tough, he was forced to move from job to job. He could never build up seniority in his companies. Although he belonged to a union, he never was able to get vested in a pension plan because he wasn't in one job long enough. When he died, his family was left with little in Social Security benefits, no insurance and no pension. However, Kathy's story has a happy ending. She found a good job with benefits and has been able to build a new life for herself. She'll probably never be rich, but she will be independent and successful.

On the other hand, things did not work so well for Dorothy. Dorothy changed jobs, moved frequently and never planned her jobs around pension benfits. She still has two years before she will be vested in her retirement plan, and the benefits she can count on in retirement are less than $200 a month. She had only $13,000 in saving. She will receive only minimal Social Security of less than $500 a month. None of this would be that bad, if Dorothy was 20 years old. Unfortunately she is 63. She will have to work probably until the day she dies.

Vesting is important, so before you change jobs, find out if you will be able to keep your retirement funds.

CHAPTER 10

Taking Your Retirement

95 WHEN SHOULD I RETIRE?

You should retire only when you are sure you will have enough assets and income from all sources to live comfortably. There is no magic number or birth date. Each person is different. You need to calculate your retirement expenses and income, including the income you can generate from your assets.

Keep in mind, the longer you wait to retire, the larger your retirement income will be. You will get more from Social Security, more from employer's retirement plans and more from your savings.

Look at the difference in retiring at age 60 versus age 65 for Henry Almost-retired. Assume Henry earns $60,000, has $100,000 in investments now and can save 10 percent of his income. Assume also he can earn 7 percent on his savings after taxes and 8 percent in his retirement accounts. He can retire today with income of $14,000 from his employer's pension and another $9,439 by taking both the interest and principal from his savings. He will not collect Social Security for a while, so for the next few years he will have an income of $23,439. When Social Security kicks in at age 62, he will have an income of $34,632. If he did not dip into his principal and lived only on the interest, his income would be just $33,193.

If he waits until age 65, he will have an additional $12,600 in IRA savings at an 8 percent return. He will have an additional $24,600 in savings outside his IRA with an after-tax return of 7 percent. His current $100,000 in savings will grow to $140,255 and so his income from these savings will be an additional $16,616 at age 65. His likely pension from his employer under a typical plan is $14,000. If he continues to work for five more years and receives a 5 percent increase in wages each year, his pension income could then be over $30,000. His total retirement income will be $60,708 at age 65 versus $33,193 at age 60. Defined-benefit plans grow tremendously in the later years because they are based on income, years in service and age.

Waiting to retire can make a big difference. Since most pension benefits are earned in the final years, there is a big incentive to continue working if you are participating in a pension plan. You may increase your pension by 25 to 100 percent by just working an extra few years.

Before you can retire you need to know:

1. The income you need.
2. The assets that you currently have, how much you can earn on these assets and any additions to them such as inheritances or gifts.
3. The retirement income from you and your employer's plan and from Social Security.
4. The kind of retirement you want: quiet and modest or active and expensive.
5. Where you want to live. Send for the AARP booklet that gives a good breakdown of costs and taxes for most states.
6. Your ability to work part-time or supplement your income. Determine where you can get a job.
7. One of the greatest expenses for retirees is insurance. Although retirees are eligible to pick up Medicare benefits for as little as $46.10 a month (1995), they have to worry about copayments, deductibles and expensive drugs. You also need to consider gaps in your medical coverage. Employers are reducing the medical coverage that fills the gap between work and retirement. Government statistics show as many as 7 percent of large companies have dropped health care coverage for future employees the past two years. Three percent of the companies have eliminated it for current retirees or are freezing the premium payments so that any inflation risk or future increase in payment cost will have to be absorbed by the employees. If you can't afford to pick up your own "gap" coverage, you may have to continue working for a

few more years. Check with Social Security before you retire to find out about Medicare benefits, Medicare supplemental insurance to fill gaps in coverage and your alternatives with HMOs.

You may want to do some research into HMOs and managed care. Write or call the following:

- The *Medicare Managed Care Directory* (Health Care Financing Administration: 800-638-6833). Free.
- *Managed Care: An AARP Guide* (American Association of Retired Persons—EE0848, No. D15595, 601 E. St. N.W., Washington, DC 22049). Free.
- *Medicare Health Maintenance Organizations: Are They Right for You?* (Medicare Beneficiaries Defense Fund, Box USHM, 1460 Broadway, 8th Floor, New York, NY 10036). Send $2.

96 WHEN SHOULD I START COLLECTING SOCIAL SECURITY?

You may want to start collecting Social Security as soon as you are eligible, if you are not working, and even if you do not need the income immediately.

One of the most important retirement questions is whether to take Social Security at age 62 or 65. You will receive 20 percent less at 62 but you will get 36 extra payments. Depending on how you invest those extra payments it can take 12 to 14 years to make up the difference.

> You will collect for 1995: 80 percent of your benefits at 62, 86 percent of your benefits at 63, 93 percent of your benefits at 64, 100 percent of your benefits at 65.

(Under new Social Security rules, the ages and percentages will change for anyone born after 1938.)

For example, if a retiree waits until age 65 to start taking Social Security, his payments are 20 percent higher than at age 62. He collects $2,400 more a year at age 65 for the rest of his life. However, if he starts taking payments at age 62, and collects $10,800 a year for three years, he is likely to have over $35,000 in savings by the time he is 65. For the rest of his life, if he earns 8 percent on his savings, he could have another $2,800 a year in income. What is better,

$2,800 from his savings or $2,400 more in Social Security? Since Social Security in the past was not taxed, it was debatable which was better, but now with as much as 85 percent of Social Security being taxed, even if your $2,800 is taxed at the maximum, you are probably better off collecting early and investing the proceeds.

If you feel comfortable investing the funds, opting for the early payout makes sense. However, if you do not feel you can earn 8 percent and think that you may live longer than age 79, you may want to wait and collect the full amount.

When you start taking Social Security also depends on whether you are still working. You may have to work part-time after retirement just to avoid poverty. If you have not been saving adequately, or if you do not have good retirement plans, you will find that Social Security alone will not give you enough income to retire completely. And if you work, Social Security will give you even less. The dilemma we face is that retirees who can barely make ends meet are faced with increasing penalties every day they work.

- ◆ **Under 65.** If you are under 65, you can earn up to $8,160 and there is no reduction in Social Security income. Any amount over that and you will have to give up some Social Security. If you are receiving $12,000 a year in Social Security and $8,160, for a total income of $20,160, that income, in most parts of the country, is not enough to live on. And if you exceed that amount, you will be penalized. If you earn more than $8,160, you will have to give up one dollar in benefits for every two dollars over that amount. The extra work you perform only nets you half of what you earn, or in effect, you are hit with the equivalent of an additional 50 percent tax.
- ◆ **Between 65 and 69.** You can earn up to $11,280 before you start losing benefits. If you earn more than that, you will lose one dollar for every three dollars you earn.
- ◆ **Over 70.** There are no earnings limits.

97 HOW CAN I CONVERT U.S. SAVINGS BONDS TAX-FREE INTO RETIREMENT INCOME?

One of the greatest tax benefits of series EE savings bonds is the fact that you can convert them to series HH.

You have three options for paying taxes on EE bonds:

1. Pay taxes each year as the interest accrues.
2. Pay taxes when you cash in the Series EE bonds.
3. Convert the Series EE to Series HH bonds and postpone taxes. You have the opportunity to pay taxes on the accrued interest each year. If you are in a very low tax bracket, this may be a good idea but it does negate one of the main reasons why you buy these bonds.

You can postpone the taxes until you sell these bonds. However, if the reason you are selling these bonds is to generate income, you may want to think again, especially if you are going to reinvest the proceeds in low-yielding money markets or CDs. You may be better off with the third alternative and convert your Series EE bonds into Series HH. You can postpone the taxes on the appreciation on these bonds for another 30 years. Your series HH bonds pay interest semi-annually. You will have income and also more principal intact.

Series HH pay low interest. In 1995 it was 4 percent. If you have been able to achieve better returns on your money than that, you may find it better to pay the taxes, convert the EE and invest the money yourself. Even money markets for most of 1995 paid more than 4 percent.

Whether you should cash in the Series EE or convert to the Series HH depends on your tax bracket and your ability to get returns better than the returns on the series HH.

If you are interested in converting your Series EE bonds, go to your local bank or savings-and-loan association for conversions. Call the Treasury Department at 1-800-872-6637 (1-800-US BONDS) for the current rates.

98 WHAT DO I NEED TO KNOW ABOUT TAKING MY RETIREMENT AND SOCIAL SECURITY BENEFITS?

Two of the most important things you must know are:

1. When to take your Social Security and retirement assets and
2. How to take them to minimize tax consequences.

◆ **Letting funds accumulate.** As we've shown previously, there is a big advantage to accumulating your money in retirement plans, especially if you don't need current income. You can legally leave money in IRAs and retirement plans until age 70½. By doing so you will not have to pay income taxes on this money until withdrawal. The tax-deferred compounding can make a huge difference. For example, if you have your funds in a retirement plan that is earning 10 percent and you take the funds out at age 70, instead of age 63, you will have twice as much money.

◆ **Tap into Social Security first.** Taking money from Social Security as soon as you are eligible is probably a good idea instead of dipping into your pension. If you take Social Security benefits and allow your money to grow tax-deferred as long as possible, assuming your investments do well, you will usually have a much larger income.

◆ **Deplete taxable assets next.** Use money that is not tax-sheltered and deplete it before dipping into your tax-deferred funds. By doing this you will be letting your retirement funds grow tax-deferred and you will be depleting assets that add to your tax burden. The two main factors to consider before depleting these funds are:

1. The tax consequences in both your retirement and your nonretirement accounts;
2. The income you can earn on the accounts.

If your retirement account is composed of assets from deductible contributions, you will have to pay taxes on the entire distribution. If the assets are a result of nondeductible contributions, then you will have to pay on all the earnings, but not the contribution.

◆ **The rich do live differently.** If you are fortunate enough to have a large amount of money set aside in 401(k)s, IRAs and other retirement plans, you may run into some tax problems by letting the money accumulate. The irony is that those retirees who need the money the least and who need the tax savings the most are the ones who are forced to withdraw the funds. If your combined pension payments exceed $150,000 a year (indexed for inflation), you may face a 15 percent excise tax on any excess distributions. That means if you take out $200,000, you will pay an extra $7,500 in taxes, in addition to any other taxes. You could be paying more than half your distribution in penalties, federal and state taxes.

◆ **Take money out on time.** Take your distributions on time from IRA and retirement plans. You must take the minimum legally required distribution in the year after you turn 70½. If you base the payments on both your and your spouse's lives, you may be able to take a smaller annual payment. This is important if taxes are a big consideration, and if you have enough money to live on without these payments.

◆ **Take your distribution every year by December 31st.** Except for the year you turn 70½, you must take your funds by December 31st of each year. If you withdraw less than required, you will have to pay as much as a 50 percent penalty.

◆ **First year grace period.** You get a grace period for withdrawing your funds the first year after you turn 70½. For example, if you turn 70½ on July 15th of 1995, you have until April 15th of 1996 to take your distributions. If your taxable income is high, this may be a good idea. However, if your income looks like it will be higher the next year, think twice, since you will have to pay taxes on two distributions the following year.

◆ **Nonqualified plans.** Many times when your employer signs you up for these plans, either you or your employer decides how benefits will be paid. For tax purposes, you may want to consider installments over many years in order to reduce your tax burden. As nice as it may seem to get the money all at once, the tax consequences on nonqualified plans can be severe. Unlike qualified plans, you do not have the option of rolling these funds over to other tax-sheltered plans, and the funds will be 100 percent taxable. So if you can take installments and minimize the tax penalty, you should consider doing so.

MOVING

Not only do Medicare benefits differ in various states but the state taxes on your pension also differ. In addition to federal taxes, you also have to be concerned about state taxes and "source" taxes.

◆ **Source taxes**: California, Kansas, Louisiana, New York, Michigan and Oregon have a "source tax" on your pension income that you accumulated during your residency in that state, even after you move out of the state. Check for changes in laws on these taxes.

◆ **State taxes**: When moving, it is important to consider state taxes. Seven states—Alaska, Florida, Nevada, South Dakota, Texas, Washington and Wyoming—do not have any state income taxes. But be careful, in your attempts to avoid state taxes you may trigger source taxes.

99 WHICH IS THE BEST CHOICE—ROLLOVERS, MY EMPLOYER'S ANNUITY OR LUMP SUM DISTRIBUTIONS?

Usually when you retire, you will have three options in taking your retirement assets.

1. You can take an annuity.
2. You can take the funds from your employer and roll them into an IRA, thereby keeping them tax-sheltered.
3. You can take a lump sum distribution and pay taxes on the entire amount. There are special tax rules such as five- and ten-year averaging to minimize these taxes.

Annuities. If you have a defined-benefit plan, you may have no choice: Your employer will set up an annuity to guarantee you an income for the rest of your life. While annuities may seem the most attractive since you are guaranteed a set income for as long as you live, consider the following, if you have a choice:

◆ The interest rate used to calculate your monthly payment may be deceiving. Because of hidden fees in annuities, you may end up with less income than if you invested in government or municipal bonds. Usually just "laddering" your bonds (buying bonds of various maturities) may provide you with better returns than annuities.

◆ When you annuitize, you use up all your principal. If you would like to leave money to your heirs, you have to take much smaller payments. If you get a higher return on a bond, you may be able to live off just the interest and leave the principal to your beneficiaries.

◆ Once you annuitize or start taking out your monthly checks, you will never be able to cash in and touch the principal.

IRA Rollover. If you have any skill at investing, usually one of the best solutions is a direct rollover into an Individual Retirement Account (IRA). Make sure you have this money rolled over directly to your IRA and do not take possession of it, even for a day. If you do you will have to pay a 20 percent tax immediately. If there is a possibility you may participate in another employer's plan, do not commingle your distributions from your retirement plan with your regular IRA. Use conduit IRA rollover instead.

Lump Sum. If your tax bracket is low, you may want to take a lump sum. This is usually the least attractive alternative, since you pay taxes on the distribution and have less money to work with. Usually your income is higher with either the annuity or with an IRA account. You should have your financial adviser or tax planner compare the different alternatives carefully. The following example shows how much you would have each year under lump sum averaging versus IRA rollovers at a 9 percent interest rate and a 33 percent tax bracket.

COMPARISON OF LUMP SUM DISTRIBUTION and IRA ROLLOVER

End of Yr.	5-Yr. Average	10-Yr. Average	IRA Rollover
5	$115,894	$118,570	$153,862
10	162,547	166,301	236,736
15	227,981	233,246	364,248
20	319,755	327,140	560,440

As you can see, the IRA rollover, even after you pay taxes, is clearly the winner.

100 HOW DO THE NEW TAX LAWS AFFECT MY SOCIAL SECURITY AND RETIREMENT?

No matter how safe your investments are, and no matter how well you and your employer do in managing your retirement assets, taxes can still destroy your retirement dreams.

In order to pay for the new global trade expenses, many new pension rules were placed in the General Agreement of Tariffs and Trade. This bill is extremely complicated, and there does not appear to be any real winner. There are some benefits for your employer, since your employer can make a lower lump sum payout to some retiring employees, or keep using pension surpluses for current medical costs of other workers. But these benefits are offset by the faster contributions your employer must make to underfunded pension plans and the higher insurance premiums now required. Overall, underfunded corporate plans are delinquent by $70 billion. For example, General Motors Corp. must now speed up funding to narrow a $20 billion underfunding deficit.

Although employees who had underfunded pension plans may feel safer, this safety comes at a cost and employees are hurt also. Part of the law is an obscure rule involving interest rate assumption. These new assumptions can cut thousands of dollars off expected lump sum retirement payments to employees. In addition, companies also have to pay more insurance and these big increases in costs might cause them to eliminate nearly all future plans. Already plans are being terminated in record numbers. IRS statistics report 42,000 employers terminated defined-benefit plans between 1989 and 1991, compared to 14,000 terminations between 1980 and 1982, a 300 percent increase. In response to the new tax bill, many retirement specialists expect new terminations to increase 500 percent!

Why do you need to know about this? Because the trend of pensions being taxed more and more is likely to continue.

HOW CAN YOU AVOID TAXES ON SOCIAL SECURITY?

There are only a few solutions, such as finding a state that doesn't tax Social Security benefits or looking into annuities. With all the negatives we mentioned previously about annuities they have one great feature: All the income that is earned on the annuity builds up tax-deferred until you take the funds. Annuities generate no "1099" income as long as you are not taking money out of the annuity and will help you keep your income as low as possible to avoid the tax on 85 percent of Social Security income.

State Exemptions on Social Security. In addition to federal taxes, you must consider state taxes. About half the states will exempt Social Security. Some states, such as Connecticut, Iowa and Wisconsin, only tax Social Security to a maximum of 50 percent. AARP's "The State Tax Laws" guidebook is a valuable resource to learn about various state taxes (1-800-322-2282, ext. 8255).

How To Avoid State Taxes. Although you have to add municipal income back when calculating taxes on Social Security, you can avoid state taxes by investing in municipals in the state in which you live or in Puerto Rico municipal bonds. (Puerto Rico's municipal income is state tax-free in all states.) Treasury securities also save on state taxes. You can purchase these securities directly from the Treasury or for a $25 charge from your broker. Stick with shorter term notes. They have been paying about 90 percent of the yield of the long bonds and are much safer, with only 20 to 30 percent of the interest rate risk. Treasuries usually are a better deal than CDs, since their rates are often higher by as much as 1 percent. They are guaranteed by the U.S. government directly, whereas CDs are guaranteed by an agency of the government. Treasuries have unlimited insurance while CD insurance is limited to $100,000. Treasuries are state tax-free and CDs are usually fully taxable.

Hold your Treasuries in your brokerage account where the interest can go into a money market or checking account directly. In case of emergency you can borrow up to 95 percent of the value of the Treasury at tax-deductible margin interest rates.

APPENDIX A

Individual Retirement Table: $1,000 Annual Contribution

Use this table to see how much $1,000 will grow to and how much income you will be able to draw for ten years or 20 years. Assume fixed rates and compounded annually and that contributions are made at the beginning of the year. If you contribute more than $1,000 annually, multiply these figures by the number of thousands you contribute. Example: If you contribute $4,000, multiply by four.

Years	Total Contribution	Interest Earned	Total Value at Retirement	Monthly Withdrawal for 10 years	Monthly Withdrawal for 20 years
			@ 6% yield		
10	$10,000	$ 3,972	$ 13,972	$ 154	$ 99
15	15,000	9,673	24,672	272	175
20	20,000	18,993	38,993	430	276
25	25,000	23,156	58,156	641	411
30	30,000	53,802	83,802	924	593
35	35,000	83,121	118,121	1,302	835
40	40,000	124,048	164,048	1,808	1,160
			@ 8% yield		
10	10,000	5,645	15,645	188	128
15	15,000	14,324	29,324	351	240
20	20,000	29,422	49,422	592	405
25	25,000	53,954	78,954	946	647
30	30,000	92,500	122,500	1,466	1,022
35	35,000	151,102	186,102	2,231	1,524
40	40,000	239,781	279,781	3,353	2,292
			@ 10% yield		
10	10,000	7,531	17,531	228	164
15	15,000	19,950	34,950	454	327
20	20,000	43,002	63,002	818	590
25	25,000	83,182	108,182	1,404	1,013
30	30,000	150,943	180,943	2,348	1,695
35	35,000	263,127	298,127	3,869	2,792
40	40,000	446,852	486,852	6,318	4,560
			@ 12% yield		
10	10,000	9,655	19,655	275	208
20	20,000	60,699	80,699	1,129	854
25	25,000	124,334	149,334	2,090	1,581
30	30,000	240,293	270,293	3,783	2,861
35	35,000	448,463	483,463	6,766	5,118
40	40,000	819,142	859,142	12,023	9,095
			@ 14% yield		
10	10,000	12,045	22,045	331	261
20	20,000	83,768	103,768	1,560	1,229
25	25,000	182,333	207,333	3,117	2,455
30	30,000	376,737	406,737	6,115	4,816
35	35,000	755,673	790,673	11,887	9,362
40	40,000	1,489,909	1,529,909	23,001	18,115

APPENDIX B

Saving for the Future Table: Monthly Savings Needed To Reach $1,000

This table shows the monthly savings required for each $1,000 you need in future years. Look down the percentage column until you reach the row showing the number of years you can hold your investment. Example: Assume you need $10,000 at the end of ten years and you can receive an 8 percent **after-tax** yield. Look down the 8 percent column until you reach the ten-year row. The number is $6. You need to save $6 for each $1,000 you need in ten years. You need $60 for $10,000 ($6 × 10). These figures are based on saving at the end of the month and have been rounded, thus giving only an approximate figure.

Yield

Years	1%	2%	3%	4%	5%	6%	7%	8%	9%	10%	11%	12%	13%	14%	15%	16%	17%	18%	19%	20%
										Monthly Savings										
1	$83	$83	$82	$82	$81	$81	$81	$80	$80	$80	$79	$79	$79	$78	$78	$77	$77	$77	$77	$76
2	41	41	40	40	40	39	39	39	38	38	37	37	37	36	36	36	35	35	35	34
3	27	27	27	26	26	25	25	25	24	24	24	23	23	23	22	22	22	21	21	21
4	20	20	20	19	19	19	18	18	17	17	17	16	16	16	15	15	15	14	14	14
5	16	16	15	15	15	14	14	14	13	13	13	13	12	12	12	11	11	11	11	10
6	13	13	13	12	12	12	11	11	11	10	10	10	9	9	9	8	8	8	8	7
7	12	11	11	10	10	10	9	9	9	8	8	8	7	7	7	7	7	6	6	6
8	10	10	9	9	9	8	8	7	7	7	7	6	6	6	6	5	5	5	5	4
9	9	8	8	8	7	7	7	6	6	6	6	5	5	5	4	4	4	4	4	4
10	8	8	7	7	6	6	6	6	5	5	5	4	4	4	4	3	3	3	3	3
11	7	7	6	6	6	5	5	5	5	4	4	4	3	3	3	3	3	2	2	2
12	7	6	6	5	5	5	4	4	4	4	3	3	3	3	3	2	2	2	2	2
13	6	6	5	5	5	4	4	4	3	3	3	3	3	2	2	2	2	2	2	2
14	6	6	5	4	4	4	4	3	3	3	3	2	2	2	2	2	2	1	1	1
15	5	5	4	4	4	3	3	3	3	2	2	2	2	2	2	1	1	1	1	.9
16	5	4	4	3	3	3	3	3	2	2	2	2	2	1	1	1	1	.9	.8	.7
17	5	4	4	3	3	3	3	2	2	2	2	2	1	1	1	1	.9	.8	.7	.6
18	4	4	4	3	3	3	2	2	2	2	2	1	1	1	.9	.8	.7	.6	.6	.5
19	4	4	3	3	3	2	2	2	2	1	1	1	1	.9	.8	.7	.6	.5	.5	.4
20	4	3	3	3	2	2	2	2	2	1	1	1	.9	.8	.7	.6	.5	.4	.4	.3
25	3	3	2	2	2	1	1	1	.9	.8	.6	.5	.5	.4	.3	.3	.2	.2	.1	.1
30	2	2	2	1	1	.9	.8	.7	.6	.4	.4	.3	.2	.2	.1	.1	.09	.07	.06	.04
35	2	2	1	1	1	.7	.6	.4	.3	.3	.2	.2	.1	.1	.07	.05	.04	.03	.02	.02
40	2	1	1	.9	.7	.5	.4	.3	.2	.2	.1	.08	.06	.04	.03	.02	.01	.01	.01	.01

APPENDIX C

Present Value Table: Saving for the Future

LUMP SUM SAVINGS (SINGLE DEPOSIT) NEEDED TO ACQUIRE $1,000

Use this table when you want to find how much you have to save today to receive $1,000 in the future. If you have specific goals that you want to achieve, such as saving for your children's college education or purchasing a new home, this table will show you how much you need to put aside now to have the money you want in future years. Example: If you need $50,000 in 20 years and you can earn 10 percent on your money, find the intersection of the number of years you can save the yield you can earn after taxes. At the intersection of the 10 percent column and 20-year row, you will find the number 148. You need $148 for each $1,000. For $50,000 you will need to set aside today $7,400 (50 × 148).

Yield

Lump Sum Savings

Years	1%	2%	3%	4%	5%	6%	7%	8%	9%	10%	11%	12%	13%	14%	15%	16%
1	$990	$980	$970	$960	$951	$942	$932	$923	$914	$905	$896	$887	$878	$869	$861	$852
2	980	961	942	923	905	887	870	853	836	820	804	788	773	758	743	728
3	970	942	915	888	863	837	813	789	766	744	722	701	681	661	642	623
4	960	923	888	854	822	792	763	735	708	683	659	636	613	592	572	552
5	951	906	863	821	784	747	713	681	650	621	594	567	543	519	497	476
6	942	887	837	790	746	705	666	630	596	564	535	507	480	456	432	410
7	932	870	813	760	711	665	623	584	547	513	482	452	425	400	376	354
8	923	853	789	731	676	627	582	540	502	466	434	404	376	351	327	305
9	914	836	766	703	645	592	544	500	460	424	391	361	333	308	284	263
10	905	820	744	676	613	558	508	463	422	386	352	322	295	270	247	227
11	896	804	722	650	585	527	475	429	388	351	317	287	261	237	215	195
12	887	788	701	624	557	497	444	397	356	319	286	257	231	208	187	168
13	878	773	681	601	530	469	415	368	326	290	258	229	204	182	163	145
14	869	758	661	577	505	442	388	341	299	263	232	205	181	160	141	125
15	861	743	641	555	481	417	362	315	275	239	209	183	160	140	123	108
16	852	728	623	534	458	394	339	292	252	218	188	163	142	123	107	93
17	844	714	605	513	436	371	317	270	231	198	170	146	125	108	93	80
18	836	700	587	494	416	350	296	250	212	180	153	130	111	95	81	69
19	827	686	570	475	396	330	277	232	195	164	138	116	98	83	70	60
20	819	673	554	456	377	312	258	215	178	148	124	104	87	73	61	51

22	803	646	522	422	342	278	226	184	150	123	101	83	68	56	46	38
24	787	622	492	392	310	247	197	158	124	102	82	66	53	43	35	28
26	772	598	464	361	281	220	172	135	106	84	66	53	42	33	26	21
28	756	574	437	333	255	196	150	116	90	69	54	42	33	26	20	16
30	742	552	412	308	231	174	131	99	75	57	44	33	26	20	15	12
32	727	531	388	285	210	155	115	85	63	47	35	27	20	15	11	9
34	712	510	366	264	190	138	100	73	53	39	29	21	16	12	9	6
36	699	490	345	244	173	123	88	63	45	32	23	17	12	9	7	5
38	685	471	325	225	157	109	76	54	38	28	19	13	10	7	5	4
40	672	453	307	208	142	97	67	46	32	22	15	11	8	5	4	3

APPENDIX D

Future Value Table: Results of Regular Savings

Often it is important to know how much you will have if you save a specified amount each year. The following table shows the future value of $1 invested at the beginning of each year. You can use this table when trying to determine the future value of any regular payments such as IRAs, pension plans and automatic savings plans.

Yield or Inflation Rate

Future Value of $1.00

Years	3%	4%	5%	6%	7%	8%	9%	10%	11%	12%
1	1.030	1.040	1.050	1.060	1.070	1.080	1.090	1.100	1.110	1.120
2	2.090	2.122	2.153	2.184	2.215	2.246	2.218	2.310	2.342	2.374
3	3.184	3.246	3.310	3.375	3.440	3.506	3.573	3.641	3.710	3.780
4	4.309	4.416	4.526	4.637	4.751	4.867	4.985	5.105	5.228	5.353
5	5.468	5.633	5.802	5.975	6.153	6.336	6.523	6.716	6.913	7.115
6	6.663	6.898	7.142	7.394	7.654	7.923	8.200	8.487	8.793	9.089
7	7.892	8.214	8.549	8.896	9.260	9.637	10.028	10.436	10.259	11.230
8	9.159	9.583	10.027	10.491	10.978	11.488	12.021	12.580	13.164	13.776
9	10.464	11.006	11.578	12.181	12.816	13.487	14.193	14.938	15.722	16.549
10	11.808	12.486	13.207	13.972	14.784	15.646	16.560	17.531	18.561	19.655
11	13.192	14.026	14.917	15.870	16.888	17.977	19.141	20.384	21.713	23.133
12	14.618	15.627	16.713	17.882	19.141	20.495	21.953	23.523	25.212	27.029
13	16.086	17.292	18.599	20.015	21.550	23.215	25.019	26.975	29.095	31.393
14	17.599	19.024	20.579	22.276	24.129	26.152	28.361	30.773	33.405	36.280
15	19.157	20.825	22.658	24.673	26.888	29.324	32.003	34.950	38.190	41.753
16	20.761	22.698	24.840	27.213	29.840	32.750	35.974	37.545	43.501	47.884
17	22.414	24.645	27.132	29.906	32.999	36.450	40.301	44.599	49.396	54.750
18	24.116	26.671	29.539	32.760	36.379	40.446	45.018	50.159	55.939	62.440
19	25.870	28.778	32.066	35.786	39.995	44.762	50.160	56.275	63.203	71.052
20	27.676	30.969	34.719	38.993	43.865	49.423	55.765	63.003	71.265	80.699
21	29.563	33.248	37.505	42.392	48.006	54.457	61.873	70.403	80.214	91.503

22	31.452	35.618	40.431	45.996	52.436	59.893	68.532	78.543	90.148	103.603
23	33.426	38.083	43.502	49.816	57.177	65.765	75.790	87.497	101.179	117.155
24	35.459	40.646	46.727	53.865	62.249	72.106	83.701	97.347	113.413	132.334
25	37.553	43.312	50.114	58.156	67.676	78.954	92.324	108.182	126.999	149.334
30	49.002	58.328	69.761	83.802	101.073	122.346	148.578	180.943	220.913	270.293
35	62.275	76.598	94.836	118.121	147.913	186.102	235.125	298.127	379.164	483.463
40	77.663	98.827	126.840	164.048	213.610	279.781	368.292	486.852	645.827	859.142

APPENDIX E

Future Value Table: Growth of Lump Sum Investment

This table shows the future value of a single investment or deposit (lump sum) of one dollar ($1). Use this table when you are trying to calculate the value of $1 invested at the yields listed as follows. Look down the column that shows the interest rate. Stop at the row that shows the number of years you can invest. Always use the yields you receive after you deduct the taxes due. If you expect to earn 6 percent, simply look down the 6 percent column until you reach the year row that shows the amount of time you can save. Use this table for inflation also. Example: What will be the inflated value of $20,000 in 15 years at 10 percent inflation? Look under the column for 10 percent and stop when you reach the 15-year row. Each dollar will need to grow to $4.18 or $20,000 will need to grow to $4.18 × 20,000 = $83,600 to keep up with inflation.

Yield or Inflation Rate

Future Value of $1.00

Years	4%	5%	6%	7%	8%	9%	10%	11%	12%	13%	14%	15%
1	1.04	1.05	1.06	1.07	1.08	1.09	1.10	1.11	1.12	1.13	1.14	1.15
2	1.08	1.10	1.12	1.14	1.16	1.18	1.21	1.23	1.25	1.27	1.29	1.32
3	1.12	1.16	1.19	1.22	1.25	1.29	1.33	1.36	1.40	1.44	1.48	1.52
4	1.17	1.22	1.26	1.31	1.36	1.41	1.46	1.51	1.57	1.63	1.68	1.74
5	1.22	1.27	1.33	1.40	1.46	1.53	1.61	1.68	1.76	1.84	1.92	2.01
6	1.27	1.34	1.41	1.50	1.58	1.67	1.77	1.87	1.97	2.08	2.19	2.31
7	1.32	1.41	1.51	1.61	1.71	1.82	1.94	2.08	2.22	2.35	2.50	2.66
8	1.37	1.47	1.59	1.72	1.85	1.99	2.14	2.30	2.47	2.66	2.85	3.05
9	1.42	1.55	1.69	1.84	1.99	2.17	2.35	2.56	2.77	3.04	3.25	3.52
10	1.48	1.63	1.79	1.96	2.16	2.37	2.59	2.84	3.11	3.39	3.70	4.05
11	1.54	1.71	1.89	2.11	2.33	2.58	2.85	3.15	3.48	3.86	4.22	4.65
12	1.60	1.80	2.01	2.25	2.52	2.81	3.14	3.49	3.90	4.34	4.81	5.35
13	1.67	1.89	2.13	2.41	2.72	3.05	3.45	3.88	4.36	4.89	5.49	6.15
14	1.73	1.98	2.26	2.57	2.94	3.34	3.80	4.31	4.89	5.55	6.26	7.08
15	1.80	2.08	2.39	2.75	3.17	3.64	4.18	4.78	5.47	6.25	7.13	8.14
16	1.87	2.18	2.54	2.92	3.43	3.97	4.60	5.31	6.13	7.06	8.13	9.36
17	1.95	2.29	2.69	3.16	3.70	4.32	5.05	5.89	6.87	7.98	9.27	10.77
18	2.03	2.41	2.85	3.38	4.00	4.72	5.56	6.54	7.68	9.02	10.57	12.38
19	2.11	2.53	3.02	3.62	4.32	5.14	6.12	7.26	8.61	10.19	12.06	14.23
20	2.19	2.65	3.20	3.87	4.66	5.60	6.73	8.06	9.65	11.52	13.74	16.31
25	2.67	3.39	4.29	5.42	6.85	8.60	10.83	13.58	17.00	21.23	26.46	32.90
30	3.24	4.32	5.74	7.61	10.06	13.27	17.45	22.89	29.96	39.11	50.95	66.22
35	3.95	5.52	7.68	10.67	14.79	20.41	28.10	38.57	52.80	72.06	98.10	133.1
40	4.80	7.04	10.29	14.97	21.72	31.41	45.26	65.00	93.05	132.8	188.9	267.9
45	5.84	8.99	13.76	21.00	31.92	48.33	72.89	109.5	164.0	244.6	363.7	538.8

APPENDIX F

Form W-4 (1995)

Want More Money In Your Paycheck?
If you expect to be able to take the earned income credit for 1995 and a child lives with you, you may be able to have part of the credit added to your take-home pay. For details, get Form W-5 from your employer.

Purpose. Complete Form W-4 so that your employer can withhold the correct amount of Federal income tax from your pay.

Exemption From Withholding. Read line 7 of the certificate below to see if you can claim exempt status. *If exempt, complete line 7; but do not complete lines 5 and 6.* No Federal income tax will be withheld from your pay. Your exemption is good for 1 year only. It expires February 15, 1996.

Note: You cannot claim exemption from withholding if (1) your income exceeds $650 and includes unearned income (e.g., interest

and dividends) and (2) another person can claim you as a dependent on their tax return.

Basic Instructions. Employees who are not exempt should complete the Personal Allowances Worksheet. Additional worksheets are provided on page 2 for employees to adjust their withholding allowances based on itemized deductions, adjustments to income, or two-earner/two-job situations. Complete all worksheets that apply to your situation. The worksheets will help you figure the number of withholding allowances you are entitled to claim. However, you may claim fewer allowances than this.

Head of Household. Generally, you may claim head of household filing status on your tax return only if you are unmarried and pay more than 50% of the costs of keeping up a home for yourself and your dependent(s) or other qualifying individuals.

Nonwage Income. If you have a large amount of nonwage income, such as interest or dividends, you should consider making

estimated tax payments using Form 1040-ES. Otherwise, you may find that you owe additional tax at the end of the year.

Two Earners/Two Jobs. If you have a working spouse or more than one job, figure the total number of allowances you are entitled to claim on all jobs using worksheets from only one Form W-4. This total should be divided among all jobs. Your withholding will usually be most accurate when all allowances are claimed on the W-4 filed for the highest paying job and zero allowances are claimed for the others.

Check Your Withholding. After your W-4 takes effect, you can use Pub. 919, Is My Withholding Correct for 1995?, to see how the dollar amount you are having withheld compares to your estimated total annual tax. We recommend you get Pub. 919 especially if you used the Two Earner/Two Job Worksheet and your earnings exceed $150,000 (Single) or $200,000 (Married). Call 1-800-829-3676 to order Pub. 919. Check your telephone directory for the IRS assistance number for further help.

Personal Allowances Worksheet

A Enter "1" for **yourself** if no one else can claim you as a dependent . . . . **A** _____

B Enter "1" if:
- You are single and have only one job; or
- You are married, have only one job, and your spouse does not work; or
- Your wages from a second job or your spouse's wages (or the total of both) are $1,000 or less.

B _____

C Enter "1" for your **spouse**. But, you may choose to enter -0- if you are married and have either a working spouse or more than one job (this may help you avoid having too little tax withheld) . . . . **C** _____

D Enter number of **dependents** (other than your spouse or yourself) you will claim on your tax return . . . . **D** _____

E Enter "1" if you will file as **head of household** on your tax return (see conditions under Head of Household above) . . **E** _____

F Enter "1" if you have at least $1,500 of **child or dependent care expenses** for which you plan to claim a credit . . **F** _____

G Add lines A through F and enter total here. **Note:** This amount may be different from the number of exemptions you claim on your return ▶ **G** _____

For accuracy, do all worksheets that apply.
- If you plan to **itemize or claim adjustments to income** and want to reduce your withholding, see the Deductions and Adjustments Worksheet on page 2.
- If you are **single** and have **more than one job** and your combined earnings from all jobs exceed $30,000 OR if you are **married** and have a **working spouse or more than one job**, and the combined earnings from all jobs exceed $50,000, see the Two-Earner/Two-Job Worksheet on page 2 if you want to avoid having too little tax withheld.
- If **neither** of the above situations applies, **stop here** and enter the number from line G on line 5 of Form W-4 below.

· · · · · · · · · · · · ✂ **Cut here and give the certificate to your employer. Keep the top portion for your records.** · · · · · · · · · · · ·

Form **W-4** Department of the Treasury Internal Revenue Service	**Employee's Withholding Allowance Certificate** ▶ For Privacy Act and Paperwork Reduction Act Notice, see reverse.	OMB No. 1545-0010 **19**95

1 Type or print your first name and middle initial	Last name	2 Your social security number

Home address (number and street or rural route)	3 ☐ Single ☐ Married ☐ Married, but withhold at higher Single rate. Note: *If married, but legally separated, or spouse is a nonresident alien, check the Single box.*
City or town, state, and ZIP code	4 If your last name differs from that on your social security card, check here and call 1-800-772-1213 for a new card . . . . . ▶ ☐

5	Total number of allowances you are claiming (from line G above or from the worksheets on page 2 if they apply) .	**5**
6	Additional amount, if any, you want withheld from each paycheck	**6** $
7	I claim exemption from withholding for 1995 and I certify that I meet **BOTH** of the following conditions for exemption: • Last year I had a right to a refund of **ALL** Federal income tax withheld because I had **NO** tax liability; **AND** • This year I expect a refund of **ALL** Federal income tax withheld because I expect to have **NO** tax liability. If you meet both conditions, enter "EXEMPT" here . . . . ▶	**7**

Under penalties of perjury, I certify that I am entitled to the number of withholding allowances claimed on this certificate or entitled to claim exempt status.

Employee's signature ▶ _____ Date ▶ _____, 19 ___

8 Employer's name and address (Employer: Complete 8 and 10 only if sending to the IRS)	9 Office code (optional)	10 Employer identification number

Cat. No. 10220Q

Form W-4 (1995)   Page **2**

Deductions and Adjustments Worksheet

Note: Use this worksheet only if you plan to itemize deductions or claim adjustments to income on your 1995 tax return.

1 Enter an estimate of your 1995 itemized deductions. These include qualifying home mortgage interest, charitable contributions, state and local taxes (but not sales taxes), medical expenses in excess of 7.5% of your income, and miscellaneous deductions. (For 1995, you may have to reduce your itemized deductions if your income is over $114,700 ($57,350 if married filing separately). Get Pub. 919 for details.) **1** $ _____

2 Enter: { $6,550 if married filing jointly or qualifying widow(er)
           $5,750 if head of household
           $3,900 if single
           $3,275 if married filing separately } . . . . **2** $ _____

3 **Subtract** line 2 from line 1. If line 2 is greater than line 1, enter -0- . . . . **3** $ _____

4 Enter an estimate of your 1995 adjustments to income. These include alimony paid and deductible IRA contributions **4** $ _____

5 **Add** lines 3 and 4 and enter the total . . . . **5** $ _____

6 Enter an estimate of your 1995 nonwage income (such as dividends or interest) . . . . **6** $ _____

7 **Subtract** line 6 from line 5. Enter the result, but not less than -0- . . . . **7** $ _____

8 **Divide** the amount on line 7 by $2,500 and enter the result here. Drop any fraction . . . . **8** _____

9 Enter the number from Personal Allowances Worksheet, line G, on page 1 . . . . **9** _____

10 **Add** lines 8 and 9 and enter the total here. If you plan to use the Two-Earner/Two-Job Worksheet, also enter this total on line 1 below. Otherwise, **stop here** and enter this total on Form W-4, line 5, on page 1 . . . . **10** _____

Two-Earner/Two-Job Worksheet

Note: Use this worksheet only if the instructions for line G on page 1 direct you here.

1 Enter the number from line G on page 1 (or from line 10 above if you used the Deductions and Adjustments Worksheet) **1** _____

2 Find the number in **Table 1** below that applies to the **LOWEST** paying job and enter it here . . . . **2** _____

3 If line 1 is **GREATER THAN OR EQUAL TO** line 2, subtract line 2 from line 1. Enter the result here (if zero, enter -0-) and on Form W-4, line 5, on page 1. **DO NOT** use the rest of this worksheet . . . . **3** _____

Note: If line 1 is **LESS THAN** line 2, enter -0- on Form W-4, line 5, on page 1. Complete lines 4–9 to calculate the additional withholding amount necessary to avoid a year end tax bill.

4 Enter the number from line 2 of this worksheet . . . . **4** _____

5 Enter the number from line 1 of this worksheet . . . . **5** _____

6 **Subtract** line 5 from line 4 . . . . **6** _____

7 Find the amount in **Table 2** below that applies to the **HIGHEST** paying job and enter it here . . . . **7** $ _____

8 **Multiply** line 7 by line 6 and enter the result here. This is the additional annual withholding amount needed **8** $ _____

9 Divide line 8 by the number of pay periods remaining in 1995. (For example, divide by 26 if you are paid every other week and you complete this form in December 1994.) Enter the result here and on Form W-4, line 6, page 1. This is the additional amount to be withheld from each paycheck . . . . **9** $ _____

Table 1: Two-Earner/Two-Job Worksheet

Married Filing Jointly				All Others	
If wages from **LOWEST** paying job are—	Enter on line 2 above	If wages from **LOWEST** paying job are—	Enter on line 2 above	If wages from **LOWEST** paying job are—	Enter on line 2 above
0 - $3,000	. . . 0	39,001 - 50,000	. . . 9	0 - $4,000	 0
3,001 - 6,000	. . . 1	50,001 - 55,000	. . . 10	4,001 - 10,000	 1
6,001 - 11,000	. . . 2	55,001 - 60,000	. . . 11	10,001 - 14,000	 2
11,001 - 16,000	. . . 3	60,001 - 70,000	. . . 12	14,001 - 19,000	 3
16,001 - 21,000	. . . 4	70,001 - 80,000	. . . 13	19,001 - 23,000	 4
21,001 - 27,000	. . . 5	80,001 - 90,000	. . . 14	23,001 - 45,000	 5
27,001 - 31,000	. . . 6	90,001 and over	. . . 15	45,001 - 60,000	 6
31,001 - 34,000	. . . 7			60,001 - 70,000	 7
34,001 - 39,000	. . . 8			70,001 and over	 8

Table 2: Two-Earner/Two-Job Worksheet

Married Filing Jointly		All Others	
If wages from **HIGHEST** paying job are—	Enter on line 7 above	If wages from **HIGHEST** paying job are—	Enter on line 7 above
0 - $50,000	. . $380	0 - $30,000	. . . $380
50,001 - 100,000	. . 700	30,001 - 60,000	. . . 700
100,001 - 130,000	. . 780	60,001 - 110,000	. . . 780
130,001 - 230,000	. . 900	110,001 - 230,000	. . . 900
230,001 and over	. . 990	230,001 and over	. . . 990

Privacy Act and Paperwork Reduction Act Notice.—We ask for the information on this form to carry out the Internal Revenue laws of the United States. The Internal Revenue Code requires this information under sections 3402(f)(2)(A) and 6109 and their regulations. Failure to provide a completed form will result in your being treated as a single person who claims no withholding allowances. Routine uses of this information include giving it to the Department of Justice for civil and criminal litigation and to cities, states, and the District of Columbia for use in administering their tax laws.

The time needed to complete this form will vary depending on individual circumstances. The estimated average time is: **Recordkeeping** 46 min., **Learning about the law or the form** 10 min., **Preparing the form** 69 min. If you have comments concerning the accuracy of these time estimates or suggestions for making this form simpler, we would be happy to hear from you. You can write to the **Internal Revenue Service**, Attention: Tax Forms Committee, PC:FP, Washington, DC 20224. **DO NOT** send the tax form to this address. Instead, give it to your employer.

✱ *Printed on recycled paper*   *U.S. Government Printing Office: 1994 — 375-119*

Glossary

age-weighted plan Special type of profit-sharing plan that allocates contributions based on age and compensation. Allows employers to give large contributions to older employees.

AMEX The American Stock Exchange handles over 20 percent of all stocks trades; usually companies are smaller in size than those that trade on the New York Stock Exchange.

blue chip A company known nationally for its quality and products and for its ability to generate profits and dividends.

broad market Term used to describe the broad market of stocks as represented by the Standard & Poor's 500. This is a much better indicator of the market than narrow indexes such as the Dow.

capital gains Profit from the sale of stocks, bonds, options, real estate or other property.

COLA Cost of living adjustments are small increases in pensions and retirement plans to adjust for inflation.

convertible securities Usually preferred stocks or bonds that can be converted into stocks.

core-plus package A type of cafeteria package that gives employees core benefits. Employee has to pay for additional benefits.

debit cards   These are similar to credit cards, but they aren't credit cards. With credit cards you are borrowing money. With debit cards you are just taking money from your account, like a "paperless check."

employee welfare benefit plan   Programs offered by an employer to provide participants with medical care and benefits in the event of sickness, death or unemployment.

ERISA   Employee Retirement Income Security ACT (1974). Sets the federal guidelines and standards for private pension plans.

excess plans   These are nonqualified plans that allow employers to contribute for higher-income employees. Since the new tax laws only allow contributions for profit-sharing money purchase, 401(k) and other retirement plans on income up to $150,000, many employees have seen their contributions decrease substantially. In the past the income limits were $236,000.

Fannie Mae (FNMA)   Securities issued by the Federal National Mortgage Association (FNMA). FNMA buys home owners' mortgages and adds guarantees, then sells these FNMA securities to investors. Although not direct obligations of the U.S. government, their high quality and the monthly payment of principal make these very attractive for income-oriented investors.

fiduciary   A person in a position of special trust and confidence who is responsible for the fiscal affairs of others.

Freddie Mac   Federal Home Loan Mortgage Corporation (FHLMC). A secondary market for conventional residential mortgages.

GNMA   Securities issued by the Government National Mortgage Association. These are some of the highest-quality obligations of the U.S. government. These securities pass through the interest and principal payments of home owners' mortgages to investors.

grace period   Group life insurance policies provide for a grace period (almost always 31 days) during which a policy owner may pay any overdue premiums.

indemnity plans   Insurance plans that usually offer the best coverage, but also the highest deductible and copayments.

integration Reducing private pension plan benefits by amounts of Social Security.

margin account An account that extends credit to an investor, using securities as collateral.

modular plan Type of cafeteria plan. Typically one of the benefits will be at no cost to the employee. Sometimes used to offer a basic package of benefits. If the employee wants more coverage, then he or she will pay for extra benefits.

money market funds Mutual funds that invest in short-term securities such as treasuries, CDs and short-term commercial paper. Must have 95 percent in securities that are rated very safe. Offer liquidity and one of safest, though lowest-yielding investments. You can use as an alternative to checking for they offer checkbook writing privileges. Can use instead of savings, since they are comparably safe in most cases.

municipal bonds Bonds issued by states, school districts, water districts, highway authorities, cities, counties or towns. The interest on these bonds may be either taxable or tax-free. Typically industrial revenue bonds are now taxable, but general obligation bonds are tax-free.

mutual fund An investment company that issues securities that are redeemable at net asset value.

Nasdaq (National Association of Security Dealers Automated Quotations) Stocks that are not qualified for one reason or another, such as credit rating, maturity or size, cannot trade on formal exchanges. Instead these stocks trade OTC, "over the counter," that is a computerized network of sophisticated "market makers," people who are willing to buy and sell shares.

New York Stock Exchange This is the market where the largest and strongest companies in America trade. In order for companies to sell their shares on this exchange, they have to meet certain criteria. Over 75 percent of all buying and selling of stocks occur in this market.

overdraft checking Allows you to write checks for money you do not have and automatically creates a loan. Easiest source for fast credit.

stop-gap policies   When you leave your current employer, you may need coverage until a new insurance plan picks up. Most group plans will either have coverage for a month after you leave your job, COBRA or interim policies.

supplemental executive retirement plans   Plans in which the employer agrees to provide death, disability and retirement benefits that he or she usually funds through insurance policies. Such insurance plans allow you to take out income without 10 percent penalties for early withdrawals, and no excise tax for excessive distributions. The income grows tax-free until received.

thrift plans   Type of retirement plan. Employer and employees contribute. The contributions are with after-tax dollars so there is no deduction from taxable income as with 401(k)s.

variable annuity   Like mutual funds in that investors can invest in several subaccounts, such as global stocks, bonds and domestic stocks. Funds build up tax-deferred. They can have high hidden fees and penalties for early withdrawal (10 percent from IRS if before age 59½ and 1 to 8 percent from annuity company).

variable life insurance   A variation of whole life insurance. These policies allow the owner to direct how the cash value or savings portion is to be invested.

whole life insurance or permanent life insurance   Whole life is made up of two parts: term insurance and a cash value "savings" vehicle. These policies can be expensive and yields are seldom as attractive as other investments, but funds build up tax-deferred and you can borrow cash value. If the employer pays, the premiums are included in your income and subject to taxation. However, the proceeds are free of income tax, and if you do not own the policies, you can avoid estate taxes.

zero-coupon bonds   Bonds similar to U.S. savings bonds in that they pay no current interest but return two or three times or a multiple of your money back at maturity. However, unlike the variable yield of U.S. savings bonds, zeros have a fixed yield and are the riskiest bonds if interest rates increase. They often have high hidden fees and if they are taxable, you will have to pay tax on income you do not receive.

Index